The
Two Hands
of God

The Two Hands of God

THE MYTHS OF POLARITY

ALAN WATTS

New World Library
Novato, California

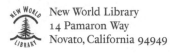

New World Library
14 Pamaron Way
Novato, California 94949

The acknowledgments on p. 245 constitute an extension of this copyright page.

Text design by Tona Pearce Myers

Library of Congress Cataloging-in-Publication Data

Names: Watts, Alan, 1915-1973, author.
Title: The two hands of god : the myths of polarity / Alan Watts.
Description: Novato, California : New World Library, 2020. | Reprint.
Originally published: New York, G. Braziller, 1963. | Includes bibliographical
    references and index. | Summary: "*The Two Hands of God* explores the
    human experience of polarity, a condition in which seemingly opposite
    qualities form part of a larger whole. The author illustrates the ways that
    different cultures express the concept of polarity through the symbolic
    language of myth, literature, and art."-- Provided by publisher.
Identifiers: LCCN 2020016961 (print) | LCCN 2020016962 (ebook) | ISBN
    9781608686865 (paperback) | ISBN 9781608686872 (epub)
Subjects: LCSH: Polarity--Religious aspects.
Classification: LCC BL325.P7 W3 2020 (print) | LCC BL325.P7 (ebook) |
    DDC 201/.4--dc23
LC record available at https://lccn.loc.gov/2020016961
LC ebook record available at https://lccn.loc.gov/2020016962

First New World Library printing, September 2020
ISBN 978-1-60868-686-5
Ebook ISBN 978-1-60868-687-2
Printed in Canada on 100% postconsumer-waste recycled paper

New World Library is proud to be a Gold Certified Environmentally
Responsible Publisher. Publisher certification awarded by Green
Press Initiative.

10   9   8   7   6   5   4   3

TO DONALD

with thanks for bones under the flesh

Let not your left hand know what your right hand doeth.

MATTHEW 6:3

Those who would have right without its correlative, wrong; or good government without its correlative, misrule,—they do not apprehend the great principles of the universe nor the conditions to which all creation is subject. One might as well talk of the existence of heaven without that of earth, or of the negative principle (*yin*) without the positive (*yang*), which is clearly absurd. Such people, if they do not yield to argument, must be either fools or knaves.

CHUANG-TZU, xvii

In biological development dualism or conflict is always super-imposed on a prior unity. The existence of an organism capable of survival implies integration, and unity is therefore always prior to inner conflict. Conflict may arise as the result of an inappropriate adaptation, and it may prove fatal or it may be overcome. But the recovery of organic health never involves the synthesis of fundamentally opposed principles, since these cannot coexist in an organism. It only seems to do so because the actual condition of the organism has been misinterpreted in using a dualistic language. The historical process does not involve the synthesis of pre-existing logical opposites, though it may appear to in the confused language of immature dialectical theories.

L.L. WHYTE, *The Next Development in Man*

Contents

List of Plates

(following page 128)

1. *Lingam* and *Yoni*. *Courtesy of the Metropolitan Museum of Art, New York.*
2. Kali. *Courtesy of the Rietberg Museum, Zürich.*
3. Black Madonna. *Private Collection. Photo courtesy of De Agostini Picture Library / Bridgeman Images.*
4. Yamantaka. *Courtesy of the Metropolitan Museum of Art, New York, gift of Mrs. Robert W. deForest, 1931.*
5. St. Michael and the Dragon. *Museo di Arte Sacra, Asciano, Italy. Photo courtesy of Scala / Art Resource, NY.*
6. The Descent of Christ into Hell. *Courtesy of the Metropolitan Museum of Art, New York.*
7. The Inferno. *Found in the Collection of Battistero di San Giovanni, Firenze. Photo courtesy of HIP / Art Resource, NY.*
8. *Detail from* The Temptation of St. Anthony. *Musee d'Unterlinden. Photo courtesy of Erich Lessing / Art Resource, NY.*
9. The Last Judgment. *Courtesy of the Metropolitan Museum of Art, New York, Fletcher Fund, 1933.*
10. Lucifer, King of Hell. *Veneranda Biblioteca Ambrosiana, Milan, Italy. Photo courtesy of De Agostini Picture Library / Bridgeman Images.*

11. The Saintly Throng in the Form of a Rose. *Private Collection. Photo courtesy of and copyright © Giancarlo Costa / Bridgeman Images.*

12. Vision of the Throne of God. *Courtesy of the Bibliothèque Nationale, Paris.*

13. St. Michael. *Courtesy of the Metropolitan Museum of Art, New York, Dick Fund, 1960.*

14. The Cross as the Tree of Life. *Basilica of San Clemente, Rome. Photo courtesy of Eye Ubiquitous / Alamy Stock Photo.*

15. Indian Tree of Life. *Courtesy of the Nelson-Atkins Gallery (Nelson Fund), Kansas City, Missouri.*

16. Vishnu sleeping on Adhi Shesha, his snake bed. *Courtesy of the Granger Historical Picture Archive.*

17. Amphisbaena. *Courtesy of the British Museum, London. Photo from the collection of Maud Oakes.*

18. Symbolic door. *Courtesy of Mrs. A. K. Coomaraswamy.*

19. Brahma. *Courtesy of the Metropolitan Museum of Art, New York, Eggleston Fund, 1927.*

20a. Four-faced Brahma, stone. *Courtesy of the Metropolitan Museum of Art, New York.*

20b. Four-faced Brahma, statue. *Rishikesh, Uttarankhand, India. Photo courtesy of agefotostock / Alamy Stock Photo.*

21. Shiva as Nataraja, King of the Dance. *Courtesy of the Rietberg Museum, Zürich.*

22. Indian map of the world. *Courtesy of the Library of Congress.*

23. Amitayus Mandala. *Courtesy of the American Museum of Natural History, New York; Anthropology Catalog No: 70.0/ 6867.*

List of Line Drawings

Preface

THIS BOOK IS THE BY-PRODUCT of many years' interest in
types of relationship which are at once difficult to express
in language and yet fundamental to the order of life itself.
I speak of the polar, reciprocal, or mutually sustaining relationship of events and forces that are usually considered to
be opposed to or basically separate from one another. These
"oppositions" include not only life and death, good and evil,
light and darkness, but also the organism and its environment, the self and the not-self, the solid and the space, and
the knower and the known. There has always been a certain
difficulty in explaining the relationship between these terms
as "transactional"—like buying and selling—such that the
one term exists only in conjunction with the other. This
points to the further insight that what is divided in terms,
that is, in thought and language, may be united in fact. To
be specific: the individual's sense of basic separation from
his universe may be a perceptual illusion based upon inadequate concepts of sensing and knowing.

I have found, however, that there are many ways in which
images, and especially mythological images, express this type

of relationship more adequately than logically descriptive language. What follows is, then, an anthology of myths and mythical images concerned with the polar relationship of opposites, together with a running commentary and a general introduction to the theme.

Not believing that mythology has yet reached the status of a science, my selection of materials is based chiefly on philosophical and literary considerations. With the exception of the materials from Milton's *Paradise Lost*, I have tried to avoid sources that would be familiar to the educated Western reader, and thus have almost entirely excluded the oft repeated Greek, Roman, and Nordic myths. For a number of most useful suggestions as to sources that I might use, I am indebted to my friend Joseph Campbell. My grateful thanks are also due to Mary Jane King, Grace Ponch, and Ruth Costello for their assistance in typing the manuscript, and to Luisa Coomaraswamy and Antoinette Gordon for providing some of the photographs for plates.

ALAN W. WATTS
Sausalito, California

Introduction

WHEN THE CRITICAL INTELLECT looks at anything carefully, it vanishes. This is as true of the solid substance of bodies as of historical generalizations, of entities such as nations, of epochs such as the Middle Ages, and of subject matters such as myth. The reason is, of course, that "things" exist only relatively—for a point of view or for convenience of description. Thus when we inspect any unit more closely we find that its structure is more complex and more differentiated than we had supposed. Its variety comes to impress us more than its unity. This is why there is something of the spirit of debunking in all scholarship and scientific inquiry. As a historian of science once put it, "Isn't it amazing how many things there are that aren't so?"

It is for this reason that no serious scholar will now propose any general definition or comprehensive theory of myth—at least, not without making numerous reservations. Nevertheless, the word "myth" remains useful. It designates a class of things which we all recognize clearly enough, provided we do not try to be too exact about it. Under the microscope, even the clean edge of a knife becomes ragged. But the stories of Hercules and Odin, the cosmologies of India and China, and the symbols of the lotus and the cross have something in common that we can call mythological—meaning by this word something very much more than the merely fanciful.

Some years ago I ventured to define myth as "a complex of stories—some no doubt fact, and some fantasy—which, for various reasons, human beings regard as demonstrations of the inner meaning of the universe and of human life."[1] Vague as this was, I should have made it yet vaguer by adding that myth includes not only stories but also symbols and images, for the yang-yin symbol of the Chinese and the neurological doctrines of Yoga are plainly mythological in the sense of my definition without being associated with any special narrative. The point is, I think, that myth is to be distinguished from religion, science, and philosophy because it consists always of concrete images, appealing to imagination, and serving in one way or another to reveal or explain the mysteries of life. Yet there is a sense in which both the poetic and the mythic image at once reveal and conceal. The meaning is divined rather than defined, implicit rather than explicit, suggested rather than stated. It is in this sense that an apocalypse is simultaneously a revelation of hidden things and a way of speaking in symbols so as to conceal them.

Beyond this I do not see how there can be any coherent theory of myth and mythogenesis. It is rather that there is some truth in almost all theories—as that myth is primitive philosophy or science, that its inner meaning is sexual, agricultural, or astrological, that it is a projection of unconscious psychic events, and that it is a consciously constructed system of allegories and parables. No one of these theories accounts for all myths, and yet I do not doubt that each accounts for some. There is, too, the special difficulty that the study of living myths is like the study of child psychology: the infant is unable to say what he thinks and feels in the terms which the psychologist wants to use. The recognition of myth as such almost invariably requires a certain sophistication; like the rainbow, myth can be seen only from a cultural or temporal distance—and as the anthropologist approaches it to find his pot of gold, the rainbow recedes and vanishes.

It is not, however, the purpose of this particular volume to explore or apply any general theories of myth beyond the rather vague assumption that myth is often a way of thinking in concrete images, in terms that are neither abstract ideas nor descriptions of tangible facts. Its less ambitious though almost paradoxical object is to show, with respect to myths of a certain type, that the mythical mode of thought is able to convey things which are difficult to express otherwise, and that therefore myth still has value for an age of science and scientific philosophy. Myth is not, furthermore, an exclusively ancient or primitive phenomenon. As Mark Schorer has said, "Myths are the instruments by which we continually struggle to make our experience intelligible to ourselves. A myth is a large controlling image that gives philosophical meaning to the facts of ordinary life; that is, which has organizing value for experience....Are not ideas, like language itself, supported by the 'submerged metaphor'? In this sense, myth is indispensable to any form of belief. And in this sense, one may even concur with Hume's offensive remark that 'there is no such passion in human minds, as the love of mankind, merely as such'; for this passion, like all others, must have an image, real or ideal, as its correlative."[2] But we may say, further, not only that the mythological image is an organizer and energizer of action, but also that it has a way of implying things that are difficult to state explicitly.

This has always been recognized with respect to the poetic image. "The moonlight steeped in silentness the steady weathercock." In "factual" language it is nonsense to say that the noise of something which, in any case, is not moving is abated by light. Does the image, then, make sense only because we read into it a series of "as ifs"—it is as if the positive presence of moonlight rather than the negative absence of wind were making the weathercock still? To put it that way is to lose something much more than elegance of expression, and, indeed, the skillful poet tends to avoid such metaphor cues as "like," "as if," or "as it were." The difference between poetic and factual language is of course that the former is associative and the latter dissociative. The one makes an active connection between moonlight and silence over and above their temporal concurrence. The other likes to keep clear distinctions between things which are not causally related. But the poetic language manages to convey something which factual language almost invariably screens out—the psychophysical involvement of the poet himself with his environment.

Factual description depends upon the convention that there can be an independent, detached observer who can regard the world objectively. But this is a convention, albeit a useful one within certain limits. The physical situation which so largely slips through the net of factual language is that there is no independent observer. Knowledge is not an encounter between two separate things—a knowing subject and a known object. Knowledge, or better, *knowing* is a relationship in which knower and known are like the poles in a magnetic field. Human beings are aware of a world because, and only because, it is the sort of world that breeds knowing organisms. Humanity is not one thing and the world another; it has always been difficult for us to see that any organism is so embedded in its environment that the evolution of so complex and intelligent a creature as man could never have come to pass without a reciprocal evolution of the environment. An intelligent man argues, without any resort to supernaturalism, an intelligent universe.

At this point, I am afraid, both the writer and the reader become aware of a certain difficulty in expressing the point. Factual language, which is what I am trying to speak, has a grammar and structure which fragment the world into quite separate things and events. But this is not the way in which the world exists physically, for there is no thing, no event, save in relation to other things and events—save in what science calls a field. True, a given thing can disappear without the disappearance of its field. The environment continues beyond the death of any organism. But the field, the environment, does not exist apart from the life-and-death of that organism. This world would be a very different world indeed if it were not the kind of world in which Socrates, or John Doe, could have lived and did in fact live.

The poet says all this much more vividly through what has been miscalled "the pathetic fallacy"—the attribution of human qualities to nature.

> The moon doth with delight look round her
> When the heavens are bare.

If we are to understand by this just that the poet looks around with delight when the moon is shining in the bare heavens, it were better said that way and let the poetry dissolve into indifferent prose. But in an image of this kind the poet divines or implies a physical truth for which the language of facts is inadequate—not that the moon has eyes of its own, but that a man's eyes are the moon's eyes, that there is light only when there are eyes, and that a world in which there is a moon goes together with a world in which there are men—inseparably. Associations which form themselves in poetic imagination are, after all, associations which exist in nature, though not along the lines of connection which factual language ordinarily describes.

At this point the poet himself may quite properly object that I have been trying to steal his thunder, that I am beginning to say in factual language what he says much better in poetry, but that, nonetheless, I have somewhat missed the point. There was more in his image than I have explained. All this is quite true, for the whole aim of this essay is, as I intimated, the almost paradoxical one of trying to say, in factual language, that poetic and mythological images can express things, even physical relationships, which are only most awkwardly expressible in other terms. And there *is* more in the image than I have explained. This is precisely the force of the image: that it is endlessly fecund, that its store of meanings is abundant for generation after generation.

Two different modes of language imply two modes of vision. Factual language obviously represents the view of nature which is held to be normal, practical, and sane—the world of science and industry, business and bureaucracy, of hard facts and cold calculations. It is a world that is rather flat, dry, and dusty—like a city parking lot—but which many of us find enormously reassuring and to which we cling as to sanity itself. But one of the most prevalent themes of myth is that this is a "fallen" world whose matter-of-fact reality is quite spurious. In differing ways the poet, the painter, and the mystic try to describe another world, or rather, this same world of nature seen in another way.

Arthur Machen quotes a curious account of this vision from Hampole's *A London Walk: Meditations in the Streets of the Metropolis*, written about the middle of the nineteenth century:

> Has it ever been your fortune, courteous reader, to rise in the earliest dawning of a summer day, ere yet the radiant beams of the sun have done more than touch with light the domes and spires of the great city?…If this has been your lot, have you not observed that magic powers have apparently been at work? The accustomed scene has lost its familiar appearance. The houses which you have passed daily, it may be for years, as you have issued forth on your business or pleasure, now seem as if you beheld them for the first time. They have suffered a mysterious change, *into something rich and strange*. Though they may have been designed with no extraordinary exertion of the art of architecture…yet you have been ready to admit that they now 'stand in glory, shine like stars, apparelled in light serene.' They have become magical habitations, supernal dwellings, more desirable to the eye than the fabled pleasure dome of the Eastern potentate, or the bejewelled hall built by the Genie for Aladdin in the Arabian tale.

Some have declared that it lies within our choice to gaze continually upon a world of equal or even greater wonder and beauty. It is said by these that the experiments of the alchemists in the Dark Ages...are, in fact, related, not to the transmutation of metals, but to the transmutation of the entire Universe....This method, or art, or science, or whatever we choose to call it (supposing it to exist, or to have ever existed), is simply concerned to restore the delights of the primal Paradise; to enable men, if they will, to inhabit a world of joy and splendour. It is perhaps possible that there is such an experiment, and that there are some who have made it.[3]

It has, of course, been supposed that this vision is a brief recapturing of the way in which we saw things in our infancy, and in this connection it is worth quoting a celebrated passage from Traherne's *Centuries of Meditations*:

"Is it not strange," he asks, "that an infant should be heir of the whole World, and see those mysteries which the books of the learned never unfold?

"The corn was orient and immortal wheat, which never should be reaped, nor was ever sown. I thought it had stood from everlasting to everlasting. The dust and stones of the street were as precious as gold: the gates were at first the end of the world. The green trees when I saw them first through one of the gates transported and ravished me, their sweetness and unusual beauty made my heart to leap, and almost mad with ecstasy, they were such strange and wonderful things. The Men! O what venerable and reverend creatures did the aged seem! Immortal Cherubims! And young men glittering and sparking Angels, and maids strange seraphic pieces of life and beauty! Boys and girls tumbling in the street, and playing, were moving jewels. I knew not that they were born or should die; but all things abided eternally as they were in their proper places.

"Eternity was manifest in the Light of Day, and something infinite behind everything appeared: which talked with my expectation and moved my desire. The city seemed to stand in Eden, or to be built in Heaven. The streets were mine, the temple was mine, the people were mine, their clothes and gold and silver were mine, as much as their sparkling eyes, fair skins and ruddy faces. The skies were mine, and so were the sun and moon and stars, and all the World was mine; and I the only spectator and enjoyer of it. I knew no churlish proprieties, nor bounds, nor divisions: but all proprieties and divisions were mine: all treasures and the possessors of them. So that with much ado I was corrupted, and made to learn the dirty devices of this world. Which now I unlearn, and become, as it were, a little child again that I may enter into the Kingdom of God."[4]

Here, two hundred years before Freud, is his idea that the infant has a sense of omnipotent oneness with all that it sees and feels. But from Freud's viewpoint any return to this state is regressive—a weak and wishful abandonment of the restrictions and responsibilities of civilized, adult manhood, despite the fact that mystics have sought and regained this consciousness through the most arduous disciplines. It seems entirely to have escaped Freud's thought that there might be an adult version of this vision, maturer than the infant's as the grown body of the baby's. It might thus be that, ordinarily, through the confusions of civilized education, this mode of vision is never cultivated and lapses, therefore, into atrophy. This way of seeing the world comes too often to people of high sensibility and culture for it to be dismissed as regression or delusion.

Furthermore, it becomes clearer and clearer even to the austere viewpoints of the physicist and biologist that the ways in which we ordinarily interpret the reports of our senses are learned and to some extent conventional—products of education rather than of the organism itself, biologically considered. If in physical fact man-and-his-environment constitute some sort of unified or polarized field, why do we not feel this to be so instead of feeling ourselves to be rather alien beings *confronting* a world?

Part of the difficulty seems to be that we educate a style of consciousness which ignores whatever is a constant sensation. Consciousness is ever upon the alert for new conditions in the environment so as to keep the rest of the organism informed about adaptations that must be made, and this style of attention comes to eclipse the more open and total style of sensitivity that we have in the beginning. In the Genesis myth, Adam and Eve fell from grace because they attained "the knowledge of good and evil," which is saying in the plainest way that they became distracted from Eden through concern with what is advantageous and disadvantageous in the environment. The Hebrew words for good and evil in this context mean precisely the useful and the useless, in other words, what is useful for survival and what is not. It would seem, then, that the Fall comes about through an obsessive and continuous preoccupation with survival, and thus it is logical for the Regainer of paradise to say, "Whosoever would save his life shall lose it."

Nothing, apparently, could be more contrary to practical good sense, especially under the conditions of a high civilization which maintains its entire business by the perpetual inculcation of competition and anxiety. But the paradox of civilization is that the more one is anxious to survive, the less survival is worth the trouble. And it looks as if, in the end, the very technology which flows from the knowledge of the useful and the useless will be the death of us all. On the other hand, there is a considerable and normally unexpected survival value in the very absence of anxiety to survive. Popular wisdom recognizes that care killed the cat because when the cat cares too much, it does not fall limply from the branch of a tree. Nothing is stronger than a certain give, or springy absence of rigidity, and this is certainly why evolution seems to favor the mammals more than the crustaceans—sensitive flesh around bone rather than insensitive bone around flesh. Without its resilient ease and looseness, the cat would certainly not have its nine lives.

The vision of the world described in factual language is therefore dim and dusty because it is a view of life deadened by concern to live. The Lord God is reported in the Bible to have said to his Chosen People, "I have set before you life and death: choose life." But the commandments of the Lord God are sometimes challenges to find out what is impossible, though plausible, by attempting to do it. As we shall see, the mythological image implies again and again that life and death are not so much alternatives as alternations, poles of a single process which may be called life-and-death. Not only is it obvious that living organisms thrive upon dead organisms; it is also only a little less obvious that the very living of any one organism is a perpetual birth, death, and elimination of its own cells. Moreover death provides for the constant renewal of life by setting limits to accumulations—of population, of property, of memories—which, beyond a certain point, tend to become static and to clog the flow of life—that is, to die! It is thus that accumulation, the building up of some relatively permanent pattern or system, is both life and death.

But in the other, paradisal, vision the individual organism has a different sense of identity. It is not merely itself, bounded rigidly by its own skin. Its identity is also its whole field, which, in mystical terms, is to say that it is one with the universe, with the system of immortal life-and-death. In the light of this awareness the overplus of concern for individual survival fades away; the dust of busy anxiety settles, and the world becomes visible in its primal, or actual, splendor.

Now this is the world of mythology, of the marvelous, for, as Aristotle said, myths are "a compact of wonders." It is not, however, a world which is good in the specifically moral sense: it is a world of gods and demons, magnificent in its wrath as in its beauty, and only the person who knows that all this is his veritable and fundamental Self can overcome the fear of it. As the Eskimo shaman Najagneq told the anthropologist Rasmussen, this Self is "the inhabitant or soul (*inua*) of the universe.... All we know is that it has a gentle voice like a woman, a voice 'so fine and gentle that even children cannot become afraid.' What it says is: *sila ersinarsinivdluge*, 'be not afraid of the universe.'"[5] This is likewise the counsel of the *Bardo Thödol*, or the Tibetan *Book of the Dead*. "At this time when the Fifty-eight Blood-Drinking Deities emanating from thine own brain come to shine upon thee, if thou knowest them to be the radiances of thine own intellect, thou wilt merge, in the state of at-one-ment, into the body of the Blood-Drinking Ones there and then, and obtain

Buddhahood. O nobly-born, by not recognizing now, and by fleeing from the deities out of fear, again sufferings will come to overpower thee."[6]

The intellectual attitude of our own time, so preponderantly antimythological, expresses our fear of the marvelous, for we have been trying to persuade ourselves that the universe is not a mystery but a somewhat stupid machine. Poetry has been regarded as a pursuit fit only for weak young men with long hair, mysticism as a refuge for the credulous and woolly-minded, and mythology as the relic of a barbarous past. Consequently the very science of mythology is, for the most part, an antiquarianism or, insofar as it is a study of existing primitive cultures, a sort of scientific game whose results will be filed in libraries and museums. The majority of works on mythology claiming any scholarly and scientific competence are thus purely historical in their approach. They are preoccupied with ferreting out the original sources of mythic themes, with archeological, philological, and literary evidences for their creation and dissemination, and with explanations of their symbolism which shall show them to be merely primitive forms of thought. There is, indeed, merit in this work because it does provide some sound evidence as to the ways in which myth is formed. Yet it is an approach which has been greatly overemphasized.

Whatever may be said against the psychological theories of Freud and, more particularly, of Jung, their work has the outstanding virtue of taking mythology seriously, of studying it as something still powerfully operative in the modern world, and, at least in Jung's case, of regarding it with all the respect due to a source of wisdom. To put it in Jung's own

words, "I can only stand in deepest awe and admiration before the depths and heights of the soul whose world beyond
space hides an immeasurable richness of images, which millions of years of living have stored up and condensed into
organic material. My conscious mind is like an eye which perceives the furthermost spaces; but the psychic non-ego is that
which fills this space in a sense beyond space. These images
are not pale shadows, but powerful and effective conditions
of the soul which we can only misunderstand but can never
rob of their power by denying them."[7]

My own approach will not be formally Jungian. I think
the hypothesis of a "collective unconscious," of a storehouse
of archaic images and memories somehow embedded in and
inherited with the structure of the brain, is plausible but quite
insufficiently proven. I do not feel that such an unconscious
is necessarily the main reason why similar types of myth
have arisen in the most widely dispersed times and places,
for evidences of their transmission by physical contacts keep
coming to light. I feel, too, that so much emphasis upon the
force of an inherited, psychoneurological unconscious gives
too little weight to the influence, also unconscious, of man's
social context—a matrix in which the individual is as deeply
involved as in the field of his natural surroundings of light,
air, water, and earth. Jung's psychology carries over too much
of the notion that the mind or soul is inside the skin as
some sort of dimension of the individual organism. Mind is
also a vast network of social intercommunication wherein
the individual is something like a transformer in an electric
power grid.

But none of this invalidates Jung's point that the mythic

image, the archetype, whether submerged in the collective unconscious or the social matrix or both, is a powerful and indispensable organizer of action and experience. Yet I do not remember any passage in which Jung suggests that, beyond this, the archetypal images reveal a vision not of the psyche alone but of the whole natural world. For Jung, the external world seems to be a somewhat indifferent screen which receives our psychic projections. He is overcareful to avoid the pathetic fallacy. For my part, I believe that these images—mythic, poetic, and artistic—reveal the outer world as well as the inner. For it is only when translated into the somewhat specialized and limited instrument of factual language that the outer world appears to be this prosaic assembly of "nobody here but just us objects." To survey and control the earth we must reduce its formations to the formal abstractions of geometry, and translate it into the flat and dry symbolism of maps. But, as Korzybski so often repeated, the map is not the territory.

Myth, too, is a symbolism and mythologies are likewise maps, and for this reason they, in their turn, are not to be taken literally. It is rather that when the dust falls from before our eyes, human beings are themselves the gods and demons, acting out, not the piddling business of worldly life, but the great archetypal situations and dramas of the myths. The gods are the archetypes, but they exist as perpetually incarnate in ourselves. In the mythic vision men appear as incarnations of the archetypal gods because the full and eternal significance of what they are doing appears. They are not just earning livings and raising families and pursuing hobbies: they are playing out, with innumerable variations, the cosmic drama of hide-and-seek, lost-and-found, which, as I shall try to show later, is the mono-plot behind all plots. In the light of this vision, the whole world of man and nature acquires an atmosphere that we may call variously divine, luminous, enchanted, timeless, archetypal, because, on the one hand, the senses—undistracted by too much concern to survive—are made available for the world as it is. On the other, every role that is played—divine or demonic—by being seen in terms of the cosmic drama is also seen as having its fit and essential place. It is this assumption into a universal wholeness which gives the individual a significance in the mythic vision far beyond anything that he may have in the factual vision. This is why the lives, the occupations, and the artifacts of so-called primitive peoples are so deeply permeated with ritual. This is not just formal politeness or good taste, just as the symbols upon their artifacts are not decoration. It is the recognition that all which happens here is a reflection, or dramatization, of what happens *in divinis.**

Schorer has said that the mythological image is what gives sense and organization to experience. A. K. Coomaraswamy went so far as to say that "myth embodies the nearest approach to absolute truth that can be stated in words."[8] All this is because the poetic, mythical, or mystical mode of vision perceives orders and relationships which, as I have tried to show, escape factual description. The factual language dissects and disintegrates experience into categories and oppositions that cannot be resolved. It is the language of either/or,

---

* Perhaps this is why, if our vision should ever have been transformed in the manner described by Hampole and Traherne, the artifacts of such peoples appear to be amazingly natural and even "realistic."

and from its standpoint all that is on the dark side of life—death, evil, and suffering—cannot be assimilated. There is nothing for it but to get rid of it. But,

> "If seven maids with seven mops
>   Swept it for half a year,
> Do you suppose," the Walrus said,
>   "That they would sweep it clear?"
> "I doubt it," said the Carpenter,
>   And shed a bitter tear.

By contrast, the language of myth and poetry is integrative, for the language of the image is *organic* language. Thus it expresses a point of view in which the dark side of things has its place, or rather, in which the light and the dark are transcended through being seen in the terms of a dramatic unity. This is the catharsis, or soul-cleansing function, of the tragic drama.

It is for this reason that I am taking as the theme of this volume the myths of polarity, myths which deal with the conflicting dualities of life and their reconciliation. And as a subordinate and logically connected motif I shall consider some representative myths of the function of the Demon, of the principle of darkness and evil. As already indicated, the polar vision or, as it is often called, the ambivalence of the mythological image implies a coincidence or reconciliation of opposites which, in the factual and practical world, would seem impossible or immoral. It is thus a theme which can hardly be introduced without some preliminary philosophical considerations.

For some reason profound and sensitive people are never content with such clear and drastic solutions to the problem of duality as that which is proposed in popular Christian orthodoxy: that the final goal of existence is the everlasting reward and perpetuation of goodness to the total exclusion of evil, and the everlasting punishment or annihilation of its perpetrators. This solution arouses the same sort of intuitive disquiet as all other forms of metaphysical dualism in that it leaves us with a picture of the world which, because it contains an element which is not integrated, fails to make sense as a whole. On the other hand, there is as much disquiet with the idea of a simple monism. We cannot quite swallow the second Isaiah's reaction to Zoroastrian dualism: "I am the Lord and there is none else. I form the light and create the darkness; I make peace and create evil. I, the Lord, do all these things." The thought is morally and practically confusing. It is just the kind of sophistry which the Devil himself would employ to blind the conscience of his victims and to spread the confusion of the witches' spell, "Fair is foul and foul is fair."

A problem which has for centuries occupied the most subtle philosophers and theologians will not, of course, be settled here. But much of this discussion may be bypassed if we realize that the problem is not answerable in the terms in which it is proposed, simply because they confuse the map with the territory. Good and evil are abstract categories like up and down, and categories do not perform their function unless they are kept distinct. It is thus perfectly proper that the *concepts* of good and evil be distinct, dualistic, and irreconcilable, that they be as firm and clear as any other measure. The "problem of duality" arises only when the abstract is confused with the concrete, when it is thought that there are as clearly distinguishable entities in the natural universe. As we have seen, factual language, in which categories of this kind belong, is never more than a strictly limited symbolism for what is happening in nature. The image, poetic or mythic, is closer than linguistic categories to events themselves, or to what I would rather call natural patterning. We pay for the exactitude of factual language with the price of being able to speak from only one point of view at a time. But the image is many-sided and many-dimensioned, and yet at the same time imprecise; here again, it is like nature itself.

The same must be said of such other duality problems as those of freedom and determinism, randomness and order, multiplicity and unity. By changing the point of view, what is actually happening may be seen as having now one aspect and now the other, and though this may be contradictory for the categories of formal thought, it is not so in actual existence. It is thus that in Christian theology Christ and Satan are irreconcilably opposed; but in the imagery of Christian mythology the Serpent does duty for both—"for as Moses lifted up the serpent in the wilderness, so also shall the Son of Man be lifted up."

What this means for practical action is that we accept the standards of logic and morals, not exactly with reservations, but with a certain humor. We will try to keep them, knowing that we shall not altogether succeed. We shall commit ourselves to positions and promises as best we may, knowing always that there must be a *Hintergedanke*—a thought far in the back of the mind which, like crossed fingers, gives us an "out" when pressed too far. We shall realize that behind our devotion to duty there is always a strong element of self-admiration, and that even in the most passionate love of others there is inevitably the aspect of personal gratification.

This attitude of gentle cynicism has always been characteristic of highly cultured and humane people, and in the fellowship of those who can "let their hair down" with each other and express the warmest friendship in such terms as, "Well, you old rascal!" The whole possibility of loving affection between human beings depends upon the recognition and acceptance of an element of irreducible rascality in oneself and others—though to parade it is just as much hypocrisy as the advertisement of one's virtues. The power of fanaticism, "effective" as it may be, is always bought at the price of unconsciousness, and whether its cause be good or evil it is invariably destructive because it works against life: it denies the ambivalence of the natural world.

But the very fact that the name of the angel of evil is Lucifer, the light-bearer, suggests that there might be something formative and creative in becoming conscious of one's own evil principle, or dark side, or innate rascality. Is it entirely a question of coming in with a bright light and a scrubbing brush to clean the darkness out? All contemporary work in psychotherapy suggests a very different attitude: to become so conscious of one's own selfishness that one begins to know what it is actually seeking, to penetrate the central core of self-love. It is the advice of the Arabian gnostic Monoimus: "Learn whence is sorrow and joy, and love and hate, and waking though one would not, and sleeping though one would not, and getting angry though one would not, and falling in love though one would not. And if thou shouldst closely investigate all these things, thou wilt find

God in thyself, one and many, just as the atom; thus finding from thyself a way out of thyself."[9] For by the principle of polarity we should find far down at the roots of the love of self the love of the other. Not to see that the two are inseparable is ignorance and unconsciousness, but in seeing this the opposition is transcended. Then it becomes clear that self and other are the terms in which love plays hide-and-seek with itself, and the wheel is set in motion of which Dante says:

> My will and my desire were both revolved,
> As is a wheel in even motion driven,
> By Love, which moves the sun and other stars.[10]

I have said that the historical approach to mythology has been overemphasized. Furthermore, it seems that there are overwhelming difficulties in the way of learning very much about mythogenesis by means of this approach—simply because the peoples and cultures we are trying to study are no longer with us, and we have therefore no direct way of studying the motivations and meanings behind their images. Nor is it safe to assume that existing "primitive" cultures are truly representative of human life in its earlier beginnings, plausible as the idea may be. Nor, alas, can we be quite sure that ontogeny repeats the patterns of phylogeny, that as the fetus seems to rehearse the stages of man's biological evolution, the growth of the child's mind rehearses the intellectual maturation of the race.

But the problem of mythogenesis is not simply a problem of the past. Today as yesterday men are still eating and breeding, and our study of digestion and reproduction is based on materials that are with us in the present. Likewise, men are still poetizing and creating myths. Perhaps, then, the most fruitful way for us to approach mythogenesis is through such disciplines as psychology, sociology, and literary and artistic criticism—keeping, however, an open mind toward all that historical evidence has to offer. As Aldous Huxley once remarked, no one would think of talking about a specifically medieval stomachache because stomachaches are in a class of nonhistorical experiences. And if this is true of stomachaches, may we not assume that the psychophysical processes of perception have undergone relatively little change throughout the past three thousand years, and that what we know about them might thus provide a point of departure for thinking about the genesis of myth? It provides a foundation, on top of which sociological and thus historical factors come into play.

According to the *Gestalt* theory of perception, we are not aware of any figure—be it an image, sound, or tactile impression—except in relation to a background. No sound or form is recognizable save in contrast with relative silence or formlessness. The reverse is also true. In experiments which attempt to expose perception to nothing but background, experiments in "sensory deprivation," the individual is compelled to supply the missing figuration by fantasy. What we perceive, then, is never a figure alone but a figure/ground relationship. The primary "unit" of perception is therefore neither the thing (figure) nor the space (ground) in which it appears: it is the field or relationship of the two. Thus it is simply impossible to conceive of a square, or other enclosed area, with nothing whatsoever outside its border.

Translating these observations into a kinesthetic language, we see that there is no awareness of motion except in relation to stillness, or of the freedom of motion except in relation to a degree of resistance. Our consciousness of the movement of the arm is precisely the sensation of muscular energy overcoming weight. Furthermore, the manifestation of any natural form whatsoever is a relationship of arrest and movement, of limited energy, and thus it might be said that consciousness is nothing other than the sensation of frustration and strife. As Heraclitus said at the dawn of Western thought, "War is both father and king of all....It should be understood that war is the common condition, that strife is justice, and that all things come to pass through the compulsion of strife. Homer was wrong in saying, 'Would that strife might perish from amongst gods and men.' For if that were to occur, then all things would cease to exist."[11]

Once stated, all this seems to be completely obvious. Yet the *Gestalt* theory of perception was at its inception a revelation or discovery, and the experimental images with which the *Gestalt* psychologists prove their points are perennially fascinating because they never fail to convey this obvious relationship without inducing in us a certain sense of shock or surprise. Consider the familiar image of a figure/ground constellation illustrated on page 24. If we attend to the enclosed white area, we see a chalice. But if we attend to the surrounding black area, we see two faces in profile, about to kiss. The point of the experiment is that we cannot see both at once—or perhaps that we find it intensely difficult to do so. Nevertheless, a single glance at the image reveals all that is there: the black and white areas are perceived simultaneously. The difficulty is that we cannot entertain the two interpretations of the image simultaneously. For our linear, one-thing-at-a-time thinking process, the image is *either* a chalice *or* kissing faces; for the logic of thought the two images are mutually exclusive (Though what happens if one thinks of the image as a loving cup?)

FIGURE 1

In other words, we think by ignoring—or by attending to one term of a relationship (the figure) and neglecting the other (the ground). Thus in the sensation of "free" movement what captures attention is the motion of the limb as distinct from the resisting weight. In looking at trees against the sky, what strikes us as significant is the area contained by the outline of the trees rather than the shape of the space containing them. Yet for the artist, whether painter or photographer, the shape of the ground is as important as that of the figure. He cannot ignore the ground without producing some unpleasing disproportion in his work. For the same reason the astronomer cannot for long study the stars without becoming preoccupied with the "properties" of space.

Surely it is now clear that this contrast between the figure/ground image, on the one hand, and our exclusive conceptual interpretations, on the other, is of the same kind which holds between the mythic image and factual language. Surely, too, our conscious ignoring of the ground is related to the psychological mechanism of repression. May not this be why myth and dream alike seem to proffer a kind of compensatory vision to that of conscious thought? They are intimations of the ignored and repressed aspects of the perceptual field—aspects to which we respond organically but not consciously.

It is not surprising, therefore, that all forms of "depth psychology" seem in some way to "take sides with the Devil" by calling attention to the aspect of things which the conscious orientation of a society ignores and devalues. For there is a point, not at all easy to determine, at which inattention and opposition to the essential ambivalence of nature becomes neurotic, becomes, in other words, an attitude against life—or life-and-death. Up to that point the selective function of consciousness, separating what is significant from what is not, is the creative and formative principle of all culture. But, needless to say, one must not go too far. If motion completely annihilates resistance, all form dissolves. If discipline altogether controls spontaneity, grace is entirely lost. This only goes to show that significant form in art and nature is not an encounter of two separate principles—motion on the one hand and resistance on the other. Form is motion/resistance. In nature they are never found apart; only in thought can they be distinguished. Hence the wisdom of the proverb, "Give the Devil his due." For the dark side of life, the principle of evil or of man's irreducible rascality, is to be "reckoned with" not merely because it may overwhelm the light, but rather because it is the condition of there being any light at all.

This recognition of the two-sidedness of the One is what makes the difference between the exoteric and esoteric aspects of a religion, and the latter is always guarded and is always mystical or "closed" (from the Greek μνειν) because of the danger that the opposites will be confused if their unity is made explicit. It is thus that mysticism is never quite orthodox, never wholly respectable. "Inside knowledge" of this kind is taboo in somewhat the same way as the exposure of the sexual organs. For as the latter is reserved for special occasions between special people, the former is reserved to an elite minority—to those who can be trusted not to spoil a game through the knowledge that it is, after all, just a game. "Don't give the show away" because "the show must go on." And "the show" here is all manifestation—the cosmic game of hide-and-seek, of God not letting his right hand know what his left is doing. Thus superb accomplishment in any art comes at the point where the beholder and the artist himself have the impression that the work is happening naturally, of itself. Though Voltaire said that if God did not exist it would be necessary to invent him, only those myths are convincing which "come to us" and are not consciously devised. For a skill is mastered to the degree that it is "othered," that is, to the extent that it is handed over to unconscious functioning and does not appear to be something that "I" am doing. So also, in mystical traditions, God "others" himself in creating the world, in creating the appearance of innumerable creatures acting on their own. Yet in his own "secret counsels" the Lord knows very well that there are no others, for "I am the Lord, and there is none beside me." Brahma, too, is "one without a second" and the appearance of the world of multiplicity is maya, which, among its numerous meanings, denotes art or skill.

Initiation into the mysteries always represents an expansion of consciousness and an overcoming of ignorance, of the maya-illusion into which the Godhead plunges to give the appearance of otherness and multiplicity. The initiate thus transcends himself, as the ego-subject, by becoming conscious of the ignored aspect of his own nature: the whole world of others which had seemed to confront him as an alien object, including also the disowned or unconscious aspects of his own organism. At this moment he sees through the game and is, one might almost say, tempted to stop playing because the possibility of desiring or choosing the good rather than the bad appears to be quite unreal. As the Buddha is reported to have exclaimed in the moment of his Awakening:

> Through birth and rebirth's endless round,
> Seeking in vain, I hastened on
> To find who framed this edifice....

> O builder, I have discovered thee!
> Never shalt thou rebuild this fabric!
> Now the rafters are all shattered,
> And the ridge-pole lies broken!
> The mind has attained Nirvana,
> Knowing the end of all desire![12]

This moment corresponds to the *pralaya* of Hindu cosmology, to Brahma's periodic withdrawal of the manifested world into his own undifferentiated essence. Correspondingly, the illuminated or awakened sage withdraws into silent contemplation.

> In the space within the heart lies the controller of all, the lord of all, the ruler of all. He does not become greater by good works nor smaller by evil works. He is the bridge that serves as the boundary to keep the different worlds apart....Verily, because they know this, the ancient (sages) did not wish for offspring. What shall we do with offspring (they said), we who have attained this Self, this world. They, having risen above the desire for sons, the desire for wealth, the desire for worlds, led the life of a mendicant....This Self is (that which has been described as) not this, not this.* He is incomprehensible for He is never comprehended. He is indestructible for He cannot be destroyed. He is unattached for He does not attach Himself. He is unfettered, He does not suffer, He is not injured. These two thoughts do not overcome him who knows this: for some reason he has done evil or for some reason he has done good. He overcomes both. What he has done or what he has not done does not burn him.[13]

---

* The formula *neti, neti*, indicating that because the supreme Self is beyond all duality, no "this" can be predicated of it, for every "this" is a defining class which must have an outside as well as an inside, i.e., an opposite.

But the Indian mind grasped a deeper solution to the problem of life than mere withdrawal. On the one hand, to withdraw is a separative and thus essentially selfish position. On the other, to choose not to play rather than to play is still to choose, and thus to remain in duality. Therefore the most truly awakened sages are represented as coming back to participate in the life of the world out of "compassion for all sentient beings," playing the game of good against evil, success against failure, in the full knowledge that it is a game (*lila*). In this sense the sage is "two-faced" like Brahma himself, for there is the *saguna* aspect of Brahma which is involved in the world and the *nirguna* aspect which remains uninvolved, the face looking outward toward the world of duality and multiplicity, and the face looking inward to the undifferentiated center.

It is not surprising, then, that various mythologies recognize a curious analogy between the divine ambivalence of God or of the savior-sage and the less respectable ambivalence of the Trickster, Joker, Conjurer, and Player. The analogy was by no means repugnant to so devout a Christian as G. K. Chesterton, who used it in his poem "The Skeleton."

> Chattering finch and water-fly
> Are not merrier than I;
> Here among the flowers I lie
> Laughing everlastingly.
> No: I may not tell the best;
> Surely, friends, I might have guessed
> Death was but the good King's jest,
> It was hid so carefully.[14]

Writing of the role of the Trickster in Amerindian and Greek mythology, Karl Kerényi says, "Archaic social hierarchies are exceedingly strict. To be archaic does not mean to be chaotic. Quite the contrary: nothing demonstrates the meaning of the all-controlling social order more impressively than the religious recognition of that which evades this order, in a figure who is the exponent and personification of the life of the body: never wholly subdued, ruled by lust and hunger, forever running into pain and injury, cunning and stupid in action. Disorder belongs to the totality of life, and the spirit of this disorder is the trickster. His function in archaic society, or rather the function of his mythology, of the tales told about him, is to add disorder to order and so make a whole, to render possible, within the fixed bounds of what is permitted, an experience of what is not permitted."[15]

In this connection one thinks, too, of the ambivalence of the carnival and the holiday, the one a *carnem levare*, a putting off of the flesh (as food) as on Shrove Tuesday, the Mardi Gras, which precedes the Lenten fast, and the other a holy day. Both are occasions for a spree, for play instead of work, license instead of law. So also the institutions of the Sabbath, the day on which God rested from creation, and the Year of Jubilee, in which all debts are canceled, are types of the *pralaya* wherein the cosmic game and the rules of the game are temporarily suspended. These are the conventional hints or cues, corresponding to the proscenium arch of the theater, that the world-order is a drama and is not to be taken with final and absolute seriousness. In their differing dimensions, aristocrat and peasant, sage and primitive, seem to have an awareness of this which is seldom characteristic of those in the middle—the unhappy bourgeoisie.

To the extent that myth is primitive philosophy, such

philosophy would have a sharper intuition of the world's ambivalence than the either/or style of more logical thinking. There are thus numerous folktales having to do with the fundamental partnership of God and the Devil. Eliade[16] cites a Bulgarian legend according to which God was one day walking all alone when he perceived his shadow and exclaimed, "Get up, friend!" Thereupon Satan rose up from the shadow of God and asked that the universe be divided between them, the earth for himself and the heavens for God, the living for God and the dead for himself. The two then signed a contract to this effect. The Mordvins of Central Asia say that one day when God was sitting alone upon a rock, he said to himself, "If I had a brother, I would create the world!" At this he spat upon the waters and from the spittle arose a mountain. God clove the mountain with his sword and out stepped the Devil, who at once proposed that they should be brothers. "We shall not be brothers," answered God, "but companions." And together they set about the creation of the world.

Citing many such examples, Eliade goes on to say, "It is enough for us to have established that, at the level of religious folklore among central Asian and European peoples long since converted to Islam or Christianity, there is still felt the necessity of making a place for the Devil; not only in the creation of the world—which would be understandable by the need to explain the origin of evil—but also in the presence of God, as a companion born of God's desire to come out of his solitude.....What is significant for us is that the popular soul should have been compelled to imagine the solitude of the Creator and his companionship with the Devil, the role of the latter as servant, of collaborator, and even as supreme counselor of God; to imagine, again, the divine origin of the Devil, for at root the spittle of God is nonetheless divine spittle; and finally to imagine a certain 'sympathy' between God and the Devil which is not without reminder of the 'sympathy' between the Creator and Mephistopheles."

At this same primitive, imagistic level of thought, language itself is sometimes as ambivalent as the image. In a celebrated essay on "The Antithetical Sense of Primal Words"[17] Freud quotes extensively from the work of the nineteenth-century German philologist Carl Abel, who pointed out that "man has not been able to acquire even his oldest and simplest conceptions otherwise than in contrast with their opposite; he only gradually learnt to separate the two sides of the antithesis and think of the one without conscious comparison with the other." Abel then cites a number of words from the earliest known forms of Egyptian which have such meanings as "strongweak," "oldyoung," "farnear," "bindloose," and "outsideinside." And there are many more recent examples:

Altus (Latin) = "high" and "deep."
Sacer (Latin) = "holy" and "accursed."
Boden (German) = "attic" and "ground floor."
Cleave (English) = "hold to" and "divide."
Compare *clamare* (Latin) "to cry" with *clam* (Latin) "softly."
Siccus (Latin) "dry" with *succus* (Latin) "juice."
Bös (German) "bad" with *bass* (German) "good."
Bat (Old Saxon) "good" with English *bad*.

The hypothesis is suggestive, but I am not aware of any more recent research that has carried it further.

The import of what has been said thus far is that, however immersed in the pursuit of success, pleasure, survival, and the good life, man retains in the back of his mind an apprehension of the figure/ground structure of all his perceptions. This apprehension expresses itself in mythic and poetic images rather than factual statement. And this "back" of the mind refers alike to what is back in time, as primitive intuition, to what is repressed to emerge only in the symbolism of "the unconscious," and to what is "recovered" in mystical wisdom by deep insight. The apprehension is simultaneously holy, or esoteric, and obscene, or unmentionable, because it subverts in one way or another the conscious ideals of the social order, intent, as they are, on achieving the victory of light over darkness. The higher subversion is the way of the monk or ascetic who sets himself apart from the life of the world. The lower subversion is the way of the libertine who defies the order of the world. But transcending both is the way of what in Buddhism is called the Bodhisattva, and in Chinese philosophy, the King-Without-and-Sage-Within: the way, that is, of the liberated soul who takes on in the spirit of play the task which others view as a matter of life *or* death. In another role he is the Fool or Jester, representing what Gerald Heard has called "meta-comedy" and Chesterton "the good King's jest," the laughter at oneself and with one's Self upon discovering play instead of battle behind the contest of Heaven and Hell. But, as Cervantes said, "The most difficult character in comedy is that of the fool, and he must be no simpleton that plays the part."

I have suggested that behind almost all myth lies the mono-plot of the game of hide-and-seek. Naturally there are excep-tions, but for the most part this theme is so obvious that it hardly needs demonstration. For, generally speaking, the very structure of a plot has the threefold form of (a) a status quo, (b) its upsetting, and (c) its restoration or transformation. Tragedy alone lacks the third stage, though one might say that it lies in the catharsis of the audience. Although this plot form might be taken from the cyclic rhythm of sun, seasons, and vegetation, its eternal fascination seems to be at the very roots of human nature. Any baby will burble with delight at the game of making one's face disappear and then appear again from behind a book. As we have seen, normal human consciousness always depends on contrasts, whether in space or in time, and tends to ignore what is constant even though it provides the necessary background for the percep-tion of change. If, then, a pleasurable state is to be conscious, it cannot be constant, for there will be no contrasting ground against which to feel it. Pleasure is thus in fact the config-uration pleasure/nonpleasure (e.g., pleasure/pain, pleasure/anxiety, pleasure/boredom, pleasure/hunger, etc.) in which the first term is the figure and the second the ground. There-fore to find or seek pleasure in the figure, it must be lost or hidden in the ground.

The truth of this does not depend on the meaningless assertion that men naturally seek pleasure. Pleasure is an abstraction from specific situations, and, as such, does not operate as the motivating cause for regarding those situa-tions as goals. (This is, no doubt, why extraneous rewards and punishments have so little effect upon the positive growth of character.) The point is that no specific situation is a constantly pleasurable figure, for whatever is constant tends to become ground.

Now in watching a drama or reading a story we know, at least in the back of our minds, that the situation is "in play." We have therefore not the least objection to there being a "villain of the piece" or other agency which upsets the initial status quo. On the contrary, this is just what we expect to see, and, at the end of the show, hero and villain alike are applauded. For the hero is the hero just because of the villain. To put it in another way, the convention of the stage or the proscenium arch enables us to see that the deeds of the villain are *grounds* for the heroism of the hero, and we recognize the necessity of the relationship. By "framing" the ground the proscenium arch makes it mutually significant with the figure.

In life, however, the situation is different. We tend to ignore the significance of the ground, as well as its necessity. Hence the restless pursuit of pleasure as if it could be a constant figure, ignoring and making no allowance for its nonpleasurable ground. But there is no way of getting rid of the ground. It impinges upon our senses however much our conscious attention may attempt to avoid it.

The ground-sensations that we try to avoid are such things as disorder, emptiness, nonpleasure, boredom, monotony, anxiety, darkness, and death. In terms of most value systems all these are meaningless. But myth, as we have seen, is a complex of images which give significance to life as a whole. It dramatizes the order/disorder of the world in such a way as to make disorder relative to order, to give the villain his part and the Devil his due. To reject the wisdom of myth we should therefore have to abandon the whole philosophy of relativity—to assert that space has no properties, that environment is a meaningless idea, and that wholes and fields are no more than empty concepts. Strange, then, as it may seem, the devaluation of myth would require a reversal of the main direction of scientific thought at the present time. We forget that a world intelligible to man is an anthropomorphic world, and that as science succeeds in making the world intelligible it moves toward myth in making it anthropomorphic. This does not mean that all ancient myths must be restored to the status of scientific fact, for the form of man, in the very act of making the universe intelligible, is changing. Man makes God in his own image, and as he comes to a clearer and more intelligible view of his own image—changing it in the process—he comes to a more intelligible view of God.

Yet as the world becomes more intelligible, it also becomes more mysterious—not, perhaps, in the sense of being problematic and baffling, but of being immeasurably grander, vaster, more complex, and, indeed, more *imaginative* than we had supposed. The world becomes intelligible through amazing reversals of common sense, and, as Whitehead saw, the notions most worth questioning are just those which are most taken for granted. Science, too, is the game of hide-and-seek, for the scientist most skillful in basic research has the peculiar flair for realizing that the best hiding places are those where no one would think of looking: they are usually right out in the open. How often an important discovery floors us with its simplicity, with the feeling of, "Well, why didn't *I* see that; it was right under my nose!" And in due course this develops the odd sensation that comprehension is near rather than far, and that what has to be kept in mind is not so much the answer as the form of the question. The hidden lies in the very process of seeking.

I cannot resist the intuition that, in some quite unexpected way, the scientist is going to find himself coming back to the truth of the ancient Hindu aphorism *tat tvam asi*—That art thou! For where, indeed, could "the Mystery" be more cleverly hidden than right in the seeking and the seeker—"nearer...than breathing, closer than hands and feet." If so, the basic mythology of the Hindu worldview may attain a new dignity; to some extent it has already done so. For this is the dramatic image of Brahma playing hide-and-seek with himself through all the ages of time, concealing himself with infinite ingenuity in the endless variety of apparently separate forms and beings, throwing himself away to recover himself with ever renewed surprise, plunging into ever more fantastically lost situations so that the finding again is all the more astounding. The image is obviously anthropomorphic, but it grows in depth and suggestiveness as one realizes that the form of man extends far, far beyond the limits of the skin and very much deeper than the conscious ego.

The image has, of course, a certain disquiet for the Christian West with its strong insistence on the otherness of God, upon the real separateness of persons, and upon the eternal gulf which is fixed between good and evil. But there is a sense in which the image includes these values, for it is all part of the game of "othering" that these distinctions should acquire intense reality. If, at root, they are a maya—a divine and cosmic fantasy—this does not make the fantasy any the less remarkable as a work of art.

Such images are likewise distasteful to the current temper of Western philosophy because they seem to be pseudo-scientific propositions—statements of fact of the same kind as that the earth revolves around the sun, but actually bereft of all meaning. But I have tried to show that statements of fact and mythological images belong to two quite different languages, and that the logic of one does not apply to the logic of the other. Atomic facts are a weft that lies upon the warp of their essential relativity. Strangely, this word which implies relatedness and unity has come to mean a kind of undependable miasma. But this is how water seems to a person who cannot swim.

One of the principal difficulties which the Westerner, and more especially the Christian, encounters in trying to understand polarity is, as we have just seen, the absolute gulf which our tradition has set between good and evil. It is inconceivable that there should be any common ground, let alone common cause, between God and Satan. The conflict here is seen to be ultimately real and serious, so much so that the suggestion that there is some profound, inner level at which God and Satan are at one seems to be the height of blasphemy. Our study of polarity can therefore profit from a special consideration of the mythology of the Devil, of the images of evil, and of the attitudes which they evoke. This must include, too, what might be called the "non-images" of evil, far more potent in their suggestion of supernatural horror than comparably abstract images of God in suggestion of divine glory. For every really sophisticated conception of the Devil is allusive: nothing is specified, but there is just the intimation that the *real* design and nature of evil is something so ghastly that ordinary people are quite unable even to imagine it.

Few writers have been able to evoke the horror of evil more imaginatively than Arthur Machen, and I am including a passage from one of his stories in which the raconteur insists that the essence of evil is not to be found in the crudities of common vice but in a kind of genius for the subtly unnatural. "If the roses and the lilies suddenly sang on this coming morning; if the furniture began to move in procession, as in De Maupassant's tale!" Evil is sensed, ultimately, in the gooseflesh and chills which arise in the presence of sorcery, of magic subverting the laws of nature. I remember the way I felt many years ago when someone gave me serious reasons for believing that a very attractive young woman was in fact an old lady of eighty. Or think of someone removing a glove to reveal, not a hand, but a bird's claw. Comic or fanciful descriptions of such things are all very well, but one has to imagine coming upon them in sober reality. We feel intimations of that pure panic which arises in absolutely unpredictable situations, the terror of believing that nature or oneself is the victim of a sinister insanity. It is sinister because these subversions of the natural are always felt to be the work of a powerful malignance whose capabilities and intentions are never precisely known.

Evil is sensed preeminently, then, in what is strangely alien—not in sheer chaos and nonsense, but in profoundly odd and unnerving disturbances of the normal. This is certainly the formula of the best horror stories. It is significant, however, that we read such tales for entertainment and find an extraordinary fascination in them—as well as in all the cruder manifestations of darkness from crime reports to public executions. Generally speaking, the fascination depends upon the experience being vicarious, but nonetheless there is a long tradition supporting the idea that the Evil One is above all alluring. The allure may be exercised in two ways: through overt beauty—notably through the charms of the opposite sex—or through the direct fascination of horror itself. On the one hand there is the baited trap or the poisoned fruit of fair and luscious form; on the other there is the vertiginous attraction of the dreadful, fascinating its victim as a snake seems to hypnotize a bird.

Only rather seldom is the good, or God, represented with allure, for of the trinity of goodness, truth, and beauty, the latter has very largely been annexed by the Devil. It is thus that literary and artistic representations of the divine rarely have the same verve and aesthetic allure as of the diabolic. Perhaps the painters of Chinese landscapes and Persian miniatures have come nearer than anyone to a persuasive vision of paradise, and the West has approached it in stained glass, in illuminated manuscripts, and in the jewelry of enamels and mosaics. All of this is, however, rather static and glistering as compared with the riots of imagination which have gone into the depiction of the Inferno. For all its splendor of detail, van Eyck's *Adoration of the Lamb* is emotionally tame in comparison with his vision of Hell in *The Last Judgment*. Is it unfair to take as representative of this point Gustave Doré's remarkable illustrations for the *Divina Commedia*? The engravings for the Inferno and the Purgatorio are rich with imagination. In contrast, those for the Paradiso are merely insipid—female angels in white nighties tripping through the skies. Reproduced here for comparison (plates 10 and 11) are his opposed visions of the central depth of Hell and the angelic choirs in the form of a rose about the light of the Godhead. Here there can be no doubt, in Dante's own words, that "vision failed the lofty fantasy." The vast icy cavern in which Satan broods with everlasting malignance is distinctly more impressive. Were it not for the dark silhouette of Beatrice and Dante upon the foreground cloud, the heavenly vision would have no character at all.

In general it seems that, in artistic representation, hell is exuberant and heaven is not. To put it in very contemporary and expressive terms, heaven does not "swing." Coming right down to the mythological images of modern times, we have but to compare the last two phases of Walt Disney's *Fantasia*. The representation of Walpurgis Night to Mussorgsky's *Night on Bald Mountain*, supervised by that splendid fantast, Kay Nielsen, was so powerfully erotic and sinister that, when I first saw it, one or two people screamed for the show to be stopped. But at the midnight bell the forces of Light took over with incomparable sentimentality. Schubert's *Ave Maria*, and a procession of shadowy figures—monks, perhaps—carrying candles through a cathedral-like forest!

(It should be noted in passing that the situation is rather different in music. There is little diabolical music of any artistic merit as compared with the magnificent tradition of sacred music from Gregorian chant, through Palestrina, Bach, and Handel, to Walton and Fauré. Nevertheless, it used to be said in early medieval times that "the Devil has all the good tunes." For the melodies of many of our traditional hymns and carols are taken from popular ballads.)

The problem of the allure of the image of evil does not permit easy generalizations. In the West, at least, the realm of the Devil has been more favorable than the divine for the projection of erotic and orgiastic themes, largely of a sado-masochistic type, since vicarious agony is suggestive of the orgasmic convulsion. Perhaps we may be helped in this puzzle by the little that we know of erotic history in the Western world. G.R. Taylor[18] has pointed out that a truly sinister and malignant image of the Devil does not appear in Christian imagery until early in the fourteenth century. Prior to that time the Devil is, in popular representation, somewhat of a buffoon, and, in theology, "a pure spirit, dangerous and tempting but not the direct enemy of man."[19]* He goes on to associate the emergence of this abysmally evil image of the Devil with that epidemic of insanity which expressed itself in the persecution of witches and heretics by the Holy Inquisition. Since these tortures were quite obviously a pretext for sadistic lust, the atmosphere of this particular passion naturally transfers itself into images of the realm of darkness. The Devil's form is, after all, that of Pan, and attendant demons are satyrs; and, as the ministers of punishment in Hell, their images reflect the motivations of their creators. The allure of demonographic literature and painting is, to a considerable extent, pornographic.

---

*   This remark must be qualified, for in both New Testament and patristic writings the Devil has become the "adversary" of God and man. But imagination had not yet filled his image with the sinister and horrendous overtones of later times.

But since the demonographer is very often the same person as the preacher, the pornographic motivation must usually be unconscious or unadmitted. It is concealed under the pretext of righteous wrath and the fear of Hell, and so, at the same time, it is concealed that the Devil is made in the image of those who imagine him. The lustful Pan or the devouring monster are aspects of man that cannot be denied. How must we seem to the animals upon whom we prey for food? The sensation of being threatened, spiritually, by a weirdly alien and incalculable power of malice is, above all, a symptom of unconsciousness—of man's alienation from himself. Furthermore, inasmuch as he is unconscious of the Devil as his own image, he is the more apt to vent upon his fellows his fear of and fury at this disowned aspect of himself. This is why the acceptance of the Devil in and as oneself is a moral obligation.

May not this, then, be why the figure of the Evil One is simultaneously horrendous and alluring: he represents the extreme of "self-othering," where, on the human level, man is most ashamed of his own organism, and, on the mythological level, Brahma has lost himself most completely in the maya of separateness. The horrendous element of the experience belongs to the motion of hiding, and the alluring to the motion of seeking—to the dawning recognition of oneself in its most unfamiliar form. At times when any sort of puritanism is dominant, or any fanatical, one-sided view of man, the ignored aspect of our nature appears as an external devil, sometimes an angel or fallen spirit, and sometimes in the form of other people, as, say, in anti-Semitism. In a culture dominated by puritan forms of Christianity, the Devil will therefore be an external caricature of our erotic, animal, and self-seeking aspects.

As we shall see, the Christian Devil is unique. No other demonic figure has ever been conceived to be so purely malicious, so sinister, and so totally opposed to the universal design. And even in Christianity this image was not conceived in its full horror until the late Middle Ages. The formation of this image is perhaps a by-product of the growth of the peculiarly Western view of personality and its values, that is, of personality as grounded and centered upon consciousness and will, of man's essence as the individual and immortal soul. This view gains an intense sharpening of consciousness at the price of ignoring a great deal that is *also* human personality. It is a unique growth of consciousness in one way and loss of consciousness in another, and what is lost appears in the image of this implacable enemy of man and all his values.

To secure this growth of consciousness we must recover the lost or hidden dimensions of our nature; we must, as Jung would say, "integrate the Evil One." But whereas much has been done to rescue the erotic sphere of life from the Devil, we are still amazingly unaware of the social and ecological dimensions of the person. We therefore treat other societies or nations as the Devil, and speak of our technical progress as the war against nature.

In other cultures man's consciousness has been more diffuse, though less brilliantly concentrated—no microscopes, no telescopes, no scientific analysis, nor anything like the same degree of the feeling of individual responsibility and freedom. In the mythologies of India and China demons are never devils in our later Western sense. Hideous as their forms and functions may be, they are always aspects or agents of universal nature, and, almost invariably, the wrathful figures of Hindu-Buddhist iconography have one hand in the gesture (mudra) of "Fear not," to indicate that the apparition is another form of maya, another of the million masks of God. Even the Biblical Satan is far from being the Devil of later Christian doctrine, for in *The Book of Job* he appears simply as a sort of counsel for the prosecution in the Court of Heaven, the Lord's attorney general. For in the Hebrew matrix of Christianity, today as yesterday, there is no place for so dangerous a brush with the insanity of ultimate dualism as is involved in the full development of Christian demonology. As Kohler has put it, "There is no evil before God, since a good purpose is served even by that which appears bad. In the life of the human body pleasure and pain, the impetus to life and its restraint and inhibition form a necessary contrast, making for health; so, in the moral order of the universe, each being who battles with evil receives new strength for the unfolding of the good. The principle of holiness... transforms and ennobles every evil."[20]

Nature appears to be a hierarchy of many grades, corresponding to what the scientist calls "levels of magnification." Thus when we adjust our lenses to watch the individual cells of an organism we see only particular successes and failures, victories and defeats in what appears to be a ruthless "dog-eat-dog" battle. But when we change the level of magnification to observe the organism as a whole, we see that what was conflict at the lower level is harmony at the higher: that the health, the ongoing life of the organism is precisely the outcome of this microscopic turmoil. Now the expansion of

consciousness is no other than extending our vision to com-
prehend many levels at once, and, above all, to grasp those
higher levels in which the discords of the lower levels are
resolved. This is the greatness of human consciousness, but
at the same time it is always posing the practical problem of
how to live upon the lower level when one's understanding
reaches to the higher. For if we discover that there is some
superior order harmonizing what seem to be conflicts at the
level of our normal, individual consciousness, may not this
new understanding upset our standards and weaken the will
to fight? If we see that the Good of the world is not the victory of good over evil but, on the contrary, the tense polarity
of good-and-evil in perpetual conflict, is it not possible that
this will lead us to a recognition of the function of evil making it difficult for us to fight and hate it?

Continuing sanity demands a successful answer to this
problem. We must be able to live simultaneously upon several levels without getting them confused. We know, for example, that the earth revolves about the sun, but in our everyday
mundane life there are still many purposes for which we
retain the old geocentric view of the sun rising and setting
and moving daily across the sky. So, too, the mundane distinction between up and down remains unconfused by the
knowledge that these directions are reversed at the antipodes and do not exist at all in outer space. Similarly, the
physicist can treat light either as waves or as a stream of
particles without the layman's sense of flat contradiction
between the two concepts. As Kurt Marek has put it, the
change of consciousness which is necessary for containing
these apparent contradictions

is vividly exemplified for us by the failure of our attempts, hitherto, to make relativity comprehensible by means of mathematical demonstrations on the blackboard. Such efforts fail, not because the relativity theory is, as we thought, the product of an extravagantly *heightened* intellect, but that of an already *transformed* intellect. "Understanding" relativity presupposes not only a rather special intelligence, but new sense perceptions. This is demonstrated by every *young* physicist or mathematician who is already *living* (not merely thinking) in the new realms of space and time, and who simply cannot understand what is supposed to make relativity so hard to "explain." …Such a sudden intuitive grasp is illustrated by the rapidity with which the theory of antipodes, utterly *inconceivable* at the time of its appearance (because it contradicted sensory experience), came to be universally understood. Since Magellan, the earth has been not only *known* but also *experienced* as round so that the theory no longer requires a labored explanation.[21]

But the transformation of man's understanding does not always or necessarily imply an abandonment of the past. It is not the kind of intellectual change in which old ideas become automatically obsolete or foolish—just because they are old. On the contrary, intellectual growth often shows that we were wiser than we knew, especially in the sense that mythological images foreshadowed ideas which, at the time of their origin, could not be expressed in some more exact or scientific symbolism. Therefore in the panorama of images which follows I am presenting man's perennial intuition of the implicit concord and harmony which underlies the explicit discord and conflict of life as he finds it with the naked eye, at the "normal" level of magnification.

It remains now to outline the plan which the rest of this book will follow, and the reader may find it convenient to refer back to this outline as he passes from chapter to chapter.

Chapters 1 and 2, "The Primordial Pair" and "The Cosmic Dance," are based on Chinese and Indian sources, on Taoist, Buddhist, and Hindu myths and images in which the principle of polarity, of the inner unity of opposites, is explicitly recognized. I begin with these, not only to clarify the principle, but also to see what will happen if we take it as a hidden background for myths which do not appear to recognize it at all.

Chapter 3, "The Two Brothers," introduces us to myths—mostly from the Middle East—having to do with the conflict of good and evil, light and darkness. The fact that the pair, e.g., Horus and Set, Ohrmazd and Ahriman, are *brothers* intimates that there is still some recognition of the basic unity of the opposed forces. But, in general, as we move westward from the Indus basin, the common ground between the two drops out of sight, and the conflict begins to be a struggle to the death, fought in absolute seriousness.

Chapter 4, "Ultimate Dualism," follows the disappearance of this inner unity to its extreme: the Christian mythology of Satan and of the Hell of everlasting damnation. We see that this *absolute* separation of good from evil renders our choice between the two an ultimately perilous adventure. While this enriches life with a dimension of earnestness and momentousness hitherto unknown, it deprives the Divinity of all humor and playfulness. However, we see that the positive values of the contest between God and Satan are preserved, and the total insanity of ultimate dualism avoided, by the assumption of a "hidden conspiracy" between the two to conceal their unity. This is related to the Hindu concept of maya—the dramatic self-deception whereby the One plays at being the Many, and the Godhead lets itself be forgotten in pretending to be each individual being.

Chapter 5, "Dismemberment Remembered," brings us back—through the separation of the opposites—to their eternally implicit union. There are myths of the creation of the world through the cutting up of some primordial being, of its division into heaven and earth, into the multiplicity of things, or into the two sexes—from which follows the generation of offspring. Thus many mythologies envisage the goal of life as the "rememberment" of this original "dismemberment." The human ideal becomes, then, the hermaphroditic or androgynous sage or "divine-man," whose consciousness transcends the opposites and who, therefore, knows himself to be one with the cosmos. We conclude with visions of the universe seen from this point of view.

1. The Primordial Pair

WHAT, EXACTLY, IS POLARITY? It is something much more than simple duality or opposition. For to say that opposites are *polar* is to say much more than that they are far apart: it is to say that they are related and joined—that they are the terms, ends, or extremities of a single whole. Polar opposites are therefore *inseparable* opposites, like the poles of the earth or of a magnet, or the ends of a stick or the faces of a coin. Though what lies between the poles is more substantial than the poles themselves—since they are the abstract "terms" rather than the concrete body—nevertheless man thinks in terms and therefore divides in thought what is undivided in nature. To think is to categorize, to sort experience into classes and intellectual pigeonholes. It is thus that, from the standpoint of thought, the all-important question is ever, "Is it this, or is it that?" Is the experience inside this class, or is it outside? By answering such questions we describe and explain the world; we make it explicit. But implicitly, in nature herself, there are no classes. We drop these intellectual nets and boxes upon the world as we weave the imaginary lines of latitude and longitude upon the face of the earth and the, likewise imaginary, firmament of the stars. It is thus the imaginary, abstract, and conceptual character of these divisions which renders them polar. The importance of a box for thought is that the inside is different from the outside. But in nature the walls of a box are what the inside and the outside have in common.

It is thus that when anyone draws attention to the implicit unity of polar opposites we feel something of a shock. For the foundations of thought are shaken by the suspicion that experiences and values which we had believed to be contrary and distinct are, after all, aspects of the same thing. At the dawn of sophisticated thought in both China and the West this ever bewildering unity of opposites was pointed out by two almost mythical sages: Heraclitus, living in Greece about 500 BC, and Lao-tzu, supposedly a contemporary of Confucius (d. 479 BC), though probably living a century or more later.

In the fragments of Heraclitus's writing that have come down to us are a set of aphorisms which, if the polarity of opposites is overlooked, seem to be shocking paradoxes:

24. Time is a child moving counters in a game; the royal power is a child's.

25. War is both father and king of all; some he has shown forth as gods and others as men, some he has made slaves and others free.

26. It should be understood that war is the common condition, that strife is justice, and that all things come to pass through the compulsion of strife.

27. Homer was wrong in saying, "Would that strife might perish from amongst gods and men." For if that were to occur, then all things would cease to exist.

98. Opposition brings concord. Out of discord comes the fairest harmony.

99. It is by disease that health is pleasant; by evil that good is pleasant; by hunger, satiety; by weariness, rest.

100. Men would not have known the name of justice if these things had not occurred.

101. Sea water is at once very pure and very foul; it is drinkable and healthful for fishes, but undrinkable and deadly for men.

106. To God all things are beautiful, good, and right; men, on the other hand, deem some things right and others wrong.

107. Doctors cut, burn, and torture the sick, and then demand of them an undeserved fee for such services.

108. The way up and the way down are one and the same.

109. In the circle the beginning and the end, are common.

111. For wool-carders the straight way and the winding way are one and the same.

112. The bones connected by joints are at once a unitary whole and not a unitary whole. To be in agreement is to differ; the concordant is the discordant. From out of all the many particulars comes oneness, and out of oneness come all the many particulars.

113. It is one and the same thing to be living or dead, awake or asleep, young or old. The former aspect in each case becomes the latter, and the latter again the former, by sudden unexpected reversal.

114. Hesiod, whom so many accept as their wise teacher, did not even understand the nature of day and night; for they are one.

115. The name of the bow is life, but its work is death.*

---

* The pun disappears in translation, but in the original the word for *bow* is βιός, with the accent on the last syllable, and the word for *life* βίος, with the accent on the first.

117. People do not understand how that which is at variance with itself agrees with itself. There is a harmony in the bending back, as in the case of the bow and the lyre.

118. Listening not to me but to the Logos, it is wise to acknowledge that all things are one.

121. God is day and night, winter and summer, war and peace, satiety and want. But he undergoes transformations, just as [a neutral base], when it is mixed with a fragrance, is named according to the particular savor [that is introduced].

124. Even sleepers are workers and collaborators in what goes on in the universe.[22]

In the history and climate of Western thought Heraclitus stands somewhat alone, for a philosophy in which "it is one and the same thing to be living or dead, awake or asleep, young or old" does not seem to offer any directives for action, that is, for making choices. For us, the master philosopher is not Heraclitus but Aristotle, who insists that all action is choice and that the will never moves into action save to choose some good in preference to some evil—even if the choice be mistaken. By and large Western culture is a celebration of the illusion that good may exist without evil, light without darkness, and pleasure without pain, and this is true of both its Christian and secular, technological phases. Here, or hereafter, our ideal is a world in which "there shall be no more death, neither sorrow, nor crying, neither shall there be any more pain; for the former things are passed away."[23]

To give credit where credit is due, it has been a *grand* illusion. Yet for those whose common sense is still based on the logic of Aristotle it is difficult to appreciate that the foundations of Chinese culture rest upon the polar view of light and darkness. Compare, then, with Heraclitus the words of Lao-tzu:

> When everyone recognizes beauty as beautiful,
>   there is already ugliness;
> When everyone recognizes goodness as good,
>   there is already evil.
> "To be" and "not to be" arise mutually;
> Difficult and easy are mutually realized;
> Long and short are mutually contrasted;
> High and low are mutually posited;...
> Before and after are in mutual sequence.[24]

A culture based on such premises was not likely to produce a heroic technology. On the other hand, the polar view of good and evil by no means led to mere stultification, to a way of life without directives for action or capacity to realize order and grace. There is no question that, prior to the Industrial Revolution, the Chinese had in several periods of their history created the most commodious and sophisticated civilization that we have known anywhere in the world.

Unlike Heraclitus, Lao-tzu did not stand alone in his culture. His view of the world had roots in a mythological tradition already ancient in his time, a tradition absolutely basic to Chinese ways of thinking and feeling. This tradition is embodied in the *I Ching* or *Book of Changes*. Although a fabulous antiquity has been claimed for this classic, dating it back anywhere from 2000 to 1300 BC, there is no clear evidence for its existence as a written document until about 400 BC. Nevertheless, the system of symbolism upon which it is based is certainly most ancient, though the work as it now stands is the compilation of centuries. Generation after generation of Chinese scholars and thinkers commented upon it and projected back into its primary forms ideas and meanings which are, historically, quite late developments.

Basically, the *Book of Changes* is a sequence of sixty-four symbols or hexagrams of the type illustrated in figure 2. Each hexagram, as the term implies, consists of six lines which may be either broken or unbroken, negative or positive, and the sixty-four symbols constitute every possible arrangement of the two types of line in the chosen pattern. Unbroken lines represent yang, the male or positive aspect of nature, and broken lines yin, the female or negative aspect. These terms are said to have been first applied to the south and north sides of mountains, the former sunny and the latter shady. As the two sides of a mountain are an inseparable polarity, yang and yin came to signify the archetypal poles of nature—plus and minus, strong and yielding, man and woman, light and darkness, rising and falling. Consequently the sequence of sixty-four sixfold combinations of the two is understood as a symbolic epitome of the basic situations of life and nature. According to the arrangement and relative strength of

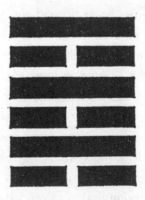

FIGURE 2

positive and negative forces, each hexagram represents the fundamental, skeletal structure of the disposition of nature at any given moment.

Each hexagram may, furthermore, be seen as composed of two trigrams, and the eight possible formations of trigrams are usually set out as illustrated in figure 3. The names assigned to each trigram, heaven, earth, water, fire, etc., stand for elemental principles in the changing pattern of nature,

and thus a hexagram having, say (earth) above

(mountain) designates a situation wherein it is propitious for greatness or power to be hidden, and for rulers and men of affairs to act with modesty.

FIGURE 3

The primary use of these symbols was for divination, and the actual text of the book is a set of oracles describing the situations represented and giving advice for appropriate action. While there are several methods for consulting the oracle, the most usual is to make random divisions of a bundle of fifty yarrow stalks which are then counted out according to a system which gives the hexagram corresponding to the present situation of the questioner. The assumption seems to be that random division of the stalks will in fact follow the order of the time at which it happens, giving a hexagram revealing the balance and disposition of natural forces operating at that particular time and place.

Tradition attributes the invention of the hexagrams to the sage-emperor Fu Hsi, reigning at the very beginnings of Chinese history.

> Anciently, when Fu Hsi had come to the rule of all under Heaven, he looked up and contemplated the forms exhibited in the sky (the constellations), and he looked down, contemplating the processes taking place on the earth. He contemplated the patterns of birds and beasts, and the properties of the various habitats and places. Near at hand, in his own body, he found things for consideration, and the same at a distance, in events in general. Thus he devised the eight trigrams, in order to enter into relations with the virtues of the Bright Spirits, and to classify the relations of the ten thousand things.[25]

The Great Appendix to the *Book of Changes* explains its general principles as follows:

> Heaven is high, earth is low; thus the *ch'ien* (heaven trigram) and *k'un* (earth trigram) are fixed. As high and low are thus

ordered, honorable and humble have their places. Movement and rest have their constancy; according to these strong and weak are differentiated. Ways coincide according to their species and things fall into classes. Hence good fortune and bad fortune come about. In the heavens phenomena appear; on earth shapes occur. Through these, change and transformation become manifest. Therefore the strong and the weak (lines in the trigrams) interplay, and the eight trigrams act and react upon each other. Things are roused by thunder and lightning; they are fertilized by wind and rain. Sun and moon revolve on their courses with a season of cold and then a season of heat. The way of the *ch'ien* constitutes the male, the way of the *k'un* constitutes the female. The *ch'ien* knows the great beginning; the *k'un* gives things their completion. The *ch'ien* knows through the easy; the *k'un* accomplishes through the simple....

Therefore the gentleman dwells securely in the emblems of the *Book of Changes* and delights in studying its explanations of the lines. When the gentleman is living quietly he observes the emblems and studies the explanations, and when he is about to act he observes their changes and studies their predictions. Therefore help comes to him from Heaven: good fortune and nothing that is not beneficial....

The successive movement of *yin* and *yang* constitutes what is called the Way (Tao). What issues from it is good, and that which brings it to completion is the individual nature. The man of humanity recognizes it and calls it humanity; the wise man recognizes it and calls it wisdom. The people use it daily and are not aware of it, for the Way of the gentleman is but rarely recognized. It manifests itself as humanity but conceals its workings. It rouses all things, but is free from the anxieties of the sage. Its glorious power and great reserve are perfect indeed! It possesses everything in abundance: this is its great reserve. It renews everything daily: this is its glorious power. It produces and reproduces, and hence it is called the Changes. As creator of the primal images, it is called *ch'ien*. As giver of forms in imitation of the images, it is called *k'un*. Because it enables one to explore the laws of number and know the future it is called divination. Because it affords the element of coherence in change it is called the course of affairs. That aspect of it which cannot be fathomed in terms of the *yin* and *yang* is called spirit.*...

Therefore in the Changes there is the Supreme Ultimate. This generates the two primary forms (the *yin* and the *yang*). The two primary forms generate the four modes.† The four modes generate the eight trigrams. The eight trigrams determine the good and bad fortune.[26]

The symbolism of the *Book of Changes* exhibits, therefore, a view of the dynamic pattern of nature constituted by the perpetual interplay of the primordial pair, yin and yang, in varying degrees of force and direction. Although the disposition of these forces is said to determine good and bad fortune, there is no hexagram in the whole book which is fundamentally bad, for wherever the negative force is in the ascendant it always contains, by implication, the seed of the positive. In Chinese thought the essential goodness of nature and human nature is precisely their good-and-bad. The two do not cancel each other out so as to make action futile: they play eternally in a certain order, and wisdom consists in the discernment of this order and acting in harmony with it. The

---

* That is, the implicit unity of the opposites, the tai chi or Supreme Ultimate—a term deriving from the ridgepole of a roof.
† The four modes are diagrams, two-line symbols, called the major and minor yin and the major and minor yang.

sage no more seeks to obliterate the negative—darkness, death, etc.—than to get rid of autumn and winter from the cycle of the seasons. There emerges, then, a view of life which sees its worth and point not as a struggle for constant ascent but as a dance. Virtue and harmony consist, not in accentuating the positive, but in maintaining a dynamic balance.

The familiar Chinese symbol of the primordial pair is the circle composed of what seem to be two stylized fishes, one black and one white, each with an "eye" of the opposite color:

FIGURE 4

The design obviously suggests rotation, and in this respect is cognate to the swastika 卍 and the triskelion 🌀 and perhaps also to the zodiacal sign of Pisces, of the ending-beginning of the year. The symbol is known as the *tai-chi* (Supreme Ultimate) or simply as the *yin-yang*, though the Supreme Ultimate is often designated by an empty circle. The significance of the circle, of the rotary character of the yin-yang symbol, is of course that the world is not seen as created, as having a temporal beginning or end. There is rather

endless beginning and ending, and the hierarchy of principles—the Supreme Ultimate (or the Tao), the yang and yin,
the four modes, the eight trigrams, the sixty-four hexagrams,
and at last the "ten thousand things"—is a sequence of rank
rather than a sequence in time.

One of the most notable forms of this hierarchy is found
in a diagram drawn and explained by the Neo-Confucian
thinker Chou Tun-yi (1017–1073). (See figure 5.) Chou thus
describes the diagram:

> That which has no Pole! And yet (itself) the Supreme Pole!
> The Supreme Pole moves and produces the *yang*. When the
> movement has reached its limit, rest (ensues). Resting, the Su-
> preme Pole produces the *yin*. When the rest has reached its
> limit, there is a return to motion. Motion and rest alternate,
> each being the root of the other. The *yin* and the *yang* take up
> their appointed functions, and so the Two Forces are estab-
> lished. The *yang* is transformed by reacting with the *yin*, and
> so water, fire, wood, metal, and earth are produced. (Desig-
> nated by the five characters under the second circle.) Then the
> five *ch'i* (matter-energies) diffuse harmoniously, and the Four
> Seasons proceed on their course....
>
> The true (principle) of that which has no Pole, and the
> essences of the Two (Forces) and the Five (Elements), unite
> (react) with one another in marvellous ways, and consolida-
> tions ensue. The Tao of the heavens perfects maleness and
> the Tao of the earth perfects femaleness. The two *ch'i* of male-
> ness and femaleness, reacting with and influencing each other,
> change and bring the myriad things into being. Generation
> follows generation, and there is no end to their changes and
> transformations.[27]

FIGURE 5

The top circle represents the Supreme Ultimate (or Pole). The second has, to the left, the words "Yang, motion," and, to the right, "Yin, quiescence." The third is marked, to the left, "The Tao (Way) of *ch'ien* perfecting the male," and, to the right, "The Tao of *k'un* perfecting the female." The fourth circle is marked, below, "The ten thousand things transforming and growing."

The use of the empty circle, and of such expressions as "the non-Pole" or "the Void," for the Supreme Ultimate is a way of saying, not that the basis of reality is mere emptiness, but that it defies all description and delineation except in terms of yang and yin. Founded, then, upon this indescribable unity the primordial pair generate a world by playful intercourse because they are implicitly one. Almost invariably, Chinese thought sees the conflicts of nature as rooted in an underlying harmony. There is thus no *serious* conflict, no ultimate threat to the universal order, no possibility of final annihilation or nonbeing because, as Lao-tzu said, "To be and not to be arise mutually."

The perennial influence of the *Book of Changes* and its dynamic, bipolar model of the course of nature led Chinese savants of all times to think of the natural elements, of seasonal changes, of geological features, of plants and animals, in terms of differing arrangements and interactions of yin and yang. According to the *Huai-nan tzu*:

> Tao begins in the Great Void, which engenders the universe, which produces the fluid. In this a separation takes place. The purer and brighter particles are thinner and finer and form heaven. The coarser and more turbid accumulate and become earth. The blending of the purer and finer parts is easy, the condensation of the heavier and turbid parts more troublesome and difficult, therefore heaven is created prior to earth. The combined essence of heaven and earth is Yin and Yang, the activity of Yin and Yang produces the four seasons, and the dispersion of the essence of the four seasons produces the ten thousand things. From the hot Yang fluid comes fire, and the essence of fire becomes the sun. From the cold Yin fluid comes water, and the essence of water forms the moon. The

sexual intercourse between the sun and the moon gives birth to the stars. Heaven harbours the sun, the moon and the stars; earth comprises water, the rivers, the soil and dust.[28]

In the *Wu-neng tzu* is described the generation of animals from the yang and yin "fluids," though the word (*ch'i*) thus translated has also the sense of a breath, a vital force, or material energy:

> Anterior to the separation of heaven and earth there was a single, chaotic fluid. This ran over and was divided into two modes, there were pure and muddy, light and heavy parts. The light and pure ones went up and formed *yang and heaven*, the heavy and muddy ones sank down and became *Yin and earth*. Heaven was hard and strong and in motion, earth was soft and yielding and in repose. This was the natural state of the fluids. After heaven and earth had taken up their positions, the Yin and Yang fluids mixed, and all animals with skin, scales, fur, feathers and shells were created thereby.[29]

It is not surprising that the generation of the world by yang and yin should have had a sexual connotation. This is brought out clearly in the following extract from the *Ch'eng-tzu*, though, as we shall see, the Chinese did not develop this symbolism to anything like the same degree as the Indians.

> One Yin and one Yang, that is the fundamental principle. The passionate union of Yin and Yang and the copulation of husband and wife is the eternal rule of the universe. If heaven and earth did not mingle, whence would all the things receive life? When the wife comes to the man, she bears children. Bearing children is the way of propagation. Man and wife cohabit and produce offspring.[30]

Observing the habits of animals, birds, and insects, Chinese naturalists again correlated them with yin and yang influences, as in the following passages from the *Ching-chi wen-chi*:

> Birds, beasts, plants and trees obtain the Yin and the Yang fluid and are determined by them. The eagle plans murder and in autumn pounces upon its prey. The mouse is full of greed and goes out at night. In the fourth and the fifth months they can transform themselves into a turtle-dove and a quail, for in the fourth and fifth months Yang is powerful and Yin can be transmuted by Yang. The sparrows brood on their eggs and congregate in spring; the pheasant searches for its mate and cries in the morning. In the 11th and 12th months they can transform themselves into frogs and shells, for in these months the Yin reaches its climax, and the Yang then can be changed by the Yin.
>
> In spring the wild geese fly to and the swallows come from the north, the former travelling from the south to the north and the latter from the north to the south. Both fly with the Yang fluid, which is to their advantage. In autumn, on the contrary, the wild geese arrive and the swallows depart, the geese going from north to south, the swallows in the opposite direction, but both make use of the convenient Yin fluid to fly upon.[31]

The text also contains this curious description of the generation of worms and other creatures from rotten plants, which, mistaken as it may be, typifies the feeling that the yang force of life is always latent in the yin situation of death and decay.

> When rotten, plants become glowworms, plants are changed into animals and inanimate things into animate things. Is that not because the brightness of Yang has reached its acme,

so that also things of the dark Yin adhere to and change into it? Generally, the two fluids Yin and Yang are immaterial and move quietly in the interior, whereas wind, rain, dew, thunder, insects and plants have form and change outwardly.[32]

Fundamental to the yang-yin symbolism is the sense of the world as a system of transformation, and this is really the importance of the passage just quoted. Yin and yang are respectively like the troughs and peaks of a wave system. The S curve dividing the yin-yang circle suggests a kind of whiplash or peristaltic motion, a continuous undulation not only of life and death, day and night, but of one living form into another.

> Certain germs, falling upon water, become duckweed. When they reach the junction of the land and water, they become lichen. Spreading up the bank, they become the dog-tooth violet. Reaching rich soil, they become *wu-tsu* (exact meaning unknown), the root of which becomes grubs, while the leaves become butterflies, or crabs. These are changed into insects, born in the chimney corner, which look like skeletons....After a thousand days it becomes a bird called *kan-yü-ku*, the spittle of which becomes the *ssu-mi* (unidentifiable). The *ssu-mi* becomes a wine-fly....The *ch'ing-ning* (insect) produces the leopard, which produces the horse, which produces man. Then man goes back to the germ, from which all things come and to which all things return.[33]

Ever differing in form, this undulation is a single process of life-death, up-down, and wisdom—at least in the Chinese Taoist and Buddhist philosophies—consists in realizing the basic identity of the two. In the words of the *Chuang-tzu*:

> Life follows upon death. Death is the beginning of life. Who knows when the end is reached?...If then life and death are

but consecutive states, what need have I to complain? Therefore all things are one. What we love is animation. What we hate
is corruption. But corruption in its turn becomes animation,
and animation once more becomes corruption. Therefore it
has been said that the world is permeated by a single vital
fluid (*ch'i*), and the sages accordingly value its unity.[34]

But the unity is not so much obscured and concealed in
the yin-yang alternation as positively revealed for those who
have the wit to see it—a point illustrated in the *Chuang-tzu*
with the following whimsical anecdote:

Therefore it is that, viewed from the standpoint of Tao, a beam
(horizontal) and a pillar (vertical) are identical. So are ugliness
and beauty, greatness, wickedness, perverseness, and strange-
ness. Separation is the same as construction; construction is
the same as destruction. Nothing is subject either to construction or destruction, for these conditions are brought together
into one. Only the truly intelligent understand this principle
of the identity of all things.... But to wear out one's intelligence in order to unify things without knowing that they
are already in agreement, this is called "Three in the Morning."... A keeper of monkeys said with regard to their rations of
chestnuts that each monkey was to have three in the morning
and four at night. But at this the monkeys were very angry, and
so the keeper said that they might have four in the morning
and three at night, with which arrangement they were all well
pleased. The actual number of chestnuts remained the same,
but there was an adaptation to the likes and dislikes of those
concerned. Thus the sages harmonize the statements "it is"
and "it is not," and rest in the natural equilibrium of Heaven.
This is called following two courses at once.[35]

In many respects the yin-yang symbolism is more of a philosophy or even a primitive science than a mythology. Though called male and female they are never personified as god and goddess progenitors of the world, nor is there the slightest hint of their being engaged in a cosmic war of light against darkness or good against evil. The Chinese never seem to have taken the personification of cosmic forces very seriously, nor to have had any strong inclination to consider the universe as the creation and dominion of a heavenly ruler. Yin-yang imagery inclined them, on the whole, to consider the universe as a self-organizing body which moves and regulates itself spontaneously, like the circulation of the blood or the legs of a centipede.

> The walrus said to the centipede, "I hop about on one leg, but not very successfully. How do you manage all those legs you have?"
>
> "I don't manage them," replied the centipede. "Have you ever seen saliva? When it is ejected, the big drops are the size of pearls, the small ones like mist. They fall promiscuously on the ground and cannot be counted. And so it is that my mechanism works naturally, without my being conscious of the fact."
>
> The centipede said to the snake, "With all my legs I do not move as fast as you with none. How is that?"
>
> "One's natural mechanism," replied the snake, "is not a thing to be changed. What need have I for legs?"[36]

A more fantastic aspect of the yang-yin theory emerges, however, in those developments of Taoism which had to do with the quest for physical immortality—that is, for attaining the same equilibrium of the forces in the individual organism as in the universe. It was thus hoped that the individual might become a system as self-perpetuating as the universe, a *hsien* or immortal. Many techniques were employed to this end—the alchemical preparation of an elixir of immortality, exercises for slowing down the breath, and particular sexual experiments to nourish the yang power of the male with the yin power of the female. The successful application of these methods was said to enable the *hsien* to shed his aging skin like a snake, and crawl out as soft-complexioned as a boy.

As with Western alchemy in its search for the stone that would turn base metals into gold, it is always difficult to judge how literally these enterprises should be taken. There is little doubt that in some instances both the end and the means were, as described, figurative representations of a process of spiritual and psychic transformation. Thus an alchemical writer of the thirteenth century, Ch'en Hsien-wei, discusses the preparation of genuine cinnabar, which, mixed with honey and made into pills, was supposed to be the medicine of immortality. He describes the process going on in the alchemical cauldron (*fu*), but associates this *fu* with the hexagram *fu* in the *Book of Changes* which designates a "turning point."

> Spiritual fire…drives away the *yang* which is inside the *yin*. This *yang* flies upwards and ascends, and at the "original position of the spiritual fire" it meets with the *yin* which is inside the *yang*. These two capture each other, control each other, have intercourse with each other, and knot each other together.…The two *ch'i* (energies), buttoning on to each other, and knotting each other together, produce change and

transformation. Sometimes the phenomena of the "lad" and "girl" appear, and sometimes the shapes of the Dragon and Tiger. With numerous changes they fly about, rising, running, and leaping, never quiet for a moment, and never coming out from the vessel and the stove....So will the true (cinnabar) medicine be condensed and aggregated. This is the Tao. The two most important things are the observant mind and the attracting spirit; both helping the efficacy of the "fire-times." The meditation methods of the Buddhists seem to be valuable but are not really so. The Taoists who take deep breaths and swallow saliva are pursuing trifles and abandoning what really matters.[37]

The last three sentences seem to indicate clearly that the "alchemical" process is actually spiritual. It is of interest that the image of the interplay of the Dragon and the Tiger was also used in connection with the dances preceding the Taoist sexual ritual. And here, again, we may be dealing with figurative language.

In other words, the immortality of the *hsien* with his continuous changing of skins may refer, not to a personal conquest of death, but to a shift in the sense of one's identity—from the ego to the universe. This would come about through a clear and complete perception of the implicit unity of the yang and yin principles, for this would include the realization of the same unity between the self and the not-self, the world inside the skin and the world outside.

Master Lü Tzu said: In comparison with Heaven and Earth, man is like a mayfly. But compared to the Great Meaning (Tao), Heaven and Earth, too, are like a bubble and a shadow. Only the primordial spirit and the true essence overcome time and space. The power of the seed (semen, i.e., biological life), like Heaven and Earth, is subject to mortality, but the primordial spirit is beyond the polar differences. Here is the place whence Heaven and Earth derive their being. When students understand how to grasp the primordial spirit they overcome the polar opposites of Light (*yang*) and Darkness (*yin*) and tarry no longer in the three worlds (of heaven, earth, and the underworld). But only he who has looked on essence in its original manifestation is able to do this.... Buddha speaks of the transient, the creator of consciousness, as being the fundamental truth of religion. And, in our Taoism, the expression "to produce emptiness" contains the whole work of completing life and essence. All...agree in the one proposition, the finding of the spiritual Elixir in order to pass from death to life. In what does this spiritual Elixir consist? It means forever tarrying in purposelessness. The deepest secret in our teaching, the secret of the bath, is confined to the work of making the heart (*hsin*, also "mind") empty. Therewith the heart is set at rest. What I have revealed here in a word is the fruit of decades of effort.[38]

The "empty heart" (*wu-hsin*) is when one's whole being seems as the head seems to the eyes—a transparent void, filled by all that one sees. So with every sense; the senser, the senses, and the things sensed become one, and the duality of the knower and the known, the inside and the outside, is transcended.

The (Heavenly) Light is not in the body alone, neither is it only outside the body. Mountains and rivers and the great Earth are lit by the sun and moon; all that is this Light. Therefore it is not only within the body. Understanding and clarity, knowing and enlightenment, and all motion (of the spirit), are likewise this Light; therefore it is not just something outside the body. The Light-flower of Heaven and Earth fills all thousand spaces (within the body). But also the Light-flower of one body passes through Heaven and covers the Earth.[39]

Here, in the symbol of the Light-flower, is what I feel to be the height of Chinese wisdom: its profound grasp of the relational character of the world, of things as "mutually arising" and "mutually interpenetrating." All things are like the rainbow, for there is no phenomenon "rainbow" except where there is a certain relationship of sun, moisture in the atmosphere, and observer. The rainbow is "void" because it has no independent existence of its own. But in Chinese thought it was seen that this is true of everything, including the observer. Eyes and light arise mutually in the same way as yin and yang. The universe is not, therefore, *composed* of independent things, that is, as human thought ordinarily fragments it: but the universe disposes itself as things. It is one body, one field, whose parts give rise to each other as inseparably as fronts and backs, but in an endlessly complex and interconnected maze. Thus to become a *hsien* was, at root, to take conscious possession of one's true and original body—the world, and this by quite literally coming to one's senses, which, after all, do the work of integration for us. Light, color, shape, weight, and texture are all states of a nervous system and a body which, in its turn, is an integral part of the rainbow-world seen in these terms. But man cuts himself off from it and loses the sense of his original body by considering himself as an "I" which *has* these experiences, standing back from them just as one looks at a picture. To empty (*wu*) the heart (*hsin*) is to stop standing back from experience and to see, not that one *has* it, but that one *is* it.

(The Master said:) "You hear not with the ears, but with the mind (*hsin*); not with the mind, but with your soul. But let hearing stop with the ears. Let the working of the mind stop with itself. Then the soul will be a negative existence, passively responsive to externals. In such a negative existence, only Tao (the Way of Nature) can abide. And that negative state is the fasting of the heart (*hsin*)."

"Then," said Yen-hui, "the reason I could not get the use of this method is my own individuality (ego). If I could get the use of it, my individuality would have gone. Is that what you mean by the negative state?"

"Exactly so," replied the Master. "Let me tell you....See that emptiness. There is light in an empty room, and there is good fortune in repose. Without repose, your mind will be rushing around even when you are sitting still. Let your eyes and ears respond within, but shut out all (idea of) knowledge with a mind."[40]*

I have devoted so much space to this quasi-mythological theory of the yin and yang because it seems to me to reflect a far deeper grasp of the polar principle than is found in any other ancient tradition. But the traditions of India, too, contain the same insight, though expressed in a far greater wealth of mythological imagery, and to these we must now turn.

---

* Cf. J. Z. Young in *Doubt and Certainty in Science*. London, 1953, p. 155. "We each probably still say, if pressed, something like, 'The central thing that I know is my mind, my experience, my consciousness.' That is to say we refer to ourselves as if we were a body occupied by a person—the old model of a circle with something inside it. Is it possible that we should convey more information if we tried to do without this whole apparatus of the words of conventional psychology? We can say everything that we want to say quite well without speaking all the time as if we were inhabited by this spirit called the mind."

2. The Cosmic Dance

WHAT IS MORE EXUBERANT than Hindu sculpture? I am
thinking of those ovoid domes of stone at Konarak, Bhu-
vaneshwar, and Khajuraho, which look, at first sight, as if
they had decomposed into the kind of squirming vitality
that one finds upon overturning a rock, as if they were alive
with anthropoid maggots, swarming together in a colossal
rout of dancing, fighting, and copulating. But close inspection reveals that the stone has come alive in figures of unbelievable grace and lilting sensuousness—at one time vividly
polychromed, but now perhaps all the better for being the
combination of drab gray rock and endlessly dancing form.
One must look at these temple figures in the light of classical
Hindu dancing—an art in which jeweled bodies move as if
they were plants suspended in water, where muscles are an
ivory liquid, and where legs, hips, belly, shoulders, and head
move quite independently in their own planes. Such exotic,
rich, and junglelike displays of human fecundity are perhaps repellent to the Western, and especially Anglo-Saxon,
taste. But to penetrate the depth and grandeur of Hindu
mythology and philosophy, one must somehow allow oneself

to enter into this seething imagery, and then feel one's way down through its bewildering variety to the simple and presiding intuition which underlies it.

In a world of intense heat, of the most startling extremes of fertility and aridity, wealth and poverty, and where life is cheap and security almost unknown, the human mind can acquire a peculiar sensitivity. Somehow the world seems lacking in solidity. External forms and surfaces are now diaphanous, and now bristling with the sharpest points. Nothing is certain but change, and change is less apt to be gradual and orderly than sudden and unforeseen. It is not surprising, then, that to the Hindu consciousness the world has seemed like an arabesque of smoke, and that its totally unreliable transitoriness has been the principal ground for considering it to be fundamentally unreal. But the word *maya*, by which this peculiar unreality is described, is not necessarily a term of contempt, as if the world were merely an illusion to be dismissed. *Maya* also means art and magic, and thus a seeming solidity evoked by divine power. But under the spell of this power the Hindu does not feel himself entirely a victim. However obscurely, he knows or feels that the source of this enchantment is in some roundabout way himself—as if being alive and human were to have got oneself deliberately lost in a labyrinth.

For the presiding intuition of the Hindu worldview is that the whole universe of multiplicity is the *lila*, or play, of a single energy known as *Paramatman*, the Supreme Self. The coming and going of all worlds, all beings, and all things is described as the eternal outbreathing and inbreathing of this One Life—eternal because it is beyond all dualities, comprising nonbeing as much as being, death as much as life, stillness as much as motion. One of the principal symbols of the *Paramatman* is the Swan, *Hamsa*, flying forth from its nest and returning, and the syllable *ham* stands for breathing out, *sa* for breathing in. As the exhalation and inhalation are repeated endlessly, *ham-sa-ham-sa-ham-sa-ham*, there is also heard *saham*, that is, *sa aham*, "He I am"—which is to say that the essential self of every being is the Supreme Self.

This in-and-out rhythm or undulation goes on endlessly through every dimension of life. It is the birth-and-death of innumerable universes, not only succeeding one another in *kalpa*-periods of 4,320,000 years, but also coexisting in untold myriads. Small universes compose great universes: our galaxies are the dust in another cosmos, and the dust in our world contains suns and stars—infinitely small or infinitely great according to the point of view. An individual is therefore a vast cosmos in his own right, and the ups and downs of his life are just the same ups and downs as those of the macrocosms beyond him and the microcosms within him. To the eye of wisdom size makes no difference: every mote, every being, every cosmos is an exemplar of the one archetypal rhythm. All beings—divine, human, demonic, or animal—are, as it were, under the spell of the Juggler, tossing and catching the multitudinous balls of the worlds with his thousands of arms and hands, simultaneously giving delight with the display of skill and terror with the thought that a ball might drop. Yet the skill and resourcefulness of the Divine Juggler are endless. The ball that seems to drop and shatter simply bursts into a million more Jugglers; the disaster turns out with unfailing astonishment to be a new tour de force, though it is all part of the game that this shall never be expected. Yet there is a clue for the wise. In all images of the many-armed divinity there is one hand raised and unmoving, with palm toward the beholder—the gesture of "Fear not." It is just a game (plate 21).

This, then, is the underlying theme of those Hindu art forms depicting the myriads of gods and goddesses in their loves and wars: it is the endless complication of a single principle, complicated by an infinite capacity for maya, for concealing the stratagem. Now you see it, now you don't.

At some time between 500 BC and AD 100 there was compiled that great epic of Hindu mythology, the *Mahabharata*. One section of this epic, *The Lord's Song* or *Bhagavad-Gita*, has been regarded for centuries as the most authoritative epitome of Hindu doctrine, taking the form of a discourse between the warrior Arjuna and Sri Krishna, the incarnation or avatar of Vishnu—one of the many names under which the Supreme Self is known. The scene of the *Gita* is a battle-field where opposing forces are encamped before their engagement. Krishna appears in the role of Arjuna's charioteer, and their conversation begins with Arjuna's despondency at the prospect of having to do battle with his own kinsmen. The battle is, of course, a symbol of the whole struggle of life-and-death, and Krishna's encouragement of his reluctant master, Arjuna, must be taken not so much as the praise of military valor as of fearlessness in the face of all life's terrors. The immediate importance of this discourse is that at one point Krishna reveals himself to Arjuna in his divine form, at which moment the *Gita* gives us the most vivid picture of the cosmic vision which I have been describing, the beautiful and terrible dance of the Divine Juggler and the maya of his innumerable forms and manifestations. Krishna says:

> I am the Self existing in the heart of all beings. I am the beginning, the middle and also the end of beings.
>
> Among purifiers, I am the wind; among warriors, I am Rama; among fishes, I am Makara (the shark); and among rivers, I am the Ganges.
>
> O Arjuna, of all creations I am the beginning, the middle and also the end; of all sciences, I am the science of Self-knowledge.
>
> Of syllables, I am "A," and Dvandva (copulative) of all compound words. I am inexhaustible Time; I am the Dispenser, facing everywhere.
>
> I am all-seizing Death; I am the origin of all that is to be; of the female I am fame, prosperity, speech, memory, intelligence, constancy and forgiveness.
>
> I am gambling among the fraudulent; I am the prowess of the powerful. I am Victory, I am Perseverance, I am the Goodness of the good.
>
> I am the Rod of disciplinarians; I am the Polity of the seekers of conquest. I am the Silence of secrets; I am the Wisdom of the wise.
>
> O Arjuna, whatever is the seed of all beings, that also am I. Without Me there is no being existent, whether moving or unmoving.
>
> There is no end to the manifestations of my Divine Power; what I have declared is only a partial statement of the vastness of my divine manifestation.
>
> Whatever being there is, glorious, prosperous or powerful, know thou that to have sprung from a portion of My splendor.
>
> O Arjuna, what need is there for thee to know these

details? I alone exist, sustaining this whole universe by a portion of Myself.

Arjuna said:

The supremely profound word regarding Self-knowledge,
spoken by Thee out of compassion for me, has dispelled this
my delusion.

O Lotus-eyed, I have heard at length from Thee of the
creation and dissolution of beings, as well as of thine inexhaustible glory.

O great Lord, as thou hast declared thyself, so it is. O
Supreme Being, I desire to see thy godly form.

O Lord, if thou thinkest me able to see that, then, O Lord
of yogis, show me thine infinite Self.

The Blessed Lord said:

Behold my various celestial forms, of different colors and
shapes, by hundreds and by thousands.

Behold in this body of mine the entire universe together,
with all that is moving and unmoving and whatever else thou
desirest to perceive.

But with these eyes of thine thou canst not see me; therefore I give thee divine sight, Behold my supreme yoga power!

Sanjaya said:

O King, having spoken thus, the great Lord of yoga, Hari,
then showed his supreme godly form.

With many faces and eyes, with many wondrous sights,
with many celestial ornaments and with many celestial weapons uplifted.

Wearing celestial garlands and garments, anointed with
celestial fragrant perfumes; the all-wonderful Deity, infinite,
facing the universe everywhere.

If the effulgence of a thousand suns were to shine at once
in the sky, that might resemble the splendor of that great Being.

Then Arjuna saw the entire universe resting together, with its manifold divisions, in the body of the God of gods.

Then (Arjuna), overpowered with wonder, and his hair standing on end, bending down his head in awe to the Deity, spoke with folded hands:

Arjuna said:

O God! in thy body I see all the gods, as well as multitudes of all kinds of beings; the Lord Brahma, seated on the lotus throne, all the Rishis (sages) and all the celestial serpents.

O Lord of the universe, O universal form, I see thee with manifold arms, bellies, mouths and eyes, boundless on every side; neither do I see thy beginning, nor middle nor end.

I see thee with diadems, maces, discus, shiningly effulgent everywhere, blazing all around like the burning fire and the sun, dazzling to the sight and immeasurable.

Thou art the imperishable, the supreme, the One to be known. Thou art the supreme refuge of this universe; thou art the ever unchanging guardian of the eternal Dharma; thou art, I know, the ancient Being.

I see thee without beginning, middle or end, with infinite power, with numberless arms, the sun and the moon as thine eyes, thy mouth as the blazing fire, heating this universe with thine own radiance.

By thee alone the space between heaven and earth and all the quarters is pervaded. O great Soul, seeing this, thy wonderful and terrifying form, the three worlds are stricken with fear.

Verily, these hosts of devas (angels) are entering into thee; some in fear, praising thee with folded hands. The host of great Rishis and Siddhas, saying "Svasti" (peace, may it be well), are singing thy glory in beautiful hymns.

O mighty-armed, seeing thine immeasurable form, with many mouths and eyes, with many arms, thighs and feet, with many loins, and fearful with many large teeth, the worlds, and I as well, are agitated with terror.

O Vishnu, seeing thee touching the sky, shining in many colors, with mouths wide open, and with large blazing eyes, my heart is terrified and I find neither peace nor tranquillity.

O Lord of gods! seeing thy mouths, terrible with long teeth, blazing like the fires of destruction, I know not the four quarters, nor do I find any peace. Have mercy, O abode of the universe!

All these sons of Dhritarashtra, with the multitude of monarchs, Bhishma, Drona and Sutaputra, as well as our own principal warriors,

Enter rushingly into thy mouths, terrible with long teeth and fearful to look at. Some are seen hanging between thy teeth, with their heads crushed to powder.

As many torrents of rivers rush toward the ocean, similarly do these heroes amongst men enter into thy mouths, blazing fiercely on all sides.

As the moths rush into the burning fire with headlong speed for destruction, in the same manner do these creatures rush into thy mouths with headlong speed, only to perish.

O Vishnu! swallowing all the worlds with thy blazing flames, thou art licking all around. Thy fierce, radiant rays, filling the whole universe, are burning.

Tell me, who art thou, in this terrible form? Salutation to thee! O supreme Deity, have mercy! O primeval One, I desire to know thee, for indeed I know not thy purpose.

The Blessed Lord said:

I am eternal, world-destroying Time, manifested here for the destruction of these people. Even without thee, none of these warriors, arrayed here in the hostile armies, shall live.

Therefore, do thou arise and acquire glory. Conquering

the enemies, enjoy the unrivalled kingdom. By me alone have they already been slain; be thou merely an instrumental cause.

Do thou kill and be not distressed by fear. Fight! and thou shalt conquer thine enemies in battle.[41]

Because the scene of the *Gita* is the battlefield, the polarity stressed in this vision of the cosmic dance is life and death, creation and destruction. But the texts represent it in other ways as well—as the peaceful and the wrathful, the male and the female, the warp and the woof—each pair a variation of the fundamental rhythm which is the very texture of life. Going back perhaps as far as 800 BC are a group of documents known as the Upanishads—a term meaning "to sit near," that is, to sit at the feet of a teacher. These are the sources from which the complex of Hindu imagery and doctrine is derived, though they, in their turn, represent a reinterpretation of the Vedas—the archaic hymns of the Aryan invaders of the Indian subcontinent, whose attitudes and institutions were slowly modified by the aboriginal population.* One of the oldest of the Upanishads is known as the *Brihadaranyaka*, in which the theme of unity-in-duality is already prominent. Here is its account of the production of the world through the bifurcation of the Supreme Self into male and female:

In the beginning this was Self alone, in the shape of a person (*purusha*). He looking round saw nothing but his Self. He first

---

*   The Aryan invasion of India, from the Northwest, is thought to have occurred between 1500 and 1000 BC. Archeological study of the earlier Indus Valley culture (second millennium BC) suggests that the basic attitudes of Hinduism as now known reflect this earlier level of civilization which, in turn, has affinities with the worldview of the Sumerians. Cf. Joseph Campbell, *The Masks of God*. vol. ii. Viking. New York, 1962.

said, "This is I"; therefore he became I by name. Therefore even now, if a man is asked, he first says, "This is I," and then pronounces the other name which he may have. And because before all this, he burnt down all evils, therefore he was a person. Verily he who knows this, burns down everyone who tries to be before him.

He feared, and therefore anyone who is lonely fears. He thought, "As there is nothing but myself, why should I fear?" Thence his fear passed away. For what should he have feared? Verily fear arises from a second only.

But he felt no delight. Therefore a man who is lonely feels no delight. He wished for a second. He was so large as man and wife together. He then made his Self to fall in two and thence arose husband and wife. Therefore Yajnavalkya said: "We two are thus (each of us) like half a shell." Therefore the void which was there, is filled by the wife. He embraced her, and men were born.

She thought, "How can he embrace me, after having produced me from himself? I shall hide myself."

She then became a cow, the other became a bull and embraced her, and hence cows were born. The one became a mare, the other a stallion; the one a male ass, the other a female ass. He embraced her, and hence one-hoofed animals were born. The one became a she-goat, the other a he-goat; the one became a ewe, the other a ram. He embraced her, and hence goats and sheep were born. And thus he created everything that exists in pairs, down to the ants.

He knew, "I indeed am this creation, for I created all this." Hence he became the creation, and he who knows this lives in this his creation.[42]

This passage contains a curious allusion to the primal guilt or shame of the sexual union. "How can he embrace me, after having produced me from himself? I shall hide myself." But it is quite obvious that the female, hiding herself in the cow, the ass, the goat, and the ewe, is hiding in order to be found. But the delight of the situation is just that she must not admit this to herself. The whole force of the cosmic game depends upon the pretense (maya) that it is not a game, upon an unconsciousness or forgetting, which will always renew the fear that the Juggler will drop the ball, that the villain will rape the heroine, and that, in short, the worst will happen. Sexual shame is thus the blushing admitting and not admitting of complicity—the secret enjoyment of what was feared so explicitly that one loses face in confessing it. Therefore the guilt or shame attaching itself to sexuality is an integral part of its pleasure, and to maintain it we will do everything possible not to "let the cat out of the bag."

Another theme of the *Brihadaranyaka* is the world as warp and woof, since, in woven cloth, the one cannot hold together without the other. The sage, Yajnavalkya, is questioned by the woman, Gargi:

> "Since all this world is woven, warp on woof, on water, on what, pray, is the water woven, warp on woof?"
>   "On wind, O Gargi."
>   "On what then, pray, is the wind woven, warp and woof?"
>   "On the atmosphere-worlds, O Gargi."

And as question follows question, Yajnavalkya explains that the woof of the atmosphere-worlds is the world of celestial musicians, that behind them is the sun, and then the moon, the stars, the gods, of Indra, Prajapati, and Brahma—and when Gargi asks upon what the world of Brahma is woven, the sage replies:

"Gargi, do not question too much, lest your head fall off. In truth, you are questioning too much about a divinity about which further questions cannot be asked. Gargi, do not over-question."

Nevertheless, the woman persists:

"As a noble youth...might rise up against you, having strung his unstrung bow and taken two foe-piercing arrows in his hand, even so, O Yajnavalkya, have I risen up against you with two questions. Answer me these."

Yajnavalkya said: "Ask, Gargi."

She said: "That, O Yajnavalkya, which is above the sky, that which is beneath the earth, that which is between these two, sky and earth, that which people call the past, the present, and the future—across what is that woven, warp and woof?"

He said: "That, O Gargi, which is above the sky, that which is beneath the earth, that which is between these two, sky and earth, that which people call the past and the present and the future—across space is that woven, warp and woof."

She said: "Adoration to you, Yajnavalkya, in that you have solved this question for me. Prepare yourself for the other."

"Ask, Gargi."

She said: "Across what then, pray, is space woven, warp and woof?"

He said: "That, O Gargi, Brahmans call the Imperishable. It is not coarse, not fine, not short, not long, not glowing, not adhesive, without shadow and without darkness, without air and without space, without stickiness, odorless, tasteless, without eye, without ear, without voice, without wind, without energy, without breath, without mouth, without measure, without inside and without outside.

It consumes nothing soever.
No one soever consumes it.

Verily, O Gargi, at the command of that Imperishable the sun and the moon stand apart. Verily, O Gargi, at the command of that Imperishable the earth and the sky stand apart. Verily, O Gargi, at the command of that Imperishable the moments, the days, the nights, the fortnights, the months, the seasons, and the years stand apart. Verily, O Gargi, at the command of that Imperishable some rivers flow from the snowy mountains to the east, others to the west, in whatever direction each flows.... Verily, O Gargi, that Imperishable is the unseen Seer, the unheard Hearer, the unthought Thinker, the ununderstood Understander. Other than It there is naught that sees...hears... thinks...understands. Across this Imperishable, O Gargi, is space woven warp and woof."[43]

The series of negations implies that if one tries to penetrate the ultimate interdependence of warp and woof, one comes to the point beyond which language cannot travel, since it is impossible to denote "this" without the contrast of "that."

Now as there is no woven cloth without the simultaneous interpenetration of warp and woof, there is no world without *both* the exhalation and inhalation of the Supreme Self. Though the image of breathing, as distinct from weaving, makes the two successive rather than simultaneous, nevertheless the one always implies the other. Successive in time, they are simultaneous in meaning—that is, *sub specie aeternitatis*, from the standpoint of eternity. Beginning and end, birth and death, manifestation and withdrawal always imply each other. In Western—that is, Judaic and Christian—imagery there has generally been a tendency to overlook this mutuality and to see each life and the creation itself as unique—as a beginning, and then an end which does not imply another beginning. Our world is linear, and the course of time is very strictly a one-way street. Nature is a clockwork mechanism which does not wind itself up in the process of running down. In Western religion and physics alike, we tend to think of all energy as expenditure and evaporation. There is no hope for a renewal of life beyond the end unless the supernatural Creator, by an act of special grace, winds things up again.

But the Indian view of time is cyclic. If birth implies death, death implies rebirth, and likewise the destruction of the world implies its recreation. The Western images are thus essentially tragic. Nature is a fall and its goal is death. There is no necessity for anything to happen beyond the end: only divine grace, operating outside the sphere of necessity, can redeem and restore the world. But the Indian imagery makes the world-drama a comedy—a sport or *lila*—in which all endings are the implicit promise of beginnings. Yet comedy must always depend on surprise. The burst of laughter is our expression of relief upon discovering that some threatened doom was an illusion—that "death was but the good King's jest."

Consider a very simple but typical comedy enacted many years ago in a London music hall. The curtain rises upon an elaborately furnished bedroom. The sleeper is at once awakened by a shrill alarm clock. Reaching under his pillow, he produces a hammer and smashes it in the face. Sitting up in bed, he glowers at his early-Monday-morning surroundings, and, hammer still in hand, slowly crawls out from the covers. Thereupon he proceeds, item by Victorian item, to smash everything in the bedroom—the bedside table, the flowered pitcher and basin on the washstand, the knickknacks on the mantel, the chocolate-colored chamber pot patterned with green leaves, the glass on the pictures, the windows, and the bed itself—leaving only a bulbous and pretentious floor lamp with a huge glass shade. Creeping stealthily across the wreckage he eyes this last and perfect object of his rage, very obviously designed to disintegrate with a spectacular explosion. Instead of smashing it with his hammer, he grasps it with both hands and flings it high into the air—and, falling to the floor, it bounces: made of rubber.

This is the vulgar archetype of the cosmic punch line, the totally unexpected anticlimax which, in Hindu mythology, follows the terrifying *tandava*—the dance in which ten-armed Shiva, wreathed in fire, destroys the universe at the end of each cycle. But Shiva is simply the opposite face of Brahma, the Creator, so that as he turns to leave the stage with the world in ruin, the scene changes with his turning, and all things are seen to have been remade under the cover of their destruction.

The polarity of Brahma and Shiva thus finds its expression in what at times seems to be the extreme ambivalence of Hindu culture—extreme in its asceticism as in its sensuality. On the one hand, there is the goal of Yoga, the meditation-discipline: to concentrate thought so as to penetrate and burn away the illusion of the world. Yoga is thus man's participation in the inhalation or withdrawal of the world breath, in the dissolution of maya, and in return to the undifferentiated unity of the Godhead. Shiva, the destructive aspect of Godhead, is therefore the archetypal yogi, the naked ascetic daubed with ashes sitting hour after hour with his consciousness in total stillness. On the other hand, there is that exuberant delight in form and flesh which is so exquisitely celebrated in Hindu dancing, music, and sculpture, in the marvelously refined eroticism of the *Kamasutra*, the scripture of love, as well as in the vision of the perfectly governed society laid out in the *Arthashastra*, the scripture of politics. One might almost say that India had set herself the problem of exploring these two attitudes to their extremes and then of finding the synthesis between them.

This problem, stated in mythological terms, is the recurrent theme of a type of popular Hindu literature known as the Puranas. Certainly much later than the Upanishads, these are texts of uncertain date,* forming a repository of myth and legend accumulated over many centuries. Notable in the Puranas is the relationship of the gods to their feminine counterparts or Shaktis, the feminine symbols of maya, the world-illusion, whereby the male god is alternatingly seduced and disenchanted. Originally the Godhead is hermaphroditic, beyond the opposites, but at the moment of creation the feminine Shakti leaps forth spontaneously, as Eve was created from the body of Adam while he slept.

The Creator, Brahma, the demiurgic, world-producing aspect of the Godhead, sat in serene meditation, bringing forth, from the enlivened depths of his own divine and all-containing substance, the universe and its multitudes of beings. A number of apparitions had already sprung into the sphere of time and space out of the abyss of his yogic state, crystal pure visions suddenly precipitated into embodied form. And these were

---

* To the continual exasperation of Western scholars, the authors of ancient Indian texts seem to have no sense whatsoever of history, and thus all attempts to date these texts are extremely vague. Manuscripts are usually late transcriptions of materials that have been memorized and handed down orally from one generation to another.

disposed around him in a serene circle, as he continued in his creative trance....Brahma, sinking still further into the limpid darkness of his own interior, struck a new depth: suddenly the most beautiful dark woman sprang from his vision, and stood naked before everyone's gaze.

She was Dawn, and she was radiant with vivid youth. Nothing like her had yet appeared among the gods; nor would her equal ever be seen, either among men, or in the depths of the waters in the jeweled palaces of the serpent queens and kings. The billows of her blue-black hair were glistening like the feathers of a peacock, and her clearly curving, dark brows formed a bow fit for the God of Love. Her eyes, like dark lotus calyxes, had the alert, questioning glance of the frightened gazelle; and her face, round as the moon, was like a purple lotus blossom. Her swelling breasts with their two dark points were enough to infatuate a saint. Trim as the shaft of a lance stood her body, and her smooth legs were like the stretched-out trunks of elephants. She was glowing with little delicate pearls of perspiration. And when she found herself in the midst of her startled audience, she stared about at them, in uncertainty, and then broke into a softly rippling laugh.

Brahma became aware of her, arose from his yogic posture, and fastened on her a long and earnest gaze. Then with his physical eyes still fixed upon her, the Creator permitted his spiritual vision to fall back again into its own profundity; and he searched to know...what the task of this apparition would be in the further unfoldment of the work of creation, and to whom she would belong.[44]

And from this second absorption there sprang a magnificent male youth, the God of Love, with his flower-tipped bow and shafts. But now Brahma has produced something almost beyond his own control.

(He) remained silent for a moment, astounded by his own production. What had slipped from him? What was this? Then he
gathered and constrained his consciousness, and brought his
mind again to center. Surprise was conquered. Again in mas-
tery, the World Creator addressed his remarkable creature and
assigned to him his field.

"You will go wandering about the earth," he said, "striking bewilderment into men and women with your flower-bow
and shafts, and in this way bring to pass the continuous creation of the world. No god, no heavenly spirit…shall be inaccessible to your aim. And I myself, as well as all-pervading
Vishnu (the Preserver of the World), even Shiva, the rocklike
immovable ascetic, steeped in his meditation, We Three, shall
be given into your power—not to speak of other breathing
existences…."

Then (Kama, the God of Love) made himself invisible.
"Right here, and without a moment's delay," he thought, "I will
prove upon these holy ones, and upon the Creator himself, the
supernal power that Brahma has assigned to me. Here they all
stand, and here is this magnificent woman, Dawn; they shall
be made—every one—the victims of my weapon…."

Having decided, he assumed the stance of an archer,
notched a flower-arrow to the flower-string, and drew the
great curve of the bow. Then there began to blow intoxi-
cating breezes, heavy with the scents of spring flowers; and
these disseminated rapture. From the Creator to the last of
his mind-born sons, the gods then were set mad, one after
another, by the shots of the disorderer, their temperaments
undergoing immediately a magnitudinous change. They continued to stare at Dawn, the woman, but with altered eyes,
and the spell of love increased in them….They were all set
wild together, and their senses thickened with lust. Indeed,

the entrancement was so strong that when the Creator's pure mind apprehended his daughter,...his awakened susceptibilities and compulsions directly opened themselves, with all their gestures and spontaneous physical manifestations, for the world to see.[45]

But suddenly there arrived in the company Shiva himself, destroyer of illusions, and, seeing the Creator and his divine sons in their unseemly infatuation, he laughed in cutting contempt.

"Well, well! Well, well!...Brahma, just what is going on here? What has brought you to this pretty pass? The sight of your own daughter? But it hardly becomes the Creator to disregard the precepts of the Vedas: 'The sister shall be as the mother, and the daughter as the sister!' That is what the Vedas declare—the laws revealed by your own mouth; and have you forgotten all this, in an excess of desire?...How did the God of Love ever do this to you all, indolent and destitute of discernment as he is? A curse on him through whose power the beauty of woman is made to purloin integrity, and the spirit is delivered to the billows of desire!"

When Brahma heard these words, his mind immediately split in two: on the one hand, his original nature again asserted itself, but on the other, the person overcome by concupiscence remained. Waves of heat streamed down his limbs. A longing to possess the incarnation of his desire groaned in him, yet he conquered this passionate modification of his character, and let the image of the woman go. At which moment, a burst of perspiration broke over his entire body, for the desire could not be destroyed, even though expelled. And from these drops then were born the so-called "Spirits of the Departed,"...the progenitors of the human race.[46]

Stung by Shiva's ridicule, Brahma thereupon declared that a time would come when Shiva, too, would be struck by the flower-arrow, though, at the same moment, the God of Love would be incinerated by the fire of Shiva's gaze. However, he promised at the same time that whensoever Shiva should take a wife to himself, the God of Love should be born in a new body. The story goes on to describe how Kama, the God of Love, became so infatuated with Dawn that he forgot Brahma's warning and set about discovering the abode of Shiva to involve even the Destroyer in his spell. Meanwhile, behind the scenes as it were, Brahma, too, is plotting the downfall of Shiva, realizing that he can do so only by evoking the ultimate embodiment of the feminine principle, Maha-maya, Vast Illusion—Mother of the World—otherwise known as Kali.

Now in Hindu myth and iconography Kali is the most ambivalent of all figures (plate 2). On the one hand, she is the embodiment of the Terrible Mother, the Spider Woman, the all-devouring maw of the abyss, image of everything of which the human soul seems to be ultimately afraid. On the other hand, she is the *Ewig Weibliche*, eternal womanhood, cherishing mother of the world, to whom that remarkable Hindu saint of modern times, Sri Ramakrishna, gave his whole life's devotion. He loved to chant the poet Ramprasad's song in her praise:

> All creation is the sport of my mad Mother Kali;
> By her maya the three worlds are bewitched.
> Mad is She and mad is her Husband; mad are her two
>   disciples!
> None can describe her loveliness, her glories, gestures,
>   moods;

> Shiva, with the agony of the poison in his throat,
> Chants her name again and again.[47]

The Primordial Power is ever at play (said Ramakrishna). She is creating, preserving, and destroying in play, as it were. This Power is called Kali. Kali is verily Brahman, and Brahman is verily Kali. It is one and the same Reality. When we think of It as inactive, that is to say, not engaged in the acts of creation, preservation, and destruction, then we call It Brahman. But when It engages in these activities, then we call It Kali or Shakti. The Reality is one and the same; the difference is in name and form.... She plays in different ways.... She is the Dispenser of boons and the Dispeller of fear.... She resides in the cremation ground, surrounded by corpses, jackals, and terrible female spirits. From her mouth flows a stream of blood, from her neck hangs a garland of human heads, and around her waist is a girdle made of human heads.

After the destruction of the universe, at the end of a great cycle, the Divine Mother garners the seeds for the next creation. She is like the elderly mistress of the house, who has a hotch-potch-pot in which she keeps different articles for household use. Oh yes! Housewives have pots like that, where they keep "seafoam" (i.e., dried cuttlefish), blue pills, small bundles of seeds of cucumber, pumpkin, and gourd, and so on. They take them out when they want them. In the same way, after the destruction of the universe, my Divine Mother, the Embodiment of Brahman, gathers together the seeds for the next creation. After the creation the Primal Power dwells in the universe itself. She brings forth this phenomenal world and then pervades it. In the Vedas creation is likened to the spider and its web. The spider brings the web out of itself and then remains in it. God is the container of the universe and also what is contained in it.

Is Kali, my Divine Mother, of a black complexion? She
appears black because she is viewed from a distance; but when
intimately known she is no longer so. The sky appears blue at
a distance; but look at it close by and you will find that it has
no color.[48]

All, then, is the play of this infinitely wily Mother—the
good and the bad, the lovely and the terrible—and the twinkle in her eye implies the unreality of both. As Ramprasad
says:

> Glory and shame, bitter and sweet, are thine alone;
> This world is nothing but thy play.
> Then why, O Blissful One, dost thou cause a rift in it?
> ...Thou hast bestowed on me this mind,
> And with a knowing wink of thine eye
> Bidden it, at the same time, to go and enjoy the world.[49]

This, then, was the ultimately Mysterious Feminine
whom Brahma evoked for the beguiling of Shiva—and to
every Hindu her image is familiar as a black and shapely
body, four-armed, and adorned with crown and bracelets of
gold, standing upon the prostrate form of Shiva. One right
hand is extended in the gesture of blessing, the other of al-
laying fear. One left hand grasps a scimitar, and the other
holds a severed head by the hair. From her mouth droops a
long blood-licking tongue. (One might compare the Black
Madonnas of the West, not, however, so frank in their spiritual realism.) According to our story, it was not in this form
that Shiva first saw her, for Brahma caused her to be born in
the shape of a baby girl with the name of Sati, or She-Who-Is.

Coming of marriageable age, Brahma and the gods led
this surpassingly exquisite being before Shiva, brought up

through all her childhood in the practice of *bhakti* or devotional Yoga toward him alone. As the eyes of Shiva opened upon her kneeling form, his heart skipped a beat for the minute fraction of time necessary for the God of Love to let fly an arrow that would reach its mark, and from that moment Shiva let his mediations and yogic austerities take care of themselves. Kali-Sati had then and there engulfed the whole withdrawal principle of the universe in her power. The Godhead could not inhale the worlds, for by the magic of the World Mother he had lost his breath.

But Hindu mythology never lets anything drop into the "then they lived happily ever after" situation. Although Shiva and Sati lived in delight for 3,600 years, the day came when the god Daksha, Sati's father, summoned all sentient beings in the world to the celebration of a great sacrifice, but neither Shiva nor Sati were invited because of Daksha's contempt for Shiva's mode of life—since he lived with Sati upon remote mountain peaks, and went naked and ash-smeared like a yogi. This would seem surprising in view of his abandonment of the ascetic life for Sati, unless we bear it in mind that certain forms of Indian Yoga, in common with Chinese Taoism, employ motionless sexual union as a form of meditative discipline, and here the symbolic implication is simply that Shiva absorbed in sexual union with Sati represents the Supreme Self enchanted and enraptured with the world-illusion. He is not invited to the sacrifice because he has thus forgotten himself and no longer "appears" among the company of the gods.

Now as soon as she became aware of this insult, Sati was possessed with an immense rage whose depths led her to the recollection of her original form as Kali, the Terrible Mother, and at this she burst from her body, leaving Sati to Shiva only as a corpse. Shiva was thus aroused to such a paroxysm of rage and grief that he went down to the sacrificial assembly and spread fire and terror from one end of the universe to the other, putting even the gods in fear for their lives, until at last Brahma soothed him, saying:

> O thou, Yogi from before the beginning, pain does not become thee. The proper object of thine inward regard is the Light Supernal, Unmitigated Majesty. Why does that regard repose now on a woman?…The same Sati who beguiled thee is Maya, the enchantress of the world. She takes from the unborn infant, while yet it lives in the mother-womb, all remembrance of its previous state of being; and she has similarly deluded thee, so that thou art racked with pain. A thousand times before hast thou been ravished of thy wit by Sati, and thou has lost her in every eon precisely as now. But just as Sati has always returned to thee, so wilt thou know her again as thou hast known her, and again cleave to her. Collect thy recollection and behold the thousand Satis, how they were snatched from thee by death, so that thou wert forsaken of them a thousand times; and then see how they are born again, and again attain to thee who art hardly accessible even to the meditations of the gods. Behold in thine inner vision how Sati is to be again thy bride.[50]

In Puranic literature the Hindu gods, like those of the Greeks, disport themselves by descending to the human condition and allowing themselves to be carried away by human passions. This is perhaps a way of saying that at every level of life—divine, human, or animal—the problem and predicament of life is the same: an eternal giving-in to the temptation of losing control of the situation, of trusting oneself to chance—the passion of the gambler. Hence the words of Krishna in the *Bhagavad-Gita*, "I am the gambling of the cheat." This goes right down to the metaphysical roots of the whole system—to the intuition that *Paramatman*, the Supreme Self, is always just beyond its own control of itself. In the words of the philosopher Shankara:

> Now a distinct and definite knowledge is possible in respect of everything capable of becoming an object of knowledge: but it is not possible in the case of That which cannot become such an object. That is Brahman, for It is the Knower, and the Knower can know other things, but cannot make Itself the object of Its own knowledge, in the same way that fire can burn other things but cannot burn itself. Neither can it be said that Brahman is able to become an object of knowledge for anything other than Itself, since outside Itself there is nothing which can possess knowledge.[51]

To be an object of knowledge is to be controlled; but the opposite pole of the controlled is the uncontrolled controller— the dimension of life which is always inaccessible to itself. It is impossible to describe something and, at the same time, describe the act of describing. This is why the known forever implies the unknown, and the found the lost. From the Supreme Self to the simplest amoeba the principle and the problem are identical, and if it were solved life would simply cease. The gambling, the game, would have come to an end.

This, then, is why the worldview of Hinduism veers now to the renunciation of the world and now to its affirmation, and why the way of the Buddha is, at one moment in history, a way of complete withdrawal from maya, the cosmic game, and, at another, the way of the Bodhisattva who lays aside the endless peace of nirvana to return into the cycle of birth-and-death to work for the final liberation of all "sentient beings"—a task as interminable as could be imagined. Every one of these alternations, these swings of the pendulum, is a manifestation in time, in succession, of the eternal inbreathing and outbreathing of the Supreme Self whereby the worlds are destroyed and recreated again and again forever. But beyond time, from the eternal standpoint of the Supreme Self, the two motions are simultaneous.

Conceive that the "field" is the round or circus of the world, that the throne of the Spectator, the Universal Man, is central and elevated and that his aquiline glance at all times embraces the whole of the field (equally before and after the enactment of any particular event) in such manner that from his point of view all events are always going on. We are to transfer our consciousness of being, from our position in the field where the games are going on, to the pavilion in which the Spectator, on whom the whole performance depends, is seated at ease.

Conceive that the right lines of vision by which the Spectator is linked to each separate performer, and along which each performer might look upward (inward) to the Spectator if only his powers of vision sufficed, are lines of force or the strings by which the puppet-master moves the puppets for himself....Each of the performing puppets is convinced of its own independent existence and of itself as one amongst others which it sees in its own immediate environment which it distinguishes by name, appearance and behavior. The Spectator does not, and cannot, see the performers as they see themselves, imperfectly, but he knows the being of each one of them as it really is—that is to say, not merely as effective in a given local position, but simultaneously at every point along the line of visual force by which the puppet is connected with himself [the Spectator], and primarily at that point at which all lines converge and where the being of all things coincides with being in itself. There the being of the puppet subsists as an eternal reason in the eternal intellect—otherwise called the Supernal Sun, the Light of lights, Spirit and Truth.

Suppose now that the Spectator goes to sleep: when he closes his eyes the universe disappears, to reappear only when he opens them again. The opening of the eyes ("Let there be light") is called in religion the act of creation, but in metaphysics it is called manifestation, utterance, or spiration...: the closing of eyes is called in religion the "end of the world" but in metaphysics it is called concealment, silence, or despiration. For us, then, there is an alternation of evolution and involution. But for the central Spectator there is no succession of events. He is always awake and always asleep,...nowever.[52]

The following passage from the *Vishnu Purana* explains, too, that the Supreme Self is primordially, i.e., externally, both spirit and body, Brahma and Rudra (Shiva), male and female:

From Brahmá...were born mind-engendered progeny, with forms and faculties derived from his corporeal nature; embodied spirits, produced from the person of that all-wise deity.... But, as they did not multiply themselves, Brahmá created other mind-born sons, like himself....But they were without desire or passion, inspired with holy wisdom, estranged from the universe, and undesirous of progeny. This when Brahmá perceived, he was filled with wrath capable of consuming the three worlds, the flame of which invested, like a garland, heaven, earth, and hell. Then from his forehead, darkened with angry frowns, sprang Rudra, radiant as the noon-tide sun, fierce, and of vast bulk, and of a figure which was half male, half female. Separate yourself, Brahmá said to him, and, having so spoken, disappeared; obedient to which command, Rudra became twofold, disjoining his male and female natures. His male being he again divided into eleven persons, of whom some were agreeable, some hideous; some fierce, some mild. And he multiplied his female nature manifold, of complexions black or white.[53]

Brahma the Creator and Shiva the Destroyer are further "synthesized" in Vishnu the Preserver. But he, too, is of double aspect, male and female.

Sri, the bride of Vishnu, the mother of the world, is eternal, imperishable. In like manner as he is all-pervading, so also is she...omnipresent. Vishnu is meaning; she is speech. Hari (Vishnu) is polity; she is prudence. Vishnu is understanding; she is intellect. He is righteousness; she is devotion. He is the creator; she is the creation. Sri is the earth; Hari, the support of it. The deity is content; the eternal Lakshmi (Sri) is resignation. He is desire; Sri is wish. He is sacrifice; she is sacrificial donation....Lakshmi is the light; and Hari, who is all, and lord of all, the lamp. She, the mother of the world, is the creeping vine; and Vishnu, the tree around which she clings. She is the night; the god who is armed with the mace and discus is the day. He, the bestower of blessings, is the bridegroom; the lotus-throned goddess is the bride. The god is one with all male, the goddess one with all female, rivers. The lotus-eyed deity is the standard; the goddess, seated on a lotus, the banner. Lakshmi is cupidity; Narayana (Vishnu), the master of the world, is covetousness....Govinda (Vishnu) is love; and Lakshmi, his gentle spouse, is pleasure. But why thus diffusely enumerate their presence? It is enough to say, in a word, that of gods, animals, and men, Hari is all that is called male; Lakshmi is all that is termed female. There is nothing else than they.[54]

The intuition of polarity, of the nondual (*advaita*) principle underlying all oppositions is so deep in the Indian mind that Hindu-Buddhist imagery contains nothing like the Christian Devil, even though it has its full share of monstrous and terrifying beings. Mara, the tempter, and Yama, the presiding judge of the purgatories, are always in the final analysis agents or aspects of the Supreme Self or, to use Buddhist terminology, of one's own mind—which is at root no other than the universal mind (*alaya-vijnana*).

Thus there is no doubt whatever of the essential divinity of both combatants in the cosmic battle between Indra, King of the Gods, and the dragon-like Vritra, as described in the *Mahabharata*:

Let us hear, O Sage, of the great dedication to virtue (*dharma*) of that immeasurably brilliant Vritra, whose wisdom was unequaled and devotion to Vishnu beyond account.

And so the tale of the cosmic tournament begins:

In those days the puissant chariot-riding King of Gods, surrounded by his army of celestials, saw before him the great titan, standing mighty as a mountain, 4,500 miles tall and in girth a full 1,500. Whereupon, perceiving that prodigious form, which the powers of all three worlds together would have been impotent to undo, the entire celestial host was paralyzed with fear, and their leader, discerning the contour of his foe, lost the use of his limbs from the waist down.

A noise of beaten drums, trumpets, and other sounding instruments went up on all sides, and the titan, taking notice of the army of the gods and its king before him, was neither astonished nor appalled. Nor did he feel that he would be called upon to make use of all his powers in this fight.

The war commenced. And it terrified all three worlds. For the entire sky was covered with the warriors of both sides, wielding swords, javelins, dirks and axes, spears and heavy clubs, rocks of various size, bows of loud sound, numerous types of celestial weapon, fires and burning brands. And there assembled to watch, gathering in their best chariots, all of those blessed seers to whom the Vedas had in times of yore been revealed, likewise yogis fully realized, and heavenly musicians in their own fair cars, wherein were also celestial mistresses; moreover, shining above all was the creator and governor of the world, the great god Brahma himself.

Then *dharma*-supporting Vritra deftly overwhelmed both the King of Gods and the entire world of air with a dense shower of rocks. And the gods, burning with anger, pouring a shower of arrows at those rocks, dissolved them. But the titan, mighty in his *māyā*-power as well as in his strength, completely stupefied the King of Gods by virtue of his *māyā*. And when the god of a hundred sacrifices, numbed by that *māyā*-power, stood without moving, the Vedic sage Vasishtha—who in contemplation had heard, and so composed, all the hymns of the seventh book of the Rig Veda—restored him to his senses by chanting at him Vedic verses. "You are the leader of the gods," said the sage. "Within you is the power of all three worlds. Why, therefore, do you falter? Brahma the Creator, Vishnu the Preserver, and Shiva the Destroyer of Illusion, as well as glorious, divine Soma, and all the Vedic seers, are watching. Do not collapse here like a mere mortal. All three of Shiva's eyes are upon you. And do you not hear the Vedic saints lauding you in your victory with hymns?"

Thus recalled to his senses, the god, becoming confident, applied himself to yoga, and so dispelled the *māyā* by which he had been stupefied. Whereupon the seers, who had now been witness to the prowess of the titan, turned to Shiva, lord of the universe, in prayer. And that Great God, in response, sent his energy into Vritra in the form of a terrific fever. Simultaneously Vishnu entered Indra's weapon. And the whole company of seers, turning to Indra, bade him attack his foe. The god Shiva himself addressed him:

"Before you is your foe, Vritra, supported by his army: the very Self (*ātman*) of the universe, ubiquitous, and of immense deluding power. For 60,000 years that titan applied himself to severe ascetic austerities for the acquisition of this strength, until, in the end, Brahma was compelled to grant the boons he wished. And these were the greatest to be gained by yoga, namely, the power of creating illusions at will, unconquerable force, and energy without end. However, I am now committing to you *my* energy and force. Therefore, with yoga to assist you, slay the enemy with your bolt."

Said the King of Gods: "O Greatest God, before thy blessed eyes, endowed with the boon of thy grace, I shall now, with this my thunderbolt, slay that invincible son of the mother of demons."

And the gods and all the saints, seeing the enemy struck with that fever, raised a roar of great joy. Rolling drums, kettle drums, conchs and trumpets, thousands upon thousands, everywhere began to beat and blow. The demons lost their wits. Their powers of delusion left them. And the form that the King of Gods then assumed, on the point of the great moment of his victory, seated in his car, amid the shouts of acclaim of the Vedic seers, was such that none could look at it without fear.

But let us tell, first, of the stricken titan. When he had

been filled with that burning fever, his immense mouth gave forth a blast of flame. His color disappeared. Everywhere he trembled, he could scarcely breathe, and each hair on his body stood erect. His mind came out through his jaws in the shape of an evil, hideous jackal, and meteors burst blazing from his sides, both right and left.

And the King of Gods, praised and worshiped by the gods, handling his bolt, watched the monster, who, when he had been ravished by that fever, yawned wide with a great howl; and while his great mouth was open still the god let fly into it his bolt, filled with no less energy than the fire that consumes the universe at the end of a cosmic cycle, which blasted Vritra prodigiously, forthwith. The gods were in ecstasy. And the King of Gods, recovering his bolt, made away in haste in his chariot toward the sky.

But that heinous crime, Brahmanicide, dreadful, ominous, striking fear into all the worlds, came forth from the body of the murdered titan with teeth projecting terribly, of an aspect furiously contorted, tawny and black, with disheveled hair, appalling eyes, and a garland of skulls around her neck, bathed in blood, clad in rags and in the bark of trees. And she went after the master of the bolt, overtook his chariot, seized him, and from that moment Brahmanicide was stuck to him. Terrified, he fled into a lotus stalk, where he stayed for years with it clinging to him still, trying every way to be quit of her. But all his attempts were in vain until, at last, with that fiend still attached, the miserable King of Gods approached in obeisance Brahma the Creator, who, knowing the crime, commenced to ponder the question of how the King of Gods might be set free.[55]

The battle here described between the angels of light and darkness, *deva* and *ashura*, is—for all its thunders—very different in spirit from the War in Heaven as we find it in the Christian apocalypses and in Milton, where the demonic power is felt to be absolutely and irredeemably bad. But here Vritra is simply the dark, obverse form of "the very Self (*atman*) of the universe," and in defeating him Indra involves himself in the guilt of Brahmanicide—priest murder, here symbolizing rather the murder of the Godhead in its unrecognized form.

One of the best sources for an understanding of the function of the dark or demonic aspect of divinity in Hindu-Buddhist mythology is a curious work known as the *Bardo Thödol*, or the Tibetan *Book of the Dead*, a text which may be as early as the seventh or eighth century AD. Based, no doubt, upon the ideas of Indian Tantric Buddhism, this document describes the various states of consciousness which are supposed to follow the moment of death, filling the intermediate period between death and rebirth. These comprise a series of visions, beatific and then horrendous, whereby the spiritual attainment of the departed is tested. To the spiritually immature person, the beatific visions are so poignant and unbearable that he slips away to sights which, though at first more tempting, turn out to be increasingly appalling, so that at last he has to seek refuge from them by fleeing to a maternal womb from which he is again born into the world. The book is cast in the form of a liturgy or ritual addressed to the departed immediately after his decease. The first vision following death is of the Clear Light of reality itself, of the "void" or undifferentiated consciousness which underlies all being, knowledge, and perception.

O nobly-born (so-and-so), listen. Now thou art experiencing the Radiance of the Clear Light of Pure Reality. Recognize it. O nobly-born, thy present intellect, in real nature void, not formed into anything as regards characteristics or colour, naturally void, is the very Reality, the All-Good.

Thine own intellect, which is now voidness, yet not to be regarded as of the voidness of nothingness, but as being the intellect itself, unobstructed, shining, thrilling, and blissful, is the very consciousness, the All-Good Buddha.

Thine own consciousness, not formed into anything, in reality void, and the intellect, shining and blissful—these two,—are inseparable. The union of them is the *Dharma-Kāya** state of Perfect Enlightenment.

Thine own consciousness, shining, void, and inseparable from the Great Body of Radiance, hath no birth, nor death, and is the Immutable Light—Buddha Amitābha.†

Knowing this is sufficient. Recognizing the voidness of thine own intellect to be Buddhahood, and looking upon it as being thine own consciousness, is to keep thyself in the [state of the] divine mind of the Buddha....

O nobly-born, when thy body and mind were separating, thou must have experienced a glimpse of the Pure Truth, subtle, sparkling, bright, dazzling, glorious, and radiantly

---

*   The *Dharma-kaya* is the first and most fundamental of the so-called *Tri-kaya*, or Three Bodies of Buddha, where "Buddha" refers not to the historic Buddha, Gautama, but to the Buddha-nature, the transcendental consciousness underlying the universe. The word Buddha is basically a title, designating one who has awakened to the true nature of the world, but it also comes to mean the reality to which such a one is awakened. The other two Bodies (*kaya*) are termed the *Sambhoga-kaya* and the *Nirmana-kaya,* and thus the three refer to the following aspects of the transcendental consciousness: (1) its original and undivided essence, (2) its blissful, joyous, and hence playful propensity, which gives rise to (3) the apparent division of itself into all the variations of individual form.

†   Amitabha, Immutable or Boundless Light, is one of the five Dhyani Buddhas, i.e., Buddhas dwelling above and beyond the manifested world and representing the five aspects of the supramundane order which correspond to the five elements of the mundane order—space, air, fire, water, and earth.

awesome, in appearance like a mirage moving across a land-scape in springtime in one continuous stream of vibrations. Be not daunted thereby, nor terrified, nor awed. That is the radiance of thine own true nature. Recognize it.

From the midst of that radiance, the natural sound of Reality, reverberating like a thousand thunders simultaneously sounding, will come. That is the natural sound of thine own real self. Be not daunted thereby, nor terrified, nor awed.

The body which thou hast now is called the thought-body of propensities. Since thou hast not a material body of flesh and blood, whatever may come,—sounds, lights, or rays,—are, all three, unable to harm thee: thou art incapable of dying. It is quite sufficient for thee to know that these apparitions are thine own thought-forms. Recognize this to be the *Bardo*.

O nobly-born, if thou dost not now recognize thine own thought-forms, whatever of meditation or of devotion thou mayst have performed while in the human world—if thou hast not met with this present teaching—the lights will daunt thee, the sounds will awe thee, and the rays will terrify thee. Shouldst thou not know this all-important key to the teachings,—not being able to recognize the sounds, lights, and rays,—thou wilt have to wander in the *Sangsāra*.[56]*

If the departed is not endowed with sufficient insight to become absorbed into the vision of the Clear Light, then and there attaining nirvana, he finds its radiance intolerable and is next exposed in succession to its beatific and horrendous aspects. First comes the beatific:

---

*   *Sangsara* or *samsara* is the wheel or round of birth-and-death through which all sentient beings wander again and again until they are awakened by becoming aware of their identity with the transcendental Buddha-consciousness, i.e., by attaining nirvana.

Then, from the Central Realm, called the Spreading Forth of the Seed, the Bhagavān Vairochana, white in colour, and seated upon a lion-throne, bearing an eight-spoked wheel in his hand, and embraced by the Mother of the Space of Heaven, will manifest himself to thee.*

It is the aggregate of matter resolved into its primordial state which is the blue light.

The Wisdom of the *Dharma-Dhātu*,† blue in colour, shining, transparent, glorious, dazzling, from the heart of Vairochana as the Father-Mother, will shoot forth and strike against thee with a light so radiant that thou wilt scarcely be able to look at it.

Along with it, there will also shine a dull white light from the *devas*,‡ which will strike against thee in thy front.

Thereupon, because of the power of bad *karma*,§ the glorious blue light of the Wisdom of the *Dharma-Dhātu* will produce in thee fear and terror, and thou wilt [wish to] flee from it. Thou wilt beget a fondness for the dull white light of the *devas*.

---

*   Bhagavan (the Lord) Vairochana is another of the five Dhyani Buddhas, usually given the supreme or central position. He is here described as appearing with his Shakti, or feminine counterpart, Mother of the Space of Heaven, because Vairochana corresponds to the mundane element of space (*akasha*).

†   The *Dharma-dhatu* designates the whole universe as a realm (*dhatu*) in which all things and events are mutually interdependent and interpenetrating like a net of jewels, in which each jewel carries the reflection of all the others, and of all the reflections in all the others. See below, pp. 226–42.

‡   *Devas* are best translated as "angels" rather than "gods." They represent the height of delight and success possible of attainment in samsara, the round of birth-and-death, but because samsara is a round the situation of the *devas* is impermanent, and must in due course give place to its opposite.

§   *Karma* (lit., "doing") is action leading necessarily to further involvement in action, and thus action in the pattern of a vicious circle (samsara). Often it is somewhat misleadingly translated as "cause-and-effect," the principle whereby good and bad deeds have their appropriate results, leading to good and bad situations upon the round of birth-and-death.

At this stage, thou must not be awed by the divine blue light which will appear shining, dazzling, and glorious; and be not startled by it. That is the light of the Tathāgata* called the Light of the Wisdom of the *Dharma-Dhātu*. Put thy faith in it, believe in it firmly, and pray unto it, thinking in thy mind that it is the light proceeding from the heart of the Bhagavān Vairochana coming to receive thee while in the dangerous ambuscade of the Bardo.† That light is the light of the grace of Vairochana.

Be not fond of the dull white light of the *devas*. Be not attached [to it]; be not weak. If thou be attached to it, thou wilt wander into the abodes of the *devas* and be drawn into the whirl of the Six *Lokas*.‡ That is an interruption to obstruct thee on the Path of Liberation. Look not at it. Look at the bright light in deep faith.[57]

But for the person who flees from the light of the beatific aspect of the Buddhas there now follows the wrathful or horrendous aspect. A Tibetan painting of such beings (plate 3) displays figures which the Westerner would at once identify as demons or devils, but the text assures the departed that they are only "the former Peaceful Deities in changed aspect." Here is plainly stated what, west of Persia and the Urals, is for the most part hidden or barely hinted—*Demon*

---

* Tathagata (he who goes or comes "thus") is a title often applied to Buddhas because they see the universe in its true state or "thus"-ness (*tathata*). Hindu and Buddhist philosophy use the word *tat* (that) or *tatha* (thus or such) to indicate reality without describing or qualifying it, to refer to the realm of reality as nonverbal or unutterable and so beyond the verbal classifications of "being" or "nonbeing," "eternal" or "temporal," etc.

† The *Bardo* is the world of the dead, i.e., the interval between death and rebirth.

‡ The six *lokas* (worlds) are the six divisions of samsara, the wheel, i.e., of humanity, of the *devas*, of the *asuras* (wrathful angels), of animals, of the purgatories, and of the frustrated ghosts (*pretas*).

est deus inversus, the Devil is God inverted: the two are the
One seen from opposite points of view. The beatific vision,
or the Clear Light itself, is terrifying to whoever would retain
his separateness, and to retain separateness, to cling to egocentric existence, is only to intensify terror—which in fact is
no other than the spasm of clinging. But the beatific and the
horrendous must alike "be recognized to be the emanations
of one's own intellect." For maya, the world-illusion, is generated by the power of thinking, of being able to divide the universe into named and classified segments called things and
events—segments which thereupon appear to be isolated
and independent. The vision of totality, of the universe as the
one body of the *Dharma-kaya*, is lost, and in its place comes
the vision of multiplicity, magnificent in its variety and terrifying in its discordance. For "there is nothing either good or
bad but thinking makes it so." The text therefore continues:

> Therefore, after the cessation [of the dawning] of the Peaceful
> and the Knowledge-Holding Deities, who come to welcome
> one, the fifty-eight flame-enhaloed, wrathful, blood-drinking
> deities come to dawn, who are only the former Peaceful De-
> ities in changed aspect—according to the place [or psychic-
> centre of the *Bardo*-body of the deceased whence they proceed];
> nevertheless, they will not resemble them....
>
> O nobly-born, the Great Glorious Buddha-Heruka, dark-
> brown of colour; with three heads, six hands, and four feet
> firmly postured; the right [face] being white, the left, red, the
> central, dark-brown; the body emitting flames of radiance;
> the nine eyes widely opened, in terrifying gaze; the eyebrows
> quivering like lightning; the protruding teeth glistening and
> set over one another; giving vent to sonorous utterances of
> "a-la-la" and "ha-ha," and piercing whistling sounds; the hair

of a reddish-yellow colour, standing on end, and emitting radiance; the heads adorned with dried [human] skulls, and the (symbols of the) sun and moon; black serpents and raw [human] heads forming a garland for the body; the first of the right hands holding a wheel, the middle one, a sword, the last one, a battle-axe; the first of the left hands, a bell, the middle one, a skull-bowl, the last one, a plough-share; his body embraced by the Mother, Buddha-Krotishaurima, her right hand clinging to his neck and her left putting to his mouth a red shell [filled with blood], [making] a palatal sound like a crackling [and] a clashing sound, and a rumbling sound as loud as thunder; [emanating from the two deities] radiant flames of wisdom, blazing from every hair-pore [of the body] and each containing a flaming *dorje*;* [the two deities together thus], standing with [one] leg bent and [the other] straight and tense, on a dais supported by horned eagles, will come forth from within thine own brain and shine vividly upon thee. Fear that not. Be not awed. Know it to be the embodiment of thine own intellect. As it is thine own tutelary deity, be not terrified. Be not afraid, for in reality it is the Bhagavān Vairochana, the Father-Mother. Simultaneously with the recognition, liberation will be obtained....

O nobly-born, the Peaceful Deities emanate from the Voidness of the *Dharma-Kāya*; recognize them. From the Radiance of the *Dharma-Kāya* emanate the Wrathful Deities; recognize them.

At this time when the Fifty-eight Blood-Drinking Deities emanating from thine own brain come to shine upon thee, if thou knowest them to be the radiances of thine own intellect,

---

* *Dorje* (Sanskrit, *vajra*) is the symbolic adamantine thunderbolt, emblem of wisdom and its power. It is represented as an object the size of a small dumbbell with claws of flame upon either end.

thou wilt merge, in the state of at-one-ment, into the body of the Blood-Drinking Ones there and then, and obtain Buddhahood.

O nobly-born, by not recognizing now, and by fleeing from the deities out of fear, again sufferings will come to overpower thee. If this be not known, fear being begotten of the Blood-Drinking Deities, [one is] awed and terrified and fainteth away: one's own thought-forms turn into illusory appearances, and one wandereth into the *Sangsāra*; if one be not awed and terrified, one will not wander into the *Sangsāra*.

Furthermore, the bodies of the largest of the Peaceful and .Wrathful Deities are equal [in vastness] to the limits of the heavens; the intermediate, as big as Mt. Meru;* the smallest, equal to eighteen bodies such as thine own body, set one upon another. Be not terrified at that; be not awed. If all existing phenomena shining forth as divine shapes and radiances be recognized to be the emanations of one's own intellect, Buddhahood will be obtained at that very instant of recognition.[58]

We leave, now, the realms of myth in which there is an explicit recognition of the basic unity of the light and dark forces. Curiously, as we move westward this recognition becomes increasingly implicit, at times vanishing altogether into a mythology of total conflict wherein the two forces are implacable and perpetual enemies.

---

*   In Hindu-Buddhist mythology Meru corresponds roughly to the Greek Olympus, the central mountain of the world, uniting heaven and earth.

3. The Two Brothers

SIBLING RIVALRY IS PROBABLY just as usual as brotherly love. But the importance of the symbol of conflict between brothers is that it keeps harmony and conflict in balance. The basic tie between the opposites is not entirely submerged, even though it may somehow aggravate the bitterness of the battle. Yet however acrimonious the conflict may be, it is impossible to disown one's own blood completely. Thus in a number of mythologies the opposition between light and darkness, good and evil, is represented as a rivalry between brothers, sometimes unresolved, though sometimes culminating in the redemption of that brother who stands for the side of the shadow.

Today the mythology of ancient Egypt seems bewildering and remote—a complex and chaotic polytheism without the unifying philosophy of Hinduism, a multitude of images emerging from a vast span of time so distant from our own that it is hard for us to realize how much history and how much variety it contains. Nevertheless, a relatively late document* gives us one of the most remarkable versions of this

---

*   The Chester Beatty Papyrus, No. 1.

fraternal combat upon the cosmic scale. Strictly speaking, Horus and Set are not brothers but nephew and uncle, Set being the brother of Horus's mother, Isis. However, they are frequently described as brothers in the texts, since Horus stands for the sky by day and Set for the sky by night, Horus for the northern division of Egypt and Set for the southern, and thus it may be assumed that the stories of their contests represent both cosmic and political rivalries.

Horus, son of Osiris and Isis, has the hawk form which allies him with Rā, god of the sun and one of the many forms of the Egyptian creator of the world. Set is usually depicted with the head of a doglike creature, perhaps a saluki, upon a human body. He is the son of the sky-goddess Nut and true brother of Osiris, but, as we shall see, Horus is in some sense a reincarnation of his father and always stands toward Set as equal and opposite. The story begins with Horus as a boy petitioning the Nine Gods for the right to occupy his father's throne. The council of the gods is presided over by Neb-er-djer, the Lord Without Limit, otherwise known as Rā Harakhti, or Rā "Horus-of-the-two-horizons," another of the many forms of the creator god.* Horus's petition is enthusiastically supported by Isis, his mother, and by Thoth, the god of wisdom, but their enthusiastic haste to reach a decision in favor of Horus displeases Neb-er-djer, the president, at which point Set asks to be allowed to settle the matter by duel. After much indecision, haggling, and intrigue, the Nine Gods

---

*   Since the text here is late and also of a slightly humorous and disrespectful attitude, the various gods appear as separate personalities without regard to the anachronism involved. For example, the creator god, known at different times and places under different names and symbols, appears here in all guises at once.

meet on the Western Delta of the Nile and command that the White Crown be set on the head of Horus, and that he be established in the office of his father Osiris. But Set cries out in fury, "Is the office to be given to my young brother whilst I, his elder brother, am in being?"* It is at this point that the president gives permission for a duel.

And Set proposed to Horus that each of them should transform himself into a hippopotamus, and then cast himself into the sea, and that he who came out of the water before the end of three months was ipso facto disqualified from the office of Osiris. So each took the form of a hippopotamus and entered the sea. Then Isis began to weep saying: "Set hath killed my son Horus," and she set to work to find a means of saving him. She fetched a hank of flax (or fibre?) and plaited (or twisted) it into a rope. And she fetched a lump of copper [weighing] a *teben*, and she beat and moulded it into a marine weapon, and having tied the rope to it she hurled it into the water at the place where Horus and Set had entered the sea. The harpoon struck Horus, and he cried out to Isis to make it drop from him; and Isis did so. A second time she hurled the harpoon, and this time it struck Set, and he cried out to Isis as his maternal sister to make the harpoon drop from him. Isis was sorry for him, and when Set entreated her not to bear enmity against her maternal brother, she commanded the harpoon to drop from his body, and it did so forthwith. Then Horus was wroth with Isis, and he became like a panther of the Sûdân. He had his axe in his hand [now it weighed sixteen *teben*], and he hacked off the head of his mother Isis, and clasping it to his bosom he went up into a mountain. Forthwith Isis transformed herself into a flint statue which had no head. Seeing

---

*   We shall note the recurrent theme of the advantage going to the younger brother.

this, Rā Harakhti said to Thoth, "What is this headless thing which hath come?" and Thoth told him that it was Isis, the mother of Horus, who had hacked off her head. Rā Harakhti cried out with a loud voice to the Nine Gods, saying, "Let us hasten and punish him severely," and he and the Nine Gods went up into the mountains to seek for Horus, the son of Isis.

Now behold Horus was lying down under a tree with dense foliage in the country of Uahet…There Set found him and he seized him, and he threw him upon his back on the stony ground. He gouged out his two *Udjats* (i.e., eyes) from their sockets, and he fastened them on the stony ground to light up the earth, and the rims (literally, the outsides) of his two eyes became two balls (?) *skharer-t*, and they grew (or sprouted) into lotuses. Then Set went back and lied to Rā Harakhti, saying "I could not find Horus."

The goddess Hathor* having, presumably, knowledge of what had happened, went and found Horus lying on the stony ground weeping. She caught a gazelle and milked it, and told Horus to open his eyes so that she might pour in milk. At her command Horus opened his eyes, first the right and then the left, and when she looked at them she found that Horus had recovered his sight. She went to Rā Harakhti and told him that she had found Horus whose eyes Set had carried away, and that she had restored them, and added, "Behold, he hath come." Thereupon the Nine Gods ordered that Horus and Set be cited to appear that sentence may be passed on them. When they appeared before the Nine Gods Neb-er-djer addressed Horus and Set, saying, "O get ye gone, and let there

---

*   Hathor or Sekhmet is a goddess usually shown with the head of a cow surmounted by the lunar disk between the horns. The name Hathor is *hethor*, i.e., "the house of Horus"—designating the eastern sky. In the fabulous muddle of Egyptian theology, she is the wife of Rā and mother of Horus, and thus perhaps an early form of Isis.

be heard by you what I am about to say to you: Eat ye, drink ye, [but] we would be at peace. Stop ye from the contention in which ye indulge every day." Then Set suggested that they should pass a happy time together (i.e., keep a feast) in his house, and Horus said unto him, "Assuredly I will do so; of course I will"; and the two went to Set's house. When evening came a *dîwân*, or couch, was prepared for them to sleep on, and the two laid themselves down on it.

During the night Set became excited sexually and attempted to violate Horus and failed because Horus caught the efflux of Set in one of his hands. Horus went to Isis and showed her his hand and its contents, and seizing her knife she hacked off the polluted hand of Horus and threw it into the water, and then fashioned a hand for him as useful as that which she had cut off. Then she fetched some sweet smelling unguent and smeared the phallus of Horus with it. This she made to swell up, and when she had placed it in a vessel Horus made his emission to fall into it. In the morning Isis took the efflux of Horus and went to the garden of Set, and asked the gardener which plant Set was in the habit of eating as an aphrodisiac. The gardener replied that the only herb there under his charge which Set ate was the *āb-t*, which some believe to have been a kind of lettuce.

Then Isis poured the efflux of Horus over these plants, and Set came day by day according to his wont, and ate them; the text adds the astonishing remark that Set became with child by the seed of Horus.*

Then Set went and told Horus that he wished to go into

---

* "This, of course, means that Set was believed to be a bisexual god like Temu or Rā. The allusion to pregnancy caused by swallowing mentioned in the *Tale of the Two Brothers* does not help us, for the person who swallowed the two splinters of wood was a woman who could conceive and not a man who could not." —Comment by A. Gardiner.

Court and plead against him, and as Horus was willing they both went and stood before the Nine Gods, who straightway ordered them to make their pleadings. Set stood up and claimed the office of Osiris because he had performed on Horus, who was there present, the deed of the victorious warrior (i.e., he claimed to have violated Horus). The Nine Gods believed his lie and retched and spat in (or in front of) the face of Horus. Horus laughed at them, and then swore an oath by God that what Set had said was a lie. And he demanded that the seed of Set and his own seed should be summoned as witnesses, so that they might see from whence each seed would respond. On this Thoth laid his hand on the arm of Horus, saying, "Come forth, O seed of Set," and it made answer to him from the water in the marsh. Then Thoth laid his hand on the arm of Set, and he said, "Come forth, O seed of Horus." The seed answered, "Where shall I come forth?" and Thoth said, "From his ear." The seed said, "Must I, being a divine essence, come forth from his ear?" And Thoth said, "Come forth from the crown of his head." And it came forth as a Disk of Gold (i.e., the solar disk) on the head of Set. At this Set was wroth and he reached out his hand to lay hold on the Gold Disk, but Thoth snatched it away from him and set it as a diadem upon his own head.

The Nine Gods who had been watching these acts decided that Horus was in the right and Set in the wrong, and when they delivered their judgment according to their opinion Set raged, and he swore an oath and refused to accept it until he had made another attempt to defeat Horus.

The contest continues until at last the Nine Gods decide to write a letter to Osiris himself in his remote kingdom of the Tuat or Underworld. Osiris replies in favor of Horus, and warns the Nine Gods that all their power derives ultimately from himself. And the narrative proceeds:

[Many days] after these happenings the letter of Osiris reached the place where Neb-er-djer was with the Nine Gods, and Thoth read it before them. When they had heard it they said, Osiris is in the right. But Set petitioned to be allowed to have one more fight, and when it had taken place on the island mentioned above Horus was declared to be the victor, and Set was made a prisoner by Isis. Atem* ordered Isis to bring Set before him, and when she did so he asked Set why he had refused to accept the judgment of the gods and had seized the office of Osiris. Set replied that such was not the fact, and he agreed that Horus should have his father's office. Horus was brought forthwith, and the White Crown was placed on his head, and he was set in the place of Osiris. The gods acclaimed him as the good king of Ta-mera (Egypt), and the good lord of every land for ever. Isis rejoiced at the triumph of her son. Then Ptah† asked what was to be done to Set, and Rā Harakhti decreed that Set should live with him and be as a son to him, and that his occupation would be to thunder in the heavens and terrify men. The gods told Rā Harakhti that Horus had become governor, and he rejoiced and he ordered the Nine Gods to "rejoice down to the ground" before Horus, the son of Isis. Isis said, "Horus standeth as Ḥeq (i.e., the hereditary Governor of Egypt), the Nine Gods celebrate a festival, heaven rejoiceth." Forthwith they placed garlands of flowers on their heads. The Nine Gods and all the earth were content when they saw Horus, the son of Osiris of Ṭeṭu, made Governor.[59]

Note that the story ends without any punishment for Set. On the contrary, the Supreme Sun, Rā Harakhti, adopts him

---

*   Atem or Temu is the divine personification of the setting sun.
†   Ptah is one of the earliest forms of the creator god, usually represented in human form as a divine craftsman.

and puts him in charge of the thunder. After all, Rā Hara-khti = Neb-er-djer = Ptah = Osiris, each having in the course of Egyptian history done duty as the Lord and Creator of the Universe. It is thus as if Horus were the right hand and Set the left of the Supreme Being, dispensing mercy in one direction and wrath in the other. Egyptian iconography gives us several examples of a Horus-Set figure with the two heads upon one and the same body. It is also noteworthy that Set becomes pregnant by Horus, giving birth to the solar disk through the crown of his head. Connected or uncon-nected, there is a comparable symbolism in Kundalini-yoga where the individual is liberated by passing out through the crown of the head in the form of a flame, and the ap-erture in the skull is taken as the microcosmic counterpart of the Sun door in the dome of the heavens—that is, the point at which the light of the Godhead shines through the firmament.

Next is a version of the two-brothers theme from the literature of Jainism, an Indian philosophy or "way of lib-eration" astonishingly akin to primitive Buddhism in doc-trine, mythology, and period of origin, approximately 526 BC, though Jaina legends take it back much earlier. The following story concerns the successive incarnations of the Lord Parsva, who is supposed to have attained the rank of Tirthankara in 772 BC. The Jaina conception of a Tirthankara is closely similar to the idea of a Buddha, namely the man who is in nirvana, the state of liberation from maya—the cosmic illu-sion. But Jainism veers even more than primitive Buddhism to the negative, world-denying pole of Indian spirituality, and thus it is hard to see how the Jaina nirvana differs from total

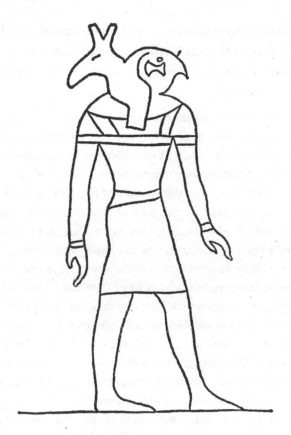

FIGURE 6
After Lanzone, *Dizionario di mitologia egiziana*.
Torino, 1881–1886. Pl. 378, 2.

extinction. But this need not concern us in the following sequence of myths:*

---

* Retold by Heinrich Zimmer and Joseph Campbell. Zimmer's notes left no clue
to the original source of this material. It is very similar to a version of the story
found in Bhavadevasuri's *Parshvanatha Caritra*, but this has not been translated
fully into English.

During the course of his many incarnations, the one who is to become the great Tirthankara, Parsva, has always an evil brother who seems to grow in vice in proportion to Parsva's growth in virtue.

The enmity between the two is represented as having begun in their ninth incarnation before the last. They had been born, that time, as the sons of Visvabhūti, the prime minister of a certain prehistoric king named Aravinda. And it so happened that their father, one day thinking: "Transitory surely is this world," went away on the path of emancipation, leaving his wife behind with the two sons and a great store of wealth. The elder son, Kamatha, was passionate and crafty, whereas the younger, Marubhūti, was eminently virtuous (the latter, of course, being the one who is to be Pārśvanātha in their final birth), and so when their king one time had to leave his kingdom on a campaign against a distant enemy, he committed the safety of the palace not to the elder brother but to the younger, Marubhūti; and the elder, in sinful anger, then seduced his brother's wife. The adultery being discovered, the king when he returned asked Marubhūti what the punishment should be. The future Tirthankara advised forgiveness. But the king, commanding that the adulterer's face should be painted black, had him seated, facing backwards, on an ass, conducted through the capital, and expelled from the realm.

Deprived thus of honor, home, property, and family, Kamatha devoted himself in the wilderness to the most extreme austerities, not in a humble spirit of renunciation or contrition, but with the intent to acquire superhuman, demonic powers with which to win revenge. When Marubhūti was apprised of these penances, he thought that his brother had at last become purified, and therefore, in spite of the warnings of the king, paid him a visit, thinking to invite him home. He discovered Kamatha standing—as had been his custom day and night—holding on his upstretched hands a great slab of stone, overcoming by that painful exercise the normal states of human weakness. But when the future Tìr-thaṅkara bowed in obeisance at his feet, the terrible hermit, beholding this gesture of conciliation, was so filled with rage that he flung down the great stone on Marubhūti's head, killing him as he bowed. The ascetics of the penance-grove, from whom the monster had learned his techniques of self-affliction, expelled him immediately from their company, and he sought refuge among a wild tribe of Bhils. He became a highwayman and murderer, and in due course died, following a life of crime....

Though both Kamatha and Marubhūti have died, this death is not to be the end of their adventure. The good king Aravinda, whom Marubhūti had served as minister, was moved, following the death of his officer, to abandon the world and take up the life of a hermit; the cause of his decision being a comparatively insignificant incident. Always pious, he was planning to build a Jaina sanctuary, when one day he beheld floating in the sky a cloud that looked like a majestic, slowly moving temple. Watching this with rapt attention, he became inspired with the idea of constructing his place of worship in just that form. So he sent in haste for brushes and paints with which to set it down; but when he turned again, the form had already changed. A weird thought then occurred to him. "Is the world," he mused, "but a series of such passing states? Why then should I call anything my own? What is the good of continuing in this career of king?" He summoned his son, installed him on the throne, and departed from the kingdom, became an aimless mendicant, and wandered from one wilderness to the next.

And so he chanced, one day, upon a great assemblage of saints in the depths of a certain forest, engaged in various forms of meditation. He joined their company, and had not been long among them when a mighty elephant, running mad, entered the grove—a dangerous event that sent most of the hermits to the four directions. Aravinda, however, remained standing rigidly, in a profound state of contemplation. The elephant, rushing about, presently came directly before the meditating king, but instead of trampling him, became suddenly calm when it perceived his absolute immobility. Lowering its trunk it went down on its great front knees in obeisance. "Why are you continuing in acts of injury?" the voice of Aravinda then was heard to ask. "There is no greater sin than that of injuring other beings. Your incarnation in this form is the result of demerits acquired at the moment of your violent death. Give up these sinful acts; begin to practice vows; a happy state will then stand in store for you."

The clarified vision of the contemplative had perceived that the elephant was his former minister, Marubhūti. Owing to the violence of the death and the distressing thoughts that had been harbored in the instant of pain, the formerly pious man was now in this inferior and rabid incarnation. His name was Vajraghosa, "Thundering Voice of the Lightning," and his mate was the former wife of his adulterous brother. Hearing the voice of the king whom he had served, he recalled his recent human life, took the vows of a hermit, received religious instruction at the feet of Aravinda, and determined to commit no further acts of nuisance. Thenceforward the mighty beast ate but a modicum of grass—only enough to keep its body and soul together; and this saintly diet, together with a program of austerities, brought it down so much in weight that it became very quiet and emaciated. Nevertheless, it never relaxed, even for a moment, from its devout contemplation of the Tìrthankaras, those "Exalted Ones" (*paramesthins*) now serene at the zenith of the universe.

Vajraghosa, from time to time, would go to the bank of a nearby river to quench his thirst, and on one of these occasions was killed by an immense serpent. This was his former brother, the perennial antagonist of his career, who, having expired in deep iniquity, had been reincarnated in this malignant form. The very sight of the saintly pachyderm proceeding piously to the river stirred the old spirit of revenge, and the serpent struck. Its deadly poison ran like fire through the loose and heavy skin. But in spite of terrific pain, Vajraghosa did not forget his hermit vows. He died the death called "the peaceful death of absolute renunciation," and was born immediately in the twelfth heaven as the god Sasi-prabha, "Splendor of the Moon."

"Splendor of the Moon," the happy deity, dwelt amidst the abundant pleasures of his heaven for sixteen oceans (*sagaras*) of time, yet did not relapse even there from the regular practice of pious acts. He was reborn, therefore, as a fortunate prince named Agnivega ("Strength of Fire"), who, on the death of his father, ascended the throne of his domain.

One day a homeless sage appeared, asking to converse with the young king, and he discoursed on the way of liberation. Immediately Agnivega experienced an awakening of the religious sense, and the world abruptly lost its charm for him. He joined his teacher's monastic following and through the regular practice of graduated penances diminished within himself both his attachment and his aversion to worldly things, until at last all was supplanted by a sublime indifference. Then he retired to a cave in the high Himalayas and there, steeped in the profoundest contemplation, lost all consciousness of the external world—but while in this state was again sharply bitten by a snake. The poison burned; but he did not lose his peaceful equilibrium. He welcomed death, and expired in a spiritual attitude of sublime submission.

The serpent, of course, was again the usual enemy, who, following his murder of the elephant, had descended to the fifth hell where the sufferings for a period of sixteen oceans of time had been indescribable. Then he had returned to the earth, still in the form of a snake, and at the sight of Agnivega committed again his characteristic sin. The hermit-king, at the very moment of his death, was elevated to the status of a god—this time for a period of twenty-two oceans of years; but the serpent descended to the sixth hell, where its torments were even greater than in the fifth....

Queen Laksmivati, the pure and lovely consort of a certain king named Vajravirya ("Having the Hero-Power of the Thunderbolt"), dreamt in one night five auspicious dreams, from which her husband deduced that some god was about to descend to become his son. Within the year she gave birth to a boy, and on his beautiful little body were found the sixty-four auspicious signs of the Cakravartin.* He was named Vajranabha ("Diamond Navel"), became proficient in every branch of learning, and in due time began to rule the realm. The world wheel (*cakra*) lay among the weapons in his royal treasury in the form of a discus of irresistible force; and he conquered the four quarters of the earth with this weapon, compelling all other kings to bow their heads before his throne. He also acquired the fourteen supernatural jewels that are the marks of the glory of the Cakravartin. And yet,

---

* Cakravartin is literally "one who turns the wheel" and is applied either to a universal monarch or to a great sage, such as a Buddha or Tirthankara, because he sets in motion the wheel of the *dharma,* the doctrine and method of liberation.

PLATE 1. *Lingam* and *Yoni*

PLATE 2. *Kali*

PLATE 3. *Black Madonna*

PLATE 4. *Yamantaka*

PLATE 5. *St. Michael and the Dragon*

PLATE 6. *The Descent of Christ into Hell*

PLATE 7. *The Inferno*

PLATE 8. Detail from *The Temptation of St. Anthony*

PLATE 9. *The Last Judgment*

PLATE 10. *Lucifer, King of Hell*

PLATE 11. *The Saintly Throng in the Form of a Rose*

PLATE 12. *Vision of the Throne of God*

PLATE 13. *St. Michael*

PLATE 14. *The Cross as the Tree of Life*

PLATE 15. *Indian Tree of Life*

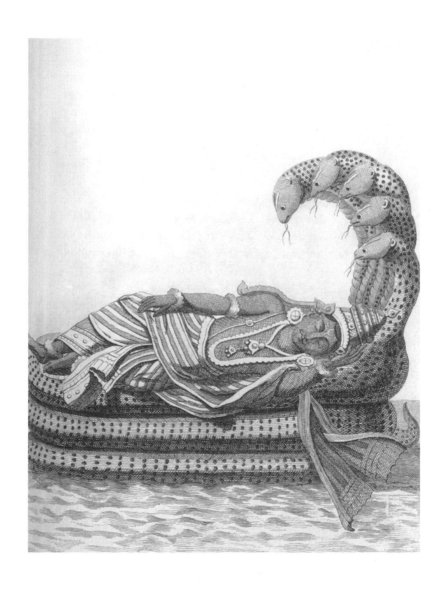

PLATE 16. *Vishnu sleeping on Adhi Shesha, his snake bed*

PLATE 17. *Amphisbaena*

PLATE 18. *Symbolic door*

PLATE 19. *Brahma*

PLATE 20a and 20b. *Two forms of the four-faced Brahma*

PLATE 21. *Shiva as Nataraja, King of the Dance*

PLATE 22. *Indian map of the world*

PLATE 23. *Amitayus Mandala*

surrounded though he was by supreme splendor, he did not forget for so much as a day the precepts of morality, but continued in his worship of the Tìrthankaras and of the living Jaina preceptors—fasting, praying, practicing vows, and performing numerous acts of mercy. A hermit whose name was Ksemankara therefore came to court; and the Cakravartin, hearing the holy man's delectable words, was released from his last attachment to the world. He renounced his throne and wealth, and departed to practice holy penances in the wilderness, absolutely fearless of the howls of the elephants, jackals, and forest goblins.

But his old enemy had returned to the world, this time as a Bhil, a wild tribesman of the jungle. And in due course the savage hunter chanced upon the place of the meditating former Cakravartin. The sight of the saintly being in meditation aroused again the ancient hatred. The Bhil remembered his last human incarnation, became fired with a passion for revenge, notched his keenest arrow to the bowstring, aimed, and let fly. Vajranabha died peacefully—absolutely unperturbed. And so he ascended to one of the very highest celestial spheres—the so-called *Madhyagraiveyaka* heaven, which is situated in the middle (*madhya*) of the neck (*griva*) of the human-shaped world-organism—and there he became an Aham-Indra ("I am Indra"); whereas the Bhil, when he died, since he was full of vile and sinful thoughts, descended to the seventh hell—again for a period of indescribable pain.

On a supremely auspicious night, the lovely Queen Vama dreamt fourteen auspicious dreams, and the moment King Asvasena was informed of them he understood that his son would be a savior—either a Cakravartin or a Tìrthankara....

When the son was born the thrones of all the Indras trembled, and the gods understood that the Lord had seen the light of day. With pomp they descended for the celebration of the Second Kalyana, "the salutary event of the Savior's birth.". . .

Now Parsva's maternal grandfather was a king named Mahipala, who, when his wife died, became so disconsolate that he renounced his throne and retired to the wilderness to practice the severest disciplines known to the penitential groves. There was, however, no real spirit of renunciation in this passionate man. He was an example of that archaic type of cruel asceticism—self-centered though directed to lofty ends—which the Jaina ideal of compassion and self-renunciation was intended to supersede. With matted locks and deerskin loincloth, full of passion and the darkness of ignorance, storing tremendous energies through self-inflicted sufferings, Mahipala moved from forest to forest, until one day he was in the neighborhood of Benares, practicing a particularly arduous spiritual exercise known as the penance of the "Five Fires." It was here that he was accidentally encountered by the grandson, the beautiful child of his lovely daughter Vama.

The boy came riding on an elephant, surrounded by the playmates with whom he had entered the jungle; and when the lively company broke upon the grim solitude of the passion-ridden old hermit among the fires, Mahipala was beside himself. He cried out to the prince, whom he immediately recognized: "Am I not your mother's father? Was I not born of an illustrious family, and have I not given up all to betake myself to the wilderness? Am I not an anchorite, practicing here the severest possible penances? What a proud little fellow you are, not to greet me with a proper salutation!"

Parsva and the company halted in amazement.

The old man then got up and seized an ax, which he prepared to bring down on a huge piece of timber—no doubt to

work off something of his temper, but ostensibly to cut fuel ·
for his great system of fires. But the boy shouted to make him
stop; then explained: "There are dwelling in that log a serpent
and his mate: do not murder them for nothing."

Mahipala's state of mind was not improved by this pe-
remptory advice. He turned and demanded with searing
scorn: "And who are you? Brahma? Visnu? Siva? I perceive
that you can see everything, no matter where." He raised his ax
and deliberately brought it down. The log was split. And there
were the two serpents, cut in half.

The boy's heart bled when he beheld the writhing, dying
creatures. "Do you not feel compassion?" he demanded of the
old man. "Grandfather, you are without knowledge. These austerities of yours are absolutely worthless."

Mahipala, at that, lost all control. "I see, I see, I see!" he
cried. "You are a sage, a very great sage. But I am your grandfather. Besides, I am a hermit. I practice the penance of the
Five Fires. I stand for days on one leg with lifted arms. I suffer
hunger; thirst; break my fast only with dry leaves. Surely it is
proper that a youngster, such as you, should call the austerities
of his grandfather fruitless and unwise!"

The little prince answered firmly, but in a sweet and won-
derfully gentle tone. "The spirit of envy," he said, "infects all of
your practices; and you are killing animals here every day with
your fires. To injure others, even if only a little, is to be guilty
of a great sin; but great suffering is the consequence even of
a little sin. Such practices as yours, divorced as they are from
right knowledge, are as barren as chaff separated from grain.
Give up this meaningless self-torture; follow the way of the
Tirthankaras and perform right acts, in right faith and right
knowledge: for that is the only road to emancipation."

The Lord Parsva then chanted a hymn to the dying

serpents and they expired to his presence calmly. He returned to his palace and they—following such a meritorious death—were immediately reborn in the underworld: the male was now Dharanendra, "Lord of the Earth" (the cosmic snake, Sesa, who supports the earth on his head), and the female, Padmavarti (the goddess Laksmi). They enjoyed unbounded delight.

Crotchety old Mahipala, it must now be told, was none other than the wicked brother. As a lion, he had slain and eaten the savior at the end of his previous incarnation, and in consequence had been hurled to the sufferings of the fifth hell, where he had remained for a period of seventeen oceans of time. After that, for a period of three oceans of time, he had passed through a number of incarnations in the forms of quadrupeds, during the last of which he performed certain meritorious acts, and in reward he was reborn as this old ruffian. But the words of the grandson bore no fruit. The hermit continued in his unproductive practices, and at last expired.

The prince grew to young manhood, and when he arrived at the age of sixteen his father wished to procure for him a bride, but the youth rejected the idea. "My life," he said, "is not to be as long as that of the first, Tìrthankara, the Lord Rsabha; for I am to live to be only one hundred. Sixteen of my short years have already been whiled away in boyish play, whereas in my thirtieth I am to enter the Order. Should I marry for a period so brief, in the hope of knowing a few pleasures, which, after all, are but imperfect?"

The king understood. His son was preparing for the Great Renunciation; all efforts to restrain him would be in vain....

The future Tìrthankara thereupon entered the "Twelve Meditations" and perceived that the chain of existences is without beginning, as well as painful and impure, and that the self is its own only friend....

The great goal, however, was not to be attained without further event; for the antagonist had yet to deal his final stroke. One day, while the Savior was standing perfectly still, erect, absorbed in meditation, the car of a god of the luminary order, Samvara by name, was stopped abruptly in its airy course— for not even a god can cut through the radiance of a saint of Parsva's magnitude, absorbed in meditation. Samvara, since he has clairvoyant knowledge, realized what had occurred; but then, suddenly, he knew that the saint was Pārśvanātha.

Now the personage in the chariot was the antagonist again—this time in the form of a minor deity, in consequence of powers gained by the penances of old Mahipala. The annoyed god determined, therefore, to resume his ancient battle, making use this time of the supernatural forces that he commanded. And so he brought down a dense and terrible darkness and conjured up a howling cyclone. Trees splintered and hurtled through the air. The earth was rent, opening with a roar, and the high peaks fell, shattering to dust; a torrential rain descended. Yet the saint remained unmoved, serene, absolutely lost in his meditation. The god, exceedingly wrathful, became as hideous as he could: face black, mouth vomiting fire, and he was like the god of death, garlanded with a necklace of human heads. When he rushed at Parsva, gleaming in the night, he fiercely shouted, "Kill! Kill!" but the saint never stirred.

The whole subterranean domain of the serpent supporting the earth began to tremble, and the great Dharanendra, "King of Earth," said to his consort, the goddess Padmavarti: "That compassionate Lord to whose sweet teachings at the time of our death we owe our present splendor is in danger." The two came up, made obeisance to the Lord, who remained unaware of the arrival, and stationing themselves at either side of him, lifting their prodigious forms, spread out their hoods, so that not a drop of the torrent touched his body. The apparitions were so large and terrifying that the god Samvara turned in his chariot and fled.

Parsva then broke the fetters of his karma one by one, and became absorbed in the White Contemplation, by which even the last and slightest traces of the human desire for advantage are dissolved. During the auspicious fourteenth day of the waning moon in the month of Caitra (March–April), the last of the sixty-three ties associated with the four modes of destructive karma broke, and the universal savior gained pure omniscience. He had entered the thirteenth stage of psychical development: he was "emancipated though embodied."* From that instant, every particle of the universe was within the purview of his mind.

His chief apostle, Svayambhu, prayed respectfully that the Tìrthankara should teach the world, and the gods prepared an assembly hall of twelve parts, which was named the "Flocking Together" (*samavasarana*), in which there was an allotted place for every species of being. The multitudes that came were tremendous. And to all without distinction—quite in contrast to the way of the Brahmans—the compassionate Lord Parsva gave his purifying instruction. His voice was a mysteriously divine sound. The highest Indra desired him to preach the true religion even to the most distant parts of India, and he consented to do so. Wherever he went a "Flocking Together" was erected, and it was immediately filled.

Samvara thought: "Is the Lord then truly such an unfailing

---

* The sixty-three ties, the four modes of karma, and the thirteenth stage of development are all technical terms associated with the Jaina disciplines of meditation, designed to eradicate the desire to go on living, or, as I would rather put it, to eradicate the compulsive necessity to go on living. These technicalities are numbered as an aid to memory in the times before writing.

source of happiness and peace?" He came to one of the vast halls and listened. Parsva was teaching. And all at once the spirit of hostility that had persisted through the incarnations was appeased. Overwhelmed with remorse, Samvara flung himself at the feet of Pārśvanātha with a cry. And the Tìrthaṅkara, inexhaustible in his kindness, gave consolation to the one who from birth to birth had been his foe. Samvara's mind, by his brother's grace, opened to right vision; he was placed on the way to liberation. Along with him, seven hundred and fifty ascetics who had been stiff-necked in their devotion to cruel penances—which, according to Jaina view, are useless— gave up their futile practices and adopted the faith of the Tìrthaṅkara.[60]

Once again, the story has a happy ending, but only in the moment of Parsva's final liberation—comparable, perhaps, to the coronation of Horus as Osiris. The sense is obviously that the implicit unity of the opposites is visible only from the throne of God, whose transcendental viewpoint is that of the Good which contains good-and-evil.

Several examples of the two-brothers theme are found in the Bible, notably the stories of Cain and Abel (Genesis 4:1–16) and of Esau and Jacob (Genesis 25:23–26, 27:1–41). These versions should be so familiar that it is, perhaps, better to present at least one of them in its greatly enriched Haggadah form—embellished, that is, with the Haggadah or legends which have accumulated around the original tale during the course of many centuries. Here follows, then, the story of Cain and Abel, constructed by the marvelous Jewish scholar Louis Ginzberg from Haggadah found in both rabbinical and patristic writings.

Wickedness came into the world with the first being born of woman, Cain, the oldest son of Adam. When God bestowed Paradise upon the first pair of mankind, He warned them particularly against carnal intercourse with each other. But after the fall of Eve, Satan, in the guise of the serpent, approached her, and the fruit of their union was Cain, the ancestor of all the impious generations that were rebellious toward God, and rose up against Him. Cain's descent from Satan, who is the angel Sammael, was revealed in his seraphic appearance. At his birth, the exclamation was wrung from Eve, "I have gotten a man through an angel of the Lord.". . .

Immediately her son was born, a radiant figure. A little while and the babe stood upon his feet, ran off, and returned holding in his hands a stalk of straw, which he gave to his mother. For this reason he was named Cain, the Hebrew word for a stalk of straw.

Now Adam took Eve and the boy to his home in the east. God sent him various kinds of seeds by the hand of the angel Michael, and he was taught how to cultivate the ground and make it yield produce and fruits, to sustain himself and his family and his posterity.

After a while, Eve bore her second son, whom she named Abel, because, she said, he was born but to die.

The slaying of Abel by Cain did not come as a wholly unexpected event to his parents. In a dream Eve had seen the blood of Abel flow into the mouth of Cain, who drank it with avidity, though his brother entreated him not to take all. When she told her dream to Adam, he said, lamenting, "O that this may not portend the death of Abel at the hand of Cain!" He separated the two lads, assigning to each an abode of his own, and to each he taught a different occupation. Cain became a tiller on the ground, and Abel a keeper of sheep. It was all in vain. In spite of these precautions, Cain slew his brother.

His hostility toward Abel had more than one reason. It began when God had respect upon the offering of Abel, and accepted it by sending heavenly fire down to consume it, while the offering of Cain was rejected. They brought their sacrifices on the fourteenth day of Nisan, at the instance of their father, who had spoken thus to his sons: "This is the day on which, in times to come, Israel will offer sacrifices. Therefore, do ye, too, bring sacrifices to your Creator on this day, that He may take pleasure in you." The place of offering which they chose was the spot whereon the altar of the Temple at Jerusalem stood later. Abel selected the best of his flocks for his sacrifice, but Cain ate his meal first, and after he had satisfied his appetite, he offered unto God what was left over, a few grains of flax seed. As though his offense had not been great enough in offering unto God fruit of the ground which had been cursed by God! What wonder that his sacrifice was not received with favor! Besides, a chastisement was inflicted upon him. His face turned black as smoke. Nevertheless, his disposition underwent no change, even when God spoke to him thus: "If thou wilt amend thy ways, thy guilt will be forgiven thee; if not, thou wilt be delivered into the power of the evil inclination. It coucheth at the door of thy heart, yet it depends upon thee whether thou shalt be master over it, or it shall be master over thee."

Cain thought he had been wronged, and a dispute followed between him and Abel. "I believed," he said, "that the world was created through goodness, but I see that good deeds bear no fruit. God rules the world with arbitrary power, else why had He respect unto thy offering, and not unto mine also?" Abel opposed him; he maintained that God rewards good deeds, without having respect unto persons. If his sacrifice had been accepted graciously by God, and Cain's not, it was because his deeds were good, and his brother's wicked.

But this was not the only cause of Cain's hatred toward

Abel. Partly love for a woman brought about the crime. To ensure the propagation of the human race, a girl, destined to be his wife, was born together with each of the sons of Adam. Abel's twin sister was of exquisite beauty, and Cain desired her. Therefore he was constantly brooding over ways and means of ridding himself of his brother.

The opportunity presented itself ere long. One day a sheep belonging to Abel tramped over a field which had been planted by Cain. In a rage, the latter called out, "What right hast thou to live upon my land and let thy sheep pasture yonder?" Abel retorted: "What right hast thou to use the products of my sheep, to make garments for thyself from their wool? If thou wilt take off the wool of my sheep wherein thou art arrayed, and wilt pay me for the flesh of the flocks, which thou hast eaten, then I will quit thy land as thou desirest, and fly into the air, if I can do it." Cain thereupon said, "And if I were to kill thee, who is there to demand thy blood of me?" Abel replied: "God, who brought us into the world, will avenge me. He will require my blood at thine hand, if thou shouldst slay me. God is the Judge, who will visit their wicked deeds upon the wicked, and their evil deeds upon the evil. Shouldst thou slay me, God will know thy secret, and He will deal out punishment unto thee."

These words but added to the anger of Cain, and he threw himself upon his brother. Abel was stronger than he, and he would have got the worst of it, but at the last moment he begged for mercy, and the gentle Abel released his hold upon him. Scarcely did he feel himself free; when he turned against Abel once more, and slew him. So true is the saying, "Do the evil no good, lest evil fall upon thee."...

Questioned by God, "Where is Abel thy brother?" Cain answered: "Am I my brother's keeper? Thou art He who holdest watch over all creatures, and yet Thou demandest account of me! True, I slew him, but Thou didst create the evil inclination in me. Thou guardest all things; why, then, didst Thou permit me to slay him? Thou didst Thyself slay him, for hadst Thou looked with a favorable countenance toward my offering as toward his, I had had no reason for envying him, and I had not slain him." But God said, "The voice of thy brother's blood issuing from his many wounds crieth out against thee, and likewise the blood of all the pious who might have sprung from the loins of Abel."...

In the obduracy of his heart, Cain spake: "O Lord of the world! Are there informers who denounce men before Thee? My parents are the only living human beings, and they know naught of my deed. Thou abidest in the heavens, and how shouldst Thou know what things happen on earth?" God said in reply: "Thou fool! I carry the whole world. I have made it, and I will bear it"—a reply that gave Cain the opportunity of feigning repentance. "Thou bearest the whole world," he said, "and my sin Thou canst not bear? Verily, mine iniquity is too great to be borne! Yet, yesterday Thou didst banish my father from Thy presence, today Thou dost banish me. In sooth, it will be said, it is Thy way to banish."

Although this was but dissimulation, and not true repentance, yet God granted Cain pardon, and removed the half of his chastisement from him. Originally, the decree had condemned him to be a fugitive and a wanderer on the earth. Now he was no longer to roam about forever, but a fugitive he was to remain. And so much was hard enough to have to suffer, for the earth quaked under Cain, and all the animals, the wild and the tame, among them the accursed serpent, gathered together and essayed to devour him in order to avenge the innocent blood of Abel. Finally Cain could bear it no longer, and, breaking out in tears, he cried: "Whither shall I go from Thy spirit? Or whither shall I flee from Thy presence?" To protect him from the onslaught of the beasts, God inscribed one letter of His Holy Name upon his forehead, and furthermore He addressed the animals: "Cain's punishment shall not be like unto the punishment of future murderers. He has shed blood, but there was none to give him instruction. Henceforth, however, he who slays another shall himself be slain." Then God gave him the dog as a protection against the wild beasts, and to mark him as a sinner, he afflicted him with leprosy....

The crime committed by Cain had baneful consequences, not for himself alone, but for the whole of nature also. Before, the fruits which the earth bore unto him when he tilled the ground had tasted like the fruits of Paradise. Now his labor produced naught but thorns and thistles. The ground changed and deteriorated at the very moment of Abel's violent end. The trees and the plants in the part of the earth whereon the victim lived refused to yield their fruits, on account of their grief over him, and only at the birth of Seth those that grew in the portion belonging to Abel began to flourish and bear again. But never did they resume their former powers. While, before, the vine had borne nine hundred and twenty-six different varieties of fruit, it now brought forth but one kind. And so it was with all other species. They will regain their pristine powers only in the world to come.[61]

Though Cain is described as the offspring of Satan, or Sammael, and is also a murderer and a deceiver, the Lord's treatment of him—in both the scriptural and Haggadah versions of the tale—is at once just and merciful. Also, Cain has the nerve to argue with the Lord, and the Lord is not yet so bereft of humor as to strike him dead or cast him forthwith into hell. For in his mythological form the Lord God is still human. It is only when the image of God becomes abstract, that is to say theological and ethical, that he begins to turn into a monster. From the human standpoint, the purely good is as monstrous as the purely evil. It is in this way that the human standpoint is the "image" of the divine and transcendental standpoint, beyond the opposites.

When and where do we get the beginnings of the myth in which this transcendental viewpoint is absent? Not, I believe, in Judaic literature until about 170 BC, the approximate date of that part of the apocryphal *Book of Enoch* which specifically refers to the *everlasting* punishment of the evil ones.* In the canonical Hebrew and Christian scriptures certain sayings of Jesus may perhaps be interpreted in this way, though his version of the two-brothers theme—the parable of the Prodigal Son—ends with reconciliation. It is in the *Apocalypse* of St. John (about AD 100) that Satan is first clearly rejected with an enmity which is metaphysical—final, implacable, and eternal.

It seems that the first real instance of the total irreconcilability of the brothers is in early Zoroastrian literature, which will take us back to the sixth century BC. It will be noted that our first text here, taken from the Zoroastrian *gathas*, refers to the principle of goodness and light by the name Ahura, which

---

*   The passage is Enoch 27:2–3. "Then Uriel, one of the holy angels who was with me, answered and said: 'This accursed valley is for those who are accursed for ever: here shall all the accursed be gathered together who utter with their lips against the Lord unseemly words and of his glory speak hard things. Here shall they be gathered together, and here shall be their place of judgement. In the last days there shall be upon them the spectacle of righteous judgement in the presence of the righteous for ever.'"[62]

is obviously the Iranian form of the Aryan (Sanskrit) *ashura*, designating the wrathful, titanic angels who fought with the angels of light (*deva*). Probably as a consequence of war between the two peoples, the terminology has been inverted. So far as we know, the Aryan and Iranian traditions have a common Indo-European source, but it is apparent that when the latter was reformed by the prophet Zoroaster (c. sixth century BC) there was a fundamental departure from the basic Aryan and Hindu conception of light and darkness, good and evil as aspects of a common, nondual principle.

1. Now will I proclaim to those who will hear the things that the understanding man should remember, for hymns unto Ahura and prayers to Good Thought; also the felicity that is with the heavenly lights, which through Right shall be beheld by him who wisely thinks.

2. Hear with your ears the best things; look upon them with clear-seeing thought, for decision between the two Beliefs, each man for himself before the Great Consummation, bethinking you that it be accomplished to our pleasure.

3. Now the two primal Spirits, who revealed themselves in vision as Twins, are the Better and the Bad in thought and word and action. And between these two the wise once chose aright, the foolish not so.

4. And when these twain Spirits came together in the beginning, they established Life and Not-Life, and that at the last the Worst Existence shall be to the followers of the Lie, but the Best Thought to him that follows Right.

5. Of these twain Spirits he that followed the Lie chose doing the worst things; the holiest Spirit chose Right, he that clothes him with the massy heavens as a garment. So likewise they that are fain to please Ahura Mazdah by dutiful actions.

6. Between these twain the demons also chose not aright, for infatuation came upon them as they took counsel together, so that they chose the Worst Thought. Then they rushed together to Violence, that they might enfeeble the world of man.

7. And to him (i.e., mankind) came Dominion, Good Thought, and Right; and Piety gave continued life of their bodies and indestructibility, so that by thy retributions through the (molten) metal he may gain the prize over those others.

8. So when there cometh the punishment of these evil ones, then, O Mazdah, at thy command shall Good Thought establish the Dominion in the Consummation, for those who deliver the Lie, O Ahura, into the hands of Right.

9. So may we be those that make this world advance! O Mazdah, and ye other Ahuras, gather together the Assembly, and thou too the Right, that thoughts may meet where Wisdom is at home.

10. Then truly on the Lie shall come the destruction of delight; but they that get them good names shall be partakers in the promised reward in the fair abode of Good Thought, of Mazdah, and of Right.

11. If, O ye mortals, ye mark those commandments that Mazdah hath ordained—of happiness and pain, the long punishment for the liars, and blessings for the righteous—then hereafter shall ye have bliss.[63]

The only hint here that there is still something in common between the two principles is the reference in verse 3 to their being twins. For an elaboration of this theme we must turn to the heterodox Zoroastrian literature of the Zurvanites, though even here is no hint of the ultimate reconciliation of the warring pair, Ohrmazd (Ahura Mazda) and Ahriman. But the Zurvanite doctrine seems to express the utter unthinkability of the two coming into being without some common root.

> Except Time all other things are created. Time is the creator; and Time has no limit, neither top nor bottom. It has always been and shall be for evermore. No sensible person will say whence Time has come. In spite of all the grandeur that surrounded it, there was no one to call it creator; for it had not brought forth creation. Then it created fire and water; and when it had brought them together, Ohrmazd came into existence, and simultaneously Time became Creator and Lord with regard to the creation it has brought forth. Ohrmazd was bright, pure, sweet-smelling, and beneficent, and had power over all good things. Then, when he looked down, he saw Ahriman ninety-six thousand parasangs away, black, foul, stinking, and maleficent; and it appeared fearful to Ohrmazd, for he was a frightful enemy.[64]

"Time" here is Zurvan—the perfectly neutral, amoral origin of things. Another text develops the origin of the twins from Zurvan in much more graphic detail:

> When absolutely nothing as yet existed, neither heaven, nor earth, nor other creatures such as might be in heaven or upon earth—there was one named Zurvan, which may be rendered "fate" or "fortune." For a thousand years he had offered sacrifice that he might perhaps have a son who would be named Ohrmazd, and who would make the heavens and the earth and all that they contain. He had thus offered sacrifice for a thousand years when he began to reflect, saying: "Of what good use is this sacrifice which I am offering? Shall I have a son, Ohrmazd? Or do I make these efforts in vain?" And as soon as he had reflected thus, Ohrmazd and Ahriman were conceived in the womb of their mother: Ohrmazd by virtue of

the offered sacrifice, and Ahriman by virtue of the aforesaid doubt. Then therefore, having taken account of this, Zurvan said: "Behold, there are two sons in the womb, and the one of them, whichever he may be, who comes to me the sooner, him will I make king."

Ohrmazd, knowing the intentions of their father, revealed them to Ahriman, saying: "Zurvan our father has planned that whichever of us comes to him the sooner shall be made king." Ahriman having heard this pierced through the womb, came forth, and presented himself before his father.*

And Zurvan, having seen him, knew not who he might be and asked, "You, who are you?" And he answered, "I am your son." Zurvan said to him, "My son is sweet smelling and radiant, and you, you are benighted and stinking." And when they had exchanged these words, Ohrmazd was born at his time, radiant and sweet smelling, and came and presented himself before Zurvan. And, having seen him, Zurvan knew that this was his son Ohrmazd for whom he had offered sacrifice. And taking the *barsom*† which he held in his hand and with which he had offered sacrifice, he gave it to Ohrmazd saying, "Until now it is I who have offered sacrifice for you; henceforth it is you who will offer it for me."

And as soon as Zurvan had given the *barsom* to Ohrmazd and blessed him, Ahriman came before Zurvan and said to him, "Have you not made the following vow: Whichever of my two sons comes to me the first, him I will make king? And Zurvan, so as not to violate his word, said to Ahriman, "O false and malicious one, the kingdom shall be accorded to you for nine thousand years, but Ohrmazd I shall make king above

---

* Thus forcing himself into the position of the older and, again, inauspicious brother.
† A bundle of twigs, being the scepter of high priesthood.

you; and after nine thousand years Ohrmazd shall reign, and
he shall do all that he wishes."

Thereupon Ohrmazd and Ahriman set themselves to the
making of creatures. And all that Ohrmazd created was good
and right, but whatever Ahriman made was evil and twisted.[65]

The peculiar interest of this story is that the responsibility for the birth of the evil one, Ahriman, is in no way shifted
to the unnamed female counterpart of Zurvan who becomes
the mother of the twins. The source of Ahriman is Zurvan's
failure of nerve, his doubt in the power of his own sacrifice,
which should here be understood in the sense of a magical
ritual as distinct from an offering to some still higher power.
In this respect the Iranian myth is strangely in agreement
with Chinese and Japanese (Zen) Buddhism where the prime
evil of "worldly attachment" is essentially to be understood
as hesitation, doubt, blocking, or general "stickiness" in action.

Another instance of a sort of hidden or *sub-rosa* unity
between Ohrmazd and Ahriman is the text in which they
collaborate in the creation of the sun and moon:

> He [Ohrmazd] created heaven and earth and the divers na-
> tures that are between them in the beauty and fairness, in
> which we see the world. But they were in darkness, and there
> was no light in them. And he was grieved, and consulted Satan
> [Ahriman] therein: and he counselled him to have intercourse
> with his mother. And he did so and had intercourse with her;
> and she conceived and bore the Sun as a light for the day. And
> (he also counselled him) to have intercourse with his sister.
> And he did so and had intercourse with her: and she con-
> ceived and bore the Moon as a light for the night.[66]

And finally one quotation from a text in which Zurvan strikes a bargain with Ahriman, and suggests that if he can get the world to love him and hate Ohrmazd, he will have demonstrated the "one principle, that the increaser and destroyer are the same."

> When first creation began to move and Zurvan for the sake of movement brought that form, the black and ashen garment to Ahriman, (he made) a treaty in this wise, "This is that implement like unto fire, blazing, harassing all creatures, that hath the very substance of Āz.* When the period of nine thousand years comes to an end, if thou hast not perfectly fulfilled that which thou didst threaten in the beginning, that thou wouldst bring all material existence to hate Ohrmazd and to love thee—*and verily this is the belief in the one principle, that the increaser and destroyer are the same*†—then by means of these weapons Āz will devour that which is thine, thy creation; and she herself will starve; for she will no longer obtain food from the creatures of Ohrmazd—like unto a frog that liveth in the water; so long as it defileth the water, it liveth by it, but when the water is withdrawn from it, it dieth parched."[67]

This is not the place to delineate the channels through which Zoroastrian dualism with its complex angelologies and demonologies has so powerfully influenced the development of both Judaism and, even more, Christianity—despite the strongest *theoretical* opposition of the two latter religions to the dualistic principle. But from the beginning of the fifth century BC, the fall of Babylon to the Persians, to the end of the Crusades, the Mediterranean and European worlds were

---

*   The principle of disorder and concupiscence.
†   Italics mine—A.W.W.

exposed to this influence in many different ways—through its infiltration of Greek religion, of Jewish apocalyptic literature, of Gnostic theologies, and through such daughter cults as Mithraism, Manichaeism, and Catharism. It should be remembered that one of the most important molders of Western Catholicism, St. Augustine of Hippo, was at first a Manichaean.

When we look at comparative dates and the successions of political hegemony and economic power in the ancient Near East, it seems more and more probable that Zoroastrianism was, at the very least, the challenge which moved the Hebrews to the development of an ethical monotheism. It was the first religion to absolutize the good, even at the cost of admitting the same status to the evil, and the appeal of its strong ethical idealism could well have moved Deutero-Isaiah, and perhaps even Hosea and Jeremiah, to see Yahweh in the same light of ethical glory as Ohrmazd.*

Despite the theoretical opposition of monotheism to dualism, the monotheism of the West became *ethical* monotheism—and evil is profoundly problematic in a universe governed by a single God both beneficent and omnipotent. If, then, one is to believe that evil is either an illusion or an expedient of the Godhead, there is no motivation for the strenuous effort against it which both Hebrew and Christian moralities demand. In a universe of ethical monotheism evil must then be considered as an effective and highly

---

* It is problematic that most scholars in this field are Jewish and Christian theologians who, liberal as they may try to be, have a special interest in giving temporal priority to the Hebrews in all matters of deep spiritual insight. For further study see *Cambridge Ancient History*,[68] Scheftclowitz,[69] and Gaster.[70]

dangerous rebellion of the creature against the Creator. But the energy with which this rebellion is hated and opposed by those on the side of light can of itself endow the rebel with godlike power. One has to be turned into a god to be eternally damned. And there is always the concurrent danger that, in such a battle, God himself may be turned into the Devil. This, then, is the paradox that the greater our ethical idealism, the darker is the shadow that we cast, and that ethical monotheism became, in attitude if not in theory, the world's most startling dualism.

4. Ultimate Dualism

WE ARE NOT GOING TO QUOTE SOURCES which present, step by step, the historical origins and development of the Christian image of the Devil and of his domain, the everlasting torture chambers of Hell. The point is rather to present the image in its fully matured enormity, and to consider what serious belief in such an image can tell us of the nature and potentialities of the human mind. As was pointed out in the Introduction, the Christian concept of the Devil is unique, marking a total break with all polarized ideas of light and darkness, life and death, good and evil, as aspects of a single reality that transcends and yet expresses itself through them. Evil from this point of view has no essential place in the universe. It need not and should not have arisen. It is therefore the diabolical parody of divine grace, the free gift of malice as the latter is the free gift of love. Yet every step that one takes in insisting on the gratuitousness of evil and the sole responsibility of the Devil for bringing it into the universe is a step in the direction of the final metaphysical dualism.*

---

*   I have discussed the philosophical and theological implications of this problem much more fully in *The Supreme Identity*,[71] and in *Myth and Ritual in Christianity*.[72]

According to the general consensus of Catholic tradition, the Devil, Satan, or Lucifer was in the beginning an angel of the highest order and beauty—an archangel, or, if one classifies these beings more precisely, a cherubim or seraphim, perhaps the head of all the angels in heaven and therefore the wisest and most beautiful creature that the Lord God had made. The story of his downfall is given by Ginzberg as follows:

> The extraordinary qualities with which Adam was blessed, physical and spiritual as well, aroused the envy of the angels. They attempted to consume him with fire, and he would have perished, had not the protecting hand of God rested upon him, and established peace between him and the heavenly host. In particular, Satan was jealous of the first man, and his evil thoughts finally led to his fall. After Adam had been endowed with a soul, God invited all the angels to come and pay him reverence and homage. Satan, the greatest of the angels in heaven, with twelve wings, instead of six like all the others, refused to pay heed to the behest of God, saying, "Thou didst create us angels from the splendor of the Shekinah,* and now Thou dost command us to cast ourselves down before the creature which Thou didst fashion out of the dust of the ground!" God answered, "Yet this dust of the ground has more wisdom and understanding than thou." Satan demanded a trial of wit with Adam, and God assented thereto, saying: "I have created beasts, birds, and reptiles. I shall have them all come before thee and before Adam. If thou art able to give them names, I shall command Adam to show honor unto thee, and thou shalt rest next to the Shekinah of My

---

* The Shekinah is the Hebrew term for the radiance or glory of God, and is sometimes identified with the divine essence.

glory. But if not, and Adam calls them by the names I have
assigned to them, then thou wilt be subject to Adam, and he
shall have a place in My garden, and cultivate it." Thus spake
God, and He betook Himself to Paradise, Satan following
Him. When Adam beheld God, he said to his wife, "O·come,
let us worship and bow down; let us kneel before the Lord our
Maker." Now Satan attempted to assign names to the animals.
He failed with the first two that presented themselves, the ox
and the cow. God led two others before him, the camel and
the donkey, with the same result. Then God turned to Adam,
and questioned him regarding the names of the same animals,
framing His questions in such wise that the first letter of the
first word was the same as the first letter of the name of the
animal standing before him. Thus Adam divined the proper
name, and Satan was forced to acknowledge the superiority
of the first man. Nevertheless he broke out in wild outcries
that reached the heavens, and he refused to do homage unto
Adam as he had been bidden. The host of angels led by him
did likewise, in spite of the urgent representations of Michael,
who was the first to prostrate himself before Adam in order to
show a good example to the other angels. Michael addressed
Satan: "Give adoration to the image of God! But if thou doest
it not, then the Lord God will break out in wrath against thee."
Satan replied: "If He breaks out in wrath against me, I will
exalt my throne above the stars of God, I will be like the Most
High!" At once God flung Satan and his host out of heaven,
down to the earth, and from that moment dates the enmity
between Satan and man.[73]

It is of interest that in this strictly mythological account,
the Lord God cheats a little in Adam's favor, giving the incident just the slightest touch of comedy. It is almost as if the
whole affair were a cosmic drama in which the parts to be

played had been prearranged. We should therefore compare this excerpt with the following, which is a very serious analysis of the Devil's motivations by Matthias Scheeben, who was in many respects one of the most sensitive and sophisticated theologians of modern times:

> If we want to emphasize a sinful act as extremely wicked, we are wont to call it a diabolical sin. By the use of this term one implies, first of all, that the specific sin was not committed out of weakness or ignorance, but with eyes wide open and with freewill, out of sheer maliciousness, as in the case of the fallen angels, and that evil was therefore intended with the same vigor and determination as of those angels when they forever and totally plunged themselves into evil. However, the essence, the real abyss of diabolical malice is not yet reached. This bottomless gulf can be gauged only when we realize that above all the angel violated God's supernatural grace; that he turned the sweetness of the Holy Spirit into the vilest poison; that, sitting at God's feet, he rebelled against Him and endeavored, as it were, to violate God's innermost being. This unfathomable maliciousness affects the action and the intention of the devil not only objectively inasmuch as the deed represents an offence against the supernatural divine ordinance—as it happens when we commit sins out of weakness or ignorance—, but it also affects him subjectively in his core, because its infamy was ignited by the very grace of God. Hence this inscrutable raging hatred of God which characterizes the devil's sin,—this terrible obstinacy and wickedness which could never have evolved on the basis of nature alone, and which occurs in men but rarely and then only in some measure when sins are committed against the Holy Spirit. It is exactly this inscrutable hatred of God, this obduracy and infamy which

give the devil's sin the specifically mysterious character which we are wont to call demonic.

Hence follows yet another interesting truth. In the super-natural order sin has a terrible repercussion on the nature of the sinner, at least if committed in sheer malice. In this case the specific perfidy of sin does not pass by his nature without leaving a trace, as if his nature could shake off grace, but leave itself undamaged. By opposing grace and hardening his heart against it as the most sublime good of nature, the creature distorts and perverts his nature in a manner otherwise impos-sible. The will becomes so twisted, so malevolent and venom-ous as to be unthinkable in mere rebellion against the natural order. And this, presumably, is the ultimate reason why a trans-formation and return of the will to good, even to the natural good, appears to be impossible for the fallen angels, and, save for a most sublime miracle of divine grace, seems also to be an impossibility for sinners against the Holy Ghost here on earth. Theologians explain the impossibility of conversion for the fallen angels out of the natural proclivity of their will; but as the natural goodness of the creature receives its sanction through grace and thus becomes *sanctitas*, so the perversion of the creature through its opposition to grace becomes more deeply embedded, more dreadful and irreversible.[74]

We shall have occasion to quote Scheeben again, upon the subject of the tortures of the damned. His peculiar combi-nation of mythological literalness, dexterity of psychological description, and maturely restrained but eloquent invective makes him one of the most accomplished horror writers of the world. He makes the evil motivation so profoundly awful that it surpasses the imagination into an inverted ineffability. It acquires thereby an infernal magnificence which begins to compel our admiration like Milton's Satan, and we begin to realize that writers who can poetize evil in this way are, in effect if unknowingly, offering worship to the Mystery of Iniquity. From Scheeben we get a distinct whiff of the bubbling-green-slime-with-teeth-in-it, of that absolute loathsomeness which we shall find so well suggested in Machen. But Milton's world is more heraldic and formal; it goes with Handel's oratorios and the Anglican Church, and thus, in its own stately way, offers unconscious worship at Satan's throne. Here, then, is the account of the Fall of Lucifer in *Paradise Lost*:

> As yet this World was not, and Chaos wild
> Reigned where these Heavens now roll, where Earth
>   now rests
> Upon her centre poised, when on a day
> (For Time, though in Eternity, applied
> To motion, measures all things durable
> By present, past, and future), on such day
> As Heaven's great year brings forth, the empyreal host
> Of Angels, by imperial summons called,
> Innumerable before the Almighty's throne
> Forthwith from all the ends of Heaven appeared
> Under their hierarchs in orders bright.
> Ten thousand thousands ensigns high advanced,
> Standards and gonfalons, 'twixt van and rear,
> Stream in the air, and for distinction serve
> Of hierarchies, of orders, and degrees,
> Or in their glittering tissues bear emblazed
> Holy memorials, acts of zeal and love
> Recorded eminent. Thus when in orbs
> Of circuit inexpressible they stood,
> Orb within orb, the Father Infinite,

By whom in bliss embosomed sat the Son,
Amidst as from a flaming moment, whose top
Brightness had made invisible, thus spake:
    "Hear all ye Angels, Progeny of Light,
Thrones, Dominations, Princedoms, Virtues, Powers,
Hear my decree, which unrevoked shall stand.
This day I have begot whom I declare
My only Son, and on this holy hill
Him have anointed, whom ye now behold
At my right hand. Your head I him appoint,
And by myself have sworn to him shall bow
All knees in Heaven, and shall confess him Lord:
Under his great vicegerent reign abide,
United as one individual soul,
Forever happy; him who disobeys,
Me disobeys, breaks union, and, that day,
Cast out from God and blessed vision, falls
Into utter darkness, deep engulfed, his place
Ordained without redemption, without end."
    So spake the Omnipotent, and with his words
All seemed well pleased; all seemed, but were not all.[75]

What, one must ask, were all those "standards and gon-
falons, 'twixt van and rear," all this military panoply, doing in
a cosmos wherein nothing had as yet gone wrong? The difficulty is that the whole notion of God as universal monarch,
King of kings, is of itself provocative and almost calculated
to stir up trouble. So, too, is the explicit prohibition against
eating the fruit of the Tree of Knowledge; this was just asking for disobedience. It will not do to argue that these military symbols represent power that is purely spiritual. For
that sort of power there could be much more appropriate

metaphors—as of sunlight and water, or of soft grasses that in growing can crack open the rocks. And is not the Lord throwing down the challenge in saying, "Hear my decree, which unrevoked shall stand"? Of course, Milton is following the most ancient imagery, but it is the imagery and not the theoretical theology which tells the tale. The tale is that this is a God who rules the universe by political violence and not by the wooing of love. Even Jesus hinted that he had at his disposal ten thousand legions of angels.

And so the story proceeds. Satan is sleepless that night, and aloof while all the good angels sit around their camp-fires and sing. The provocation in Milton's story seems to be different: it is not the creation of Adam that wounds Satan's pride, but the elevation of God the Son to the post of second-in-command. Yet it comes, in a way, to the same thing, for the angels have the power to look into God's foreknowledge, and they know that God the Son is to become Man, the Second Adam.

> But not so waked
> Satan—so call him now; his former name*
> Is heard no more in Heaven: he, of the first,
> If not the first Archangel, great in power,
> In favour, and pre-eminence, yet fraught
> With envy against the Son of God that day
> Honoured by his great Father and proclaimed
> Messiah, King Anointed, could not bear
> Through pride, that sight, and thought himself impaired.
> Deep malice thence conceiving and disdain,
> Soon as midnight brought on the dusky hour

---

*   That is, Lucifer, the Light-Bearer.

Friendliest to sleep and silence, he resolved
With all his legions to dislodge, and leave
Unworshipped, unobeyed, the Throne supreme,
Contemptuous, and, his next subordinate
Awakening, thus to him in secret spake:
  "Sleep'st thou, companion dear? what sleep can
    close
Thy eyelids? and rememberest what decree
Of yesterday, so late has passed the lips
Of Heaven's Almighty? Thou to me thy thoughts
Was wont, I mine to thee was wont, to impart;
Both waking we were one; how then can now
Thy sleep dissent? New laws thou seest imposed;
New laws from him who reigns new minds may raise
In us who serve, new counsels, to debate
What doubtful may ensue. More in this place
To utter is not safe. Assemble thou
Of all those myriads which we lead the chief;
Tell them that, by command, ere yet dim Night
Her shadowy cloud withdraws, I am to haste,
And all who under me their banners wave,
Homeward with flying march where we possess
The quarters of the North, there to prepare
Fit entertainment to receive our King,
The great Messiah, and his new commands,
Who speedily through all the hierarchies
Intends to pass triumphant, and give laws."[76]

Thereupon Satan and his legions of attendant angels, "thrones, dominations, princedoms, virtues, powers," take flight toward the heavenly citadel which he occupies in the symbolic North of the divine realm. The story is now being told to Adam by the archangel Raphael.

Satan with his Powers
Far was advanced on winged speed, an host
Innumerable as the stars at night,
Or stars of morning, dewdrops which the sun
Impearls on every leaf and every flower.
Regions they passed, the mighty regencies
Of Seraphim and Potentates and Thrones
In their triple degrees, regions to which
All thy dominion, Adam, is no more
Than what this garden is to all the earth
And all the sea, from one entire globose
Stretched into longitude; which having passed,
At length into the limits of the North
They came, and Satan to his royal seat
High on a hill, far-blazing, as a mount
Raised on a mount, with pyramids and towers
From diamond quarries hewn and rocks of gold,
The palace of great Lucifer (so call
That structure, in the dialect of men
Interpreted) which, not long after, he
Affecting all equality with God,
In imitation of that mount whereon
Messiah was declared in sight of Heaven,
The Mountain of the Congregation called;
For thither he assembled all his train,
Pretending so commanded to consult
About the great reception of their King
Thither to come, and with calumnious art
Of counterfeited truth thus held their ears:
"Thrones, Dominations, Princedoms, Virtues, Powers,*

---

*   These are some of the names of the nine orders of angels. The full list is as follows: Cherubim, Seraphim, Thrones; Dominations, Princedoms, Virtues; Powers,
Archangels, and Angels.

If these magnific titles yet remain
Not merely titular, since by decree
Another now hath to himself engrossed
All power, and us eclipsed under the name
Of King Anointed; for whom all this haste
Of midnight march, and hurried meeting here,
This only to consult, how we may best,
With what may be devised of honours new,
Receive him coming to receive from us
Knee-tribute yet unpaid, prostration vile,
Too much to one, but double how endured,
To one and to his image now proclaimed?
But what if better counsels might erect
Our minds, and teach us to cast off this yoke?
Will ye submit your necks and choose to bend
The supple knee? ye will not, if I trust
To know ye right, or if ye know yourselves
Natives and Sons of Heaven possessed before
By none, and, if not equal all, yet free,
Equally free; for orders and degrees
Jar not with liberty, but well consist.
Who can in reason, then, or right, assume
Monarchy over such as live by right
His equals—if in power and splendour less,
In freedom equal; or can introduce
Law and edict on us, who without law
Err not? Much less for this to be our Lord,
And look for adoration, to the abuse
Of those imperial titles which assert
Our being ordained to govern, not to serve!"[77]

Satan's points are well taken, and, it must be admit-
ted, accord fairly well with Milton's own political views,

democratic, antimonarchical. Thereupon the War in Heaven begins: Satan defies the triune Godhead, and God the Son, at the head of his legions of angels, commands them to move into battle:

> So spake the Son, and into terror changed
> His countenance, too severe to be beheld,
> And full of wrath bent on his enemies.
> At once the Four* spread out their starry wings
> With dreadful shade contiguous, and the orbs
> Of his fierce chariot rolled, as with the sound
> Of torrent floods, or of a numerous host.
> He on his impious foes right onward drove,
> Gloomy as Night. Under his burning wheels
> The steadfast empyrean shook throughout,
> All but the throne of God. Full soon
> Among them he arrived, in his right hand
> Grasping ten thousand thunders, which he sent
> Before him, such as in their souls infixed
> Plagues. They, astonished, all resistance lost,
> All courage, down their idle weapons dropped;
> O'er shields, and helms, and helmed heads he rode
> Of Thrones and mighty Seraphim prostrate,
> That wished the mountains now might be again
> Thrown on them as a shelter from his ire.
> Nor less on either side tempestuous fell
> His arrows, from the fourfold visaged Four,

---

*   These are the four cherubim described by Ezekiel as in constant attendance upon the throne of God. Each has six wings, and their heads are respectively those of a bull, a lion, an eagle, and a man, figures that were later associated with the Four Evangelists—Luke, Mark, John, and Matthew. But they are obviously the so-called fixed signs of the Zodiac—Taurus, Leo, Scorpio (often a phoenix), and Aquarius.

Distinct with eyes, and from the living wheels,
Distinct alike with multitude of eyes;
One spirit in them ruled, and every eye
Glared lightning and shot forth pernicious fire
Among the accursed, that withered all their strength
And of their wonted vigour left them drained,
Exhausted, spiritless, afflicted, fallen.
Yet half his strength he put not forth, but checked
His thunder in mid-volley, for he meant
Not to destroy but root them out of Heaven.
The overthrown he raised, and, as a herd
Of goats or timorous flock together thronged,
Drove them before him thunderstruck, pursued
With terrors and with furies to the bounds
And crystal wall of Heaven, which, opening wide,
Rolled inward, and a spacious gap disclosed
Into the wasteful Deep. The monstrous sight
Struck them with horror backward, but far worse
Urged them behind: headlong themselves they threw
Down from the verge of Heaven; eternal wrath
Burnt after them to the bottomless pit.

    Hell heard the unsufferable noise; Hell saw
Heaven ruining from Heaven, and would have fled
Affrighted; but strict Fate had cast too deep
Her dark foundations, and too fast had bound.
Nine days they fell; confounded Chaos roared,
And felt tenfold confusion in their fall
Through his wild anarchy, so huge a rout
Encumbered him with ruin. Hell at last,
Yawning, received them whole, and on them closed—
Hell, their fit habitation, fraught with fire
Unquenchable, the house of woe and pain.[78]

"But I say unto you which hear, Love your enemies, do good to them that hate you, bless them that curse you, pray for them that despitefully use you."

It has often been observed that the ethical behavior ascribed to the Lord God himself is vastly inferior to the ideals which he preaches for men. The reason, as already suggested, is that we have tendency to make our images of God insufficiently anthropomorphic. In our attempts to imagine the superhuman and the supernatural we create something subhuman. "De Lawd" of *Green Pastures* is much nearer to the point, for he wears a top hat and smokes a big cigar. Of course we cannot take such an image quite seriously, but so much the better, because it prevents us from idolatry.

Milton now goes on to describe the condition of the fallen Satan in hell:

> Him the Almighty Power
> Hurled headlong flaming from the ethereal sky,
> With hideous ruin and combustion down
> To bottomless perdition, there to dwell
> In adamantine chains and penal fire,
> Who durst defy the Omnipotent to arms.
> Nine times the space that measures day and night
> To mortal men, he with his horrid crew
> Lay vanquished, rolling in the fiery gulf,
> Confounded, though immortal; but his doom
> Reserved to him more wrath, for now the thought
> Both of lost happiness and lasting pain
> Torments him: round he throws his baleful eyes,
> That witnessed huge affliction and dismay,
> Mixed with obdurate pride and steadfast hate;
> At once, as far as angel's ken, he views

The dismal situation waste and wild;
A dungeon horrible, on all sides round,
As one great furnace flamed, yet from those flames
No light, but rather darkness visible
Served only to discover sights of woe,
Regions of sorrow, doleful shades, where peace
And rest can never dwell, hope never comes
That comes to all, but torture without end
Still urges, and a fiery deluge, fed
With ever-burning sulphur unconsumed.
Such place Eternal Justice had prepared
For those rebellious, here their prison ordained
In utter darkness, and their portion set,
As far removed from God and light of Heaven
As from the centre thrice to the utmost pole.[79]

And, finally, the speech of the defeated archangel in which, intentionally or otherwise, Milton has made him the true hero of the drama:

"Is this the region, this the soil, the clime,"
Said then the lost Archangel, "this the seat
That we must change for Heaven, this mournful gloom
For that celestial light? Be it so, since he
Who now is sovran can dispose and bid
What shall be right: farthest from him is best,
Whom reason hath equalled, force hath made supreme
Above his equals. Farewell, happy fields,
Where joy for ever dwells! Hail, horrors! hail,
Infernal World! and thou, profoundest Hell,
Receive thy new possessor—one who brings
A mind not to be changed by place or time.
The mind is its own place, and in itself

Can make a Heaven of Hell, a Hell of Heaven.
What matter where, if I be still the same,
And what I should be, all but less than he
Whom thunder hath made greater? Here at least
We shall be free; the Almighty hath not built
Here for his envy, will not drive us hence;
Here we may reign secure, and, in my choice,
To reign is worth ambition, though in Hell:
Better to reign in Hell than serve in Heaven."[80]

If it was Milton's intention to make a convincing image of the ultimately Evil One, he did not succeed. He depicted instead a proud, stubborn, but most courageous warrior. The villain in this story is really God the Son, as William Blake observed, for in his omnipotence he runs no real risks, and yet he is described as moving into battle with a supercolossal display of fury.

The depiction of utter and abysmal evil is immensely difficult. Once I sat for hours with an artist friend attempting to draw perfectly evil faces, but all turned out to be merely angry, sad, or comic. The face of evil is actually as unimaginable as the face of God, and it is thus that the only way of suggesting it is to use masks or veils such as those worn by the Spanish Inquisitors or the Ku Klux Klan—pointed and featureless head-coverings with slits for the eyes. Scheeben uses a comparable technique: he suggests the unimaginably depraved depths of Satan's malice, but is never specific about anything. The same device is used, still more effectively, in the following extract from Arthur Machen's story, "The White People," where everything is suggested without being specified, where the final point is that the Mystery of Iniquity is as indescribable as the Vision of God.

"Sorcery and sanctity," said Ambrose, "these are the only realities. Each is an ecstasy, a withdrawal from the common life."

Cotgrave listened, interested. He had been brought by a friend to this mouldering house in a northern suburb, through an old garden to the room where Ambrose the recluse dozed and dreamed over his books.

"Yes," he went on, "magic is justified of her children. There are many, I think, who eat dry crusts and drink water, with a joy infinitely sharper than anything within the experience of the 'practical' epicure."

"You are speaking of the saints?"

"Yes, and of the sinners, too. I think you are falling into the very general error of confining the spiritual world to the supremely good; but the supremely wicked, necessarily, have their portion in it. The merely carnal, sensual man can no more be a great sinner than he can be a great saint. Most of us are just indifferent, mixed-up creatures; we muddle through the world without realizing the meaning and the inner sense of things, and, consequently, our wickedness and our goodness are alike second-rate, unimportant."

"And you think the great sinner, then, will be an ascetic, as well as the great saint?"

"Great people of all kinds forsake the imperfect copies and go to the perfect originals. I have no doubts but that many of the very highest among the saints have never done a 'good action' (using the words in their ordinary sense). And, on the other hand, there have been those who have sounded the very depths of sin, who all their lives have never done an 'ill deed.'"

He went out of the room for a moment, and Cotgrave, in high delight, turned to his friend and thanked him for the introduction.

"He's grand," he said. "I never saw that kind of lunatic before."

Ambrose returned with more whisky and helped the two men in a liberal manner. He abused the teetotal sect with ferocity, as he handed the seltzer, and pouring out a glass of water for himself, was about to resume his monologue, when Cotgrave broke in—

"I can't stand it, you know," he said, "your paradoxes are too monstrous. A man may be a great sinner and yet never do anything sinful! Come!"

"You're quite wrong," said Ambrose. "I never make paradoxes; I wish I could. I merely said that a man may have excellent taste in Romanée Conti, and yet never have even smelt sour ale. That's all, and it's more like a truism than a paradox, isn't it? Your surprise at my remark is due to the fact that you haven't realized what sin is. Oh, yes, there is a sort of connexion between Sin with the capital letter, and actions which are commonly called sinful: with murder, theft, adultery, and so forth. Much the same connexion that there is between the A, B, C and fine literature. But I believe that the misconception—it is all but universal—arises in great measure from our looking at the matter through social spectacles. We think that a man who does evil to *us* and to his neighbors must be very evil. So he is, from a social standpoint; but can't you realize that Evil in its essence is a lonely thing, a passion of the solitary, individual soul? Really, the average murderer, *qua* murderer, is not by any means a sinner in the true sense of the word. He is simply a wild beast that we have to get rid of to save our own necks from his knife. I should class him rather with tigers than with sinners."

"It seems a little strange."

"I think not. The murderer murders not from positive

qualities, but from negative ones; he lacks something which nonmurderers possess. Evil, of course, is wholly positive—only it is on the wrong side. You may believe me that sin in its proper sense is very rare; it is probable that there have been far fewer sinners than saints. Yes, your standpoint is all very well for practical, social purposes; we are naturally inclined to think that a person who is very disagreeable to us must be a very great sinner! It is very disagreeable to have one's pocket picked, and we pronounce the thief to be a very great sinner. In truth, he is merely an undeveloped man. He cannot be a saint, of course; but he may be, and often is, an infinitely better creature than thousands who have never broken a single commandment. He is a great nuisance to *us*, I admit, and we very properly lock him up if we catch him; but between his troublesome and unsocial action and evil—Oh, the connexion is of the weakest."

It was getting very late. The man who had brought Cotgrave had probably heard all this before, since he assisted with a bland and judicious smile, but Cotgrave began to think that his "lunatic" was turning into a sage.

"Do you know," he said, "you interest me immensely? You think, then, that we do not understand the real nature of evil?"

"No, I don't think we do. We over-estimate it and we under-estimate it. We take the very numerous infractions of our social 'bye-laws'—the very necessary and very proper regulations which keep the human company together—and we get frightened at the prevalence of 'sin' and 'evil.' But this is really nonsense. Take theft, for example. Have you any *horror* at the thought of Robin Hood, of the Highland caterans of the seventeenth century, of the moss-troopers, of the company promoters of our day?

"Then, on the other hand, we underrate evil. We attach

such an enormous importance to the 'sin' of meddling with our pockets (and our wives) that we have quite forgiven the awfulness of real sin."

"And what is sin?" said Cotgrave.

"I think I must reply to your question by another. What would your feelings be, seriously, if your cat or your dog began to talk to you, and to dispute with you in human accents? You would be overwhelmed with horror. I am sure of it. And if the roses in your garden sang a weird song, you would go mad. And suppose the stones in the road began to swell and grow before your eyes, and if the pebble that you noticed at night had shot out stony blossoms in the morning?

"Well, these examples may give you some notion of what sin really is."

"Look here," said the third man, hitherto placid, "you two seem pretty well wound up. But I'm going home. I've missed my tram, and I shall have to walk."

Ambrose and Cotgrave seemed to settle down more profoundly when the other had gone out into the early misty morning and the pale light of the lamps.

"You astonish me," said Cotgrave. "I had never thought of that. If that is really so, one must turn everything upside down. Then the essence of sin really is—"

"In the taking of heaven by storm, it seems to me," said Ambrose. "It appears to me that it is simply an attempt to penetrate into another and higher sphere in a forbidden manner. You can understand why it is so rare. There are few, indeed, who wish to penetrate into other spheres, higher or lower, in ways allowed or forbidden. Men, in the mass, are amply content with life as they find it. Therefore there are few saints, and sinners (in the proper sense) are fewer still, and men of genius, who partake sometimes of each character are rare also. Yes;

on the whole, it is, perhaps, harder to be a great sinner than a great saint."

"There is something profoundly unnatural about sin? Is that what you mean?"

"Exactly. Holiness requires as great, or almost as great, an effort; but holiness works on lines that *were* natural once; it is an effort to recover the ecstasy that was before the Fall. But sin is an effort to gain the ecstasy and the knowledge that pertain alone to angels, and in making this effort man becomes a demon. I told you that the mere murderer is not *therefore* a sinner; that is true, but the sinner is sometimes a murderer. Gilles de Rais is an instance. So you see that while the good and the evil are unnatural to man as he now is—to man the social, civilized being—evil is unnatural in a much deeper sense than good. The saint endeavours to recover a gift which he has lost; the sinner tries to obtain something which was never his. In brief, he repeats the Fall."

"But are you a Catholic?" said Cotgrave.

"Yes; I am a member of the persecuted Anglican Church."

"Then, how about those texts which seem to reckon as sin that which you would set down as a mere trivial dereliction?"

"Yes; but in one place the word 'sorcerers' comes in the same sentence, doesn't it? That seems to me to give the key-note. Consider: can you imagine for a moment that a false statement which saves an innocent man's life is a sin? No; very good, then, it is not the mere liar who is excluded by those words; it is, above all, the 'sorcerers' who use the material life as instruments to obtain their infinitely wicked ends. And let me tell you this: our higher senses are so blunted, we are so drenched with materialism, that we should probably fail to recognize real wickedness if we encountered it."

"But shouldn't we experience a certain horror—a terror

such as you hinted we would experience if a rose tree sang—in the mere presence of an evil man?"

"We should if we were natural: children and women feel this horror you speak of, even animals experience it. But with most of us convention and civilization and education have blinded and deafened and obscured the natural reason. No, sometimes we may recognize evil by its hatred of the good— one doesn't need much penetration to guess at the influence which dictated, quite unconsciously, the 'Blackwood' review of Keats—but this is purely incidental; and, as a rule, I suspect that the Hierarchs of Tophet pass quite unnoticed, or, perhaps, in certain cases, as good but mistaken men."

"But you used the word 'unconscious' just now, of Keats' reviewers. Is wickedness ever unconscious?"

"Always. It must be so. It is like holiness and genius in this as in other points; it is a certain rapture or ecstasy of the soul; a transcendent effort to surpass the ordinary bounds. So, surpassing these, it surpasses also the understanding, the faculty that takes note of that which comes before it. No, a man may be infinitely and horribly wicked and never suspect it. But I tell you, evil in this, its certain and true sense, is rare, and I think it is growing rarer."

"I am trying to get hold of it all," said Cotgrave. "From what you say, I gather that the true evil differs generically from that which we call evil?"

"Quite so. There is, no doubt, an analogy between the two; a resemblance such as enables us to use, quite legitimately, such terms as the 'foot of the mountain' and the 'leg of the table'. And, sometimes, of course, the two speak, as it were, in the same language. The rough miner, or 'puddler,' the untrained, undeveloped 'tiger-man,' heated by a quart or two above his usual measure, comes home and kicks his irritating and injudicious wife to death. He is a murderer. And Gilles de Rais was a murderer. But you see the gulf that separates the two? The 'word,' if I may so speak, is accidentally the same in each case, but the 'meaning' is utterly different. It is flagrant 'Hobson Jobson' to confuse the two, or rather, it is as if one supposed that Juggernaut and the Argonauts had something to do etymologically with one another. And no doubt the same weak likeness, or analogy, runs between all the 'social' sins and the real spiritual sins, and in some cases, perhaps, the lesser may be 'schoolmaster' to lead one on to the greater—from the shadow to the reality. If you are anything of a theologian, you will see the importance of all this."

"'I am sorry to say," remarked Cotgrave, "that I have devoted very little of my time to theology. Indeed, I have often wondered on what grounds theologians have claimed the title of Science of Sciences for their favourite study; since the 'theological' books I have looked into have always seemed to me to be concerned with feeble and obvious pieties, or with the kings of Israel and Judah. I do not care to hear about those kings."

Ambrose grinned.

"We must try to avoid theological discussion," he said. "I perceive that you would be a bitter disputant. But perhaps the 'dates of the kings' have as much to do with theology as the hobnails of the murderous puddler with evil."

"Then, to return to our main subject, you think that sin is an esoteric, occult thing?"

"Yes. It is the infernal miracle as holiness is the supernal. Now and then it is raised to such a pitch that we entirely fail to suspect its existence; it is like the note of the great pedal pipes of the organ, which is so deep that we cannot hear it. In other cases it may lead to the lunatic asylum, or to still stranger issues. But you must never confuse it with mere social mis-doing. Remember how the Apostle, speaking of the 'other side,' distinguishes between 'charitable' actions and charity. And as one may give all one's goods to the poor, and yet lack charity; so, remember, one may avoid every crime and yet be a sinner."

"Your psychology is very strange to me," said Cotgrave, "but I confess I like it, and I suppose that one might fairly de-duce from your premises the conclusion that the real sinner might very well strike the observer as a harmless personage enough?"

"Certainly; because the true evil has nothing to do with social life or social laws, or if it has, only incidentally and acci-dentally. It is a lonely passion of the soul—or a passion of the lonely soul—whichever you like. If, by chance, we understand it, and grasp its full significance, then, indeed, it will fill us with horror and with awe. But this emotion is widely distin-guished from the fear and the disgust with which we regard the ordinary criminal, since this latter is largely or entirely founded on the regard which we have for our own skins or purses. We hate a murderer, because we know that we should hate to be murdered, or to have any one that we like murdered. So, on the 'other side,' we venerate the saints, but we don't 'like' them as we like our friends. Can you persuade yourself that you would have 'enjoyed' St. Paul's company? Do you think that you and I would have 'got on' with Sir Galahad?

"So with the sinners, as with the saints. If you met a very evil man, and recognized his evil; he would, no doubt, fill you with horror and awe; but there is no reason why you should 'dislike' him. On the contrary, it is quite possible that if you could succeed in putting the sin out of your mind you might find the sinner capital company, and a little while you might have to reason yourself back into horror. Still, how awful it is. If the roses and the lilies suddenly sang on this coming morning; if the furniture began to move in procession, as in De Maupassant's tale!"[81]

Machen never becomes more specific, in his suggestion of ultimate evil, than using such images as swelling stones and talking flowers. But what is it all about? Why would anyone want to make stones swell? The point is that if we *knew* it would cease to horrify. For nothing is more horrendous than disturbances of the order and regularity of events which make it impossible to predict and to chart rational courses of conduct. If I saw a stone swelling, I would believe that I was going insane, or, what almost comes to the same thing, that the world was going insane. When the environment abandons those day-to-day regularities that we take most for granted there comes panic, and in panic we take measures for self-protection that are inappropriate and extreme.

The same is true of our reaction to people who bash in the heads of babies, make lampshades out of human skin, and put electric wires into prisoners' testicles. Our emotions panic; no punishment is enough for such devils, and we want to see them screaming in boiling oil forever. But panic of this kind has nothing whatsoever to do with justice, much less with the prevention of future outrages. At this point, judge and criminal alike are in a common field of deranged communication and neurological pandemonium. It is out of this tortured, panic-ridden, "screaming meemies," pole of human experience that there have arisen the awesome fantasies of Hell and everlasting damnation. Postmortem hells, both hot and cold, are found in the popular mythologies of Hinduism and Buddhism, described, and often painted, in vivid detail.

But these oriental hells are really purgatories, for even though one may remain in them for eons of time there is always an end. The evil *karma*, or destiny, generated by the evil deed eventually works itself out. For the energy of *karma* generates a cyclic process of continual rebirth through six realms: (1) of men, (2) of angels, (3) of titans or dark angels, (4) of animals, (5) of the hot and cold hells, and (6) of the frustrated ghosts. Hell is thus described in the (Hindu) *Vishnu Purana*:

> Men are bound, when they die, by the servants of the king of Tartarus, with cords, and beaten with sticks, and have, then, to encounter the fierce aspect of Yama,* and the horrors of their terrible route. In the different hells there are various intolerable tortures with burning sand, fire, machines, and weapons: some are severed with saws; some, roasted in forges; some are chopped with axes; some, buried in the ground; some are mounted on stakes; some, cast to wild beasts (to be devoured); some are gnawed by vultures; some, torn by tigers; some are boiled in oil; some, rolled in caustic slime; some are precipitated from great heights; some, tossed (upwards) by engines. The number of punishments inflicted in hell, which are the consequences of sin, is infinite.
>
> But not in hell alone do the souls of the deceased undergo pain: there is no cessation, even in heaven; for its temporary inhabitant is ever tormented with the prospect of descending again to earth...[82]

In the long run, hell and heaven are both seen to be traps, and final liberation comes with realizing that there is nothing to choose between them.

But in the Hell of the West there is neither escape nor

---

* Yama is the ruler of the Naraka (Purgatorial) realm and judge of the dead.

cessation. The following is an early (third century) account from the Apocalypse of Peter:

21 And I saw also another place over against that one, very squalid; and it was a place of punishment, and they that were punished and the angels that punished them had their raiment dark, according to the air of the place.

22 And some there were there hanging by their tongues; and these were they that blasphemed the way of righteousness, and under them was laid fire flaming and tormenting them.

23 And there was a great lake full of flaming mire, wherein were certain men that turned away from righteousness; and angels, tormentors, were set over them.

24 And there were also others, women, hanged by their hair above that mire which boiled up; and these were they that adorned themselves for adultery.

And the men that were joined with them in the defilement of adultery were hanging by their feet, and had their heads hidden in the mire, and said: We believed not that we should come unto this place.

25 And I saw the murderers and them that were consenting to them cast into a strait place full of evil, creeping things, and smitten by those beasts, and so turning themselves about in that torment. And upon them were set worms like clouds of darkness. And the souls of them that were murdered stood and looked upon the torment of those murderers and said: O God, righteous is thy judgement.

26 And hard by that place I saw another strait place wherein the discharge and stench of them that were in torment ran down, and there was as it were a lake there. And there sat women up to their necks in that liquor, and over against them many children which were born out of due time

sat crying: and from them went forth rays of fire and smote the women in the eyes: and these were they that conceived out of wedlock (?) and caused abortion.

27 And other men and women were being burned up to their middle and cast down in a dark place and scourged by evil spirits, and having their entrails devoured by worms that rested not. And these were they that had persecuted the righteous and delivered them up.

28 And near to them again were women and men gnawing their lips and in torment, and having iron heated in the fire set against their eyes. And these were they that did blaspheme and speak evil of the way of righteousness.

29 And over against these were yet others, men and women, gnawing their tongues and having flaming fire in their mouths. And these were the false witnesses.

30 And in another place were gravel-stones sharper than swords or any spit, heated with fire, and men and women clad in filthy rags rolled upon them in torment.* And these were they that were rich and trusted in their riches, and had no pity upon orphans and widows but neglected the commandments of God.

31 And in another great lake full of foul matter (pus) and blood and boiling mire stood men and women up to their knees. And these were they that lent money and demanded usury upon usury.

32 And other men and women being cast down from a great rock (precipice) fell (came) to the bottom, and again were driven by them that were set over them, to go up upon the rock, and thence were cast down to the bottom and had

---

*   This is suggested by the Septuagint [i.e., the Greek version of the Old Testament] of two passages in Job: xli. 30, his bed is of sharp spits; viii. 17, on an heap of stones doth he rest, and shall live in the midst of gravel-stones.

no rest from this torment. And these were they that did defile their bodies, behaving as women: and the women that were with them were they that lay with one another as a man with a woman.

33 And beside that rock was a place full of much fire, and there stood men which with their own hands had made images for themselves instead of God, [And beside them other men and women]* having rods of fire and smiting one another and never resting from this manner of torment....

34 And yet others near unto them, men and women, burning and turning themselves about and roasted as in a pan. And these were they that forsook the way of God....

Furthermore the angel Ezraël shall bring children and maidens, to show them those that are tormented. They shall be chastised with pains, with hanging up (?) and with a multitude of wounds which flesh-devouring birds shall inflict upon them. These are they that boast themselves (trust) in their sins, and obey not their parents and follow not the instruction of their fathers, and honor not them that are more aged than they.

Beside them shall be girls clad in darkness for a garment, and they shall be sore chastised and their flesh shall be torn in pieces. These are they that kept not their virginity until they were given in marriage, and with these torments shall they be punished, and shall feel them.

And again, other men and women, gnawing their tongues without ceasing, and being tormented with everlasting fire. These are the servants (slaves) which were not obedient unto their masters; and this then is their judgement for ever.

And hard by this place of torment shall be men and

* The bracketed words are intrusive.

women dumb and blind, whose raiment is white. They shall crowd one upon another, and fall upon coals of unquenchable fire. These are they that give alms and say: We are righteous before God: whereas they have not sought after righteousness.

Ezraël the angel of God shall bring them forth out of this fire and establish a judgement of decision. This then is their judgement. A river of fire shall flow and all they that are judged shall be drawn down into the middle of the river. And Uriel shall set them there.

And there are wheels of fire, and men and women hung thereon by the strength of the whirling *thereof*. And they that are in the pit shall burn: now these are the sorcerers and sorceresses. Those wheels shall be in all decision (judgement, punishment) by fire without number.

Thereafter shall the angels bring mine elect and righteous which are perfect in all uprightness, and bear them in their hands, and clothe them with the raiment of the life that is above. They shall see their desire on them that hated them, and the torment of every one shall be for ever according to his works.

And all they that are in torment shall say with one voice: Have mercy upon us, for now know we the judgement of God, which he declared unto us aforetime, and we believed not. And the angel Tatirokos (Tartaruchus, keeper of hell: a word corresponding in formation to Temeluchus) shall come and chastise them with yet greater torment, and say unto them: Now do ye repent, when it is no longer the time for repentance, and naught of life remaineth. And they shall say: Righteous is the judgement of God, for we have heard and perceived that his judgement is good; for we are recompensed according to our deeds.[83]

As if this were not bad enough, the conception is strangely increased in horror when described by writers both

emotionally sensitive and intellectually gifted. The mere
narrative of the Apocalypse of Peter might be the description
of a nightmare, but let us listen to the celebrated Jesuit theologian, Cardinal Bellarmine:

> It remaineth that we consider the justice which God will use
> in punishing sinners in the uttermost depths of hell. Where-
> fore if we mark with attention and diligence, we shall indeed
> understand that it is most true which the Apostle teaches "It
> is a fearful thing to fall into the hands of the living God" (Heb.
> 10:31).
>
> For God the just judge will punish all sins though ever so
> small, as, for example, an idle word, for so we read in the Gos-
> pel: "Every idle word that men shall speak, they shall render
> an account of it in the day of judgement" (Matt. 12:36).
>
> Neither shall all sins be punished only, but so horribly
> punished that scarcely any man can imagine it. For as no eye
> hath seen, nor ear heard; neither hath it entered into the heart
> of man, what things God hath prepared for them that love
> him (1 Cor. 2:9), so no eye hath seen nor ear heard, neither has
> it entered into the heart of man what things God has prepared
> for those who hate him.
>
> The punishments of sinners in hell shall be very great,
> very many and very pure, to wit, mixed with no comforts and
> which shall increase their misery everlasting. They shall be
> many because every power of the soul and every sense shall
> be tormented. Weigh the words of the highest Judge's sen-
> tence "Get ye away from me, ye cursed, into everlasting fire
> which has been prepared for the devil and his angels" (Matt.
> 25:41). Get ye away, He saith, depart ye from the company of
> the blessed, being forever deprived of the sight of God, which
> is the highest essential happiness and best end for which you
> were created. Ye cursed, He saith, that is, hope not hereafter

for any benediction for ye are deprived of the life of grace and all hope of salvation; the water of wisdom and dew of divine inspiration shall not rain upon you; neither the grace of repentance nor the flower of charity, nor the fruits of good works shall grow in you. Neither shall ye lose only spiritual and eternal goods, but also corporal and temporal; ye shall have no riches, no delights, no comforts, but shall be like the fig tree which being cursed by me withered from the root all over (Matt. 21:19). Into fire, that is, into the furnace of burning and unquenchable fire (Matt. 13:42) which shall not consume one member alone but all the members together with horrible punishment. Everlasting, that is, into a fire which is blown by the breath of the Almighty and therefore needeth no fuel to make it always to burn, that as your fault shall still remain, so your punishment shall forever endure. Therefore I can truly exclaim "Which of you can dwell with devouring fire? Which of you shall dwell with everlasting burnings?" (Isa. 33:14). For there shall be the worm of conscience and remembrance of this life wherein they might easily, if they would, have escaped their punishment and obtained eternal joys....

But if all these things which we have said of the loss of all goods both celestial and terrestrial and of most unsufferable dolours, ignominies and disgraces were to have end, or at least some kind of comfort or mitigation as all miseries in this life have, they might in some sort be thought tolerable; *but since it is most certain and undeniable that the happiness of the blessed shall continue forever without mixture of misery, so likewise shall the unhappiness of the damned continue forever without mixture of comfort.**

Lastly, if the sin of the damned were not eternal, we might

---

*   Italics mine. Compare with the passage similarly italicized in the following
      extract from Scheeben.—A.W.W.

marvel that the punishment thereof should be eternal but seeing that the obstinacy of the damned is eternal, why should
we wonder if their punishment is also eternal? And this wilful
obstinacy in wickedness, which is in both the damned and the
devils, I say, this perverse will, which is in them averted from
God the chief happiness, and shall so forever remain, maketh
holy men more to fear a mortal sin than hell fire.[84]

And, as a final description of hell, here is Matthias
Scheeben again, writing in a modern idiom and with full sin-
cerity and intellectual profundity, and for that very reason
achieving what is possibly the highest masterpiece of subtle
ghastliness in all religious literature:

> It is the punishment by fire in particular which distinguishes
> the state of the damned as the reverse of a mysterious order,
> and thus is in itself truly a mystery which in its horror sur-
> passes the grasp of natural reason no less than the inexpress-
> ible magnificence of salvation.
>
> The mysterious aspect of infernal punishment entails, es-
> pecially for man, corporal punishment and defines its nature.
>
> The fact that man must suffer his everlasting punishment
> also in his body has at least a de facto relation to the super-
> natural order. For the miraculous resurrection of the flesh and
> its unrelenting preservation for eternal punishment is undeni-
> ably related to the resurrection and preservation of the body
> for eternal reward. *If the latter did not occur, the former would
> not be relevant; but where the latter happens, the former must
> happen too, if the manner and extent of the punishment is to
> correspond to that of the reward.*[*] Since the latter is fully moti-
> vated only in the divine ordinance, the former, therefore, must

---

[*]   Italics mine.—A.W.W.

be considered as the specific consequence of the violation of this ordinance.

As for the punishment itself, it clearly must be seen on the one hand as analogous to the chastisement of the spirit, and on the other hand as a state which corresponds inversely to the transfiguration of the bodies of the blessed.

It must stem from a supernatural power which permeates the body without destroying it and, through the body, most dreadfully tortures the soul; it must stem from a supernatural power because otherwise the punishment of the body would not correspond to the punishment of the soul nor, for that matter, to the glory of the transfigured body, and, finally, because natural forces can consume only while they simultaneously destroy. By the same divine power, by which He dignifies and exalts soul and body in man's glorification, God must now debase and torture soul and body, but in reverse order. Because God achieves the body's transfiguration through the fact that he causes it to be governed and spiritualized by the soul, He uses the degradation of the body, on the other hand, as a means to a much deeper abasement of the soul; the body is to draw the soul along to its perdition. It is precisely the fact that the soul loses its superiority over the body and falls under its dominance which constitutes the soul's well deserved punishment, while, on the other hand, the soul's most precious reward lies in its fullest dominance over the body.

In consequence of the body's glorification a light that was induced by divine power and can be perceived by the senses, endows the body with an unearthly beauty: so, in a similar way, a physical affliction must be connected with the degradation of the body—an affliction which, though caused by divine power and therefore supernatural, but for that reason no less discernible, devours and tortures the body; or rather, it is this very same affliction which similar to the natural fire brings the body to the brink of destruction and causes the soul in this body the same, only much more intense, suffering than it would endure from the natural fire at the height of its destructiveness.

The material agent by which God reduces the body to this state of all-consuming heat, thereby inflicting the torture of burning upon the soul which experiences this torture as the life principle of the body, is of course much more similar to earthly fire than that agent which tortures the spirit in itself. But it differs from natural fire inasmuch as its flame is not caused by a natural chemical process: it is maintained by divine power and therefore does not disintegrate the body which it assails, but keeps it forever suspended in a state of agonizing heat; it is, after all, supernatural fire in its origin, in its efficacy and in the immeasurable intensity of pain it causes.

From this then follows that the fire of hell has a different effect on the body, and on the soul as the life-principle of the body, than it has on the soul not yet rejoined with the body, or on the pure spirits. In the first instance it can create a true agony of burning; in the latter, however, it can, as previously stated, neither burn the soul in an actual sense nor create in it the sensation which our soul experiences when the body is exposed to the tortures of burning; it can only, by divine power, create an analogous, but for that reason no less immense destruction and torture in the spirit. Therefore the Savior could designate as one and the same this fire which, on the one hand, was prepared for the resurrected condemned human being and on the other hand for the devil and his angels because in both instances it is the same agent applied by the force of divine wrath, but it acts differently according to the different susceptibility of the subject.[85]

The words italicized in both of the foregoing quotations are rather startling, considering the general viewpoint of their authors. In attempting a logical justification of the existence of so excruciating a Hell in the same universe that contains the Beatific Vision of Love Itself, they have let slip the inevitable conclusion that Heaven and Hell are polar and thus mutually sustaining. The sine qua non of absolute goodness is absolute evil. And neither Bellarmine nor Scheeben leave room for the least doubt that Hell is unqualified, absolute, and unimaginable evil.

But if Heaven and Hell, and thus also the Lord and the Devil, are polar, the reality of the two is the unity which lies implicitly between them. In this light the War in Heaven begins to look like a conspiracy, an immense cosmic drama, an ultimate "big act" whereby the universe scares itself stiff for the thrill of it. For it is as if in the far-off beginnings, behind the scenes, before the world-drama began, the Lord and the Devil had *agreed* to have a battle, like Tweedledum and Tweedledee—their agreement being their inexpressible, unmanifest, and ineffable unity.

To be an orthodox Christian is therefore to enter into an intense adventure. It is comparable to joining in with a gambling game like Russian roulette, where the stakes are life and death. Only here the stakes are eternal bliss and eternal torture—the issue to be decided irrevocably in one short human life which may end at any minute. Furthermore, one lives in continual uncertainty as to the outcome because salvation depends upon avoiding the opposing sins of presumption and despair. The former is being sure that one is saved, and the latter being sure that one is damned. For once there is certainty, the essential suspense and thrill of the gambling game has been destroyed. What is more, it is of the essence of this game that one does not know that it is a game, that the original conspiracy between the Lord and the Devil be kept secret. But it is also part of the whole *mystique* of such games that there be occasional cracks in the wall, occasional opportunities to look behind the scenes and become disillusioned. In the traditional Christian world these opportunities were made all the rarer, and thus all the more valuable, because the mystic was in constant danger of being accused of heresy. Just as one must not be certain as to one's eventual salvation or damnation, there must also be doubt as to whether mystical vision is of the Lord or of the Devil. For without doubt there is no gambling. The guardian of the game's secret, who, when it finally comes down to it, is oneself, will outface you until the very last moment. Let not your left hand know what your right hand doeth. Thus if Christ sits at the right hand of God, who sits at the left?

To see through the game, then, requires somewhat more heroism than playing it, than taking quite seriously the stakes of Heaven and Hell. It involves the risk of the most awful blasphemy of saying that the Lord and the Devil are one—*demon est deus inversus*. The test of heroism in this case is that one must be able to find one's way out of Hell from its ultimate bottom, and the clue is given in the concluding canto of Dante's *Inferno*. Dante, with Virgil as his guide, has come to the deepest pit of Hell—the region where Satan himself sits locked in ice. The way out—down and out—lies through climbing down the back of the Fiend himself, first waiting for the moment when his batlike wings are most widely opened.

At his command, I clasped him round the neck.
He took advantage of the time and place,
And when the wings were opened wide enough,
He laid firm hold upon the shaggy flanks.
From shag to shag he now went slowly down,
Between the matted hair and crusts of ice.
When we had reached that point just where the thigh
Doth turn upon the thickness of the haunch,
My leader, with fatigue and labored breath
Brought round his head to where his legs had been,
And grasped the hair like one who clambers up,
So that I thought our way lay back to hell.
"Hold fast! For it is by such stairs as these,"
My master said to me with panting breath,
"We must depart from such great wickedness!"
Now through a rocky cleft he issued forth,
And made me seat myself upon its edge;
He then walked carefully up to my side.
I raised my eyes, believing I should look
On Lucifer as I had seen him last:
But lo! I saw his legs were uppermost.
And if, indeed, I then became perplexed,
Let me be judged in ignorance by those
Who fail to see what point it was I passed!
"Rise to your feet," the master said to me,
"Long is the way, and difficult the road:
The sun returns already to mid-tierce."
It was no palace hallway where we were,
But rather a vast dungeon in the rock;
Uneven was its floor, and dim the light.
"Before I turn my steps from the abyss,
Dear master," I said now that I had risen,

"Say a few words to lead me from my error.
Where is the ice? And how is Lucifer
Thus fastened upside down? How has the sun
So quickly moved from evening into morn?"
And he replied: "You still must think yourself
Beyond the center, where I grasped the hide
Of that fell worm who perforates the world.
You were upon that side when I went down;
But when I turned around, we passed the point
To which all weights are drawn from everywhere.
Now that you have come beneath the hemisphere
Facing the region where dry land prevails,
Below whose culminating point was slain
The Man who lived and died without one sin,
Your feet now rest upon the little sphere
That forms the other aspect of Giudecca.
Here it is morn when there the evening falls;
And he whose hair has served us for a ladder
Still remains fixed as he was fixed before.
It was upon this side he fell from heaven:
The earth, which first projected outward here,
For dread of him, made of the sea a veil,
Retreating to your hemisphere. Perhaps
The land where we now are, in fear of him
Rushed upward too, and left this vacant space."
A place as distant from Beelzebub
As his whole tomb's extent, lies there below.
It is not known by sight, but by the sound
Of a small rivulet that there descends
Along the hollow of a rock, carved out
By its long, twisting course and slight incline.
Upon this secret path my guide and I

> Now trod, to seek again the world of light;
> And caring not for rest, we mounted upward,
> He first and I behind, until I saw
> Some of those lovely gems that heaven wears,
> Through a round opening far above our heads:
> Thence we came forth, again to see the stars.[86]

It will be recognized that in Dante's Ptolemaic cosmology the bottom of Hell is the narrow end of a conical pit, reaching to the center of the earth, and that antipodal to this pit is the Mountain of Purgatory. Satan's abode is therefore the very center of the cosmos. It seems, then, highly probable that the symbolism of the stream and the secret path are initiatic. The stream that is known by sound but not by sight recalls St. Thomas's hymn:

> Taste and touch and vision to discern Thee fail;
> Faith, which comes by hearing, pierces through the veil.

Furthermore the long, twisting course of the stream's path is reminiscent of the recurrent theme of the labyrinth through which the hero or neophyte must find his way to freedom. To discover the secret path is to discover that as the center implies the circumference, so Hell implies Heaven, and Satan implies the Lord. And implication is the unity of opposites. The Roman Catholic liturgy also contains one point at which the veil is lifted, when, at the Blessing of the Paschal Candle on Holy Saturday, the deacon sings, "O truly necessary sin of Adam which the death of Christ has blotted out! O happy fault which merited such and so great a Redeemer!" So, too, Christ and Satan are at one as the Serpent—Satan as the serpent coiled around the Tree of Knowledge, and Christ as the serpent on the Cross, prefigured by the *nehushtan* or bronze serpent which Moses "lifted up" for the healing of a plague of snakes.* There is, furthermore, the celebrated Legend of the Cross in which it is told that the Cross was made from beams which Adam had cut from the Tree of Knowledge, thus making one the Tree of Salvation and the Tree of Perdition. *Paradise Lost* has also its hint of this fundamental polarity:

> There is a cave
> Within the Mount of God, fast by his throne,
> Where Light and Darkness in perpetual round
> Lodge and dislodge by turns, which makes through
>   Heaven
> Grateful vicissitude, like day and night;
> Light issues forth, and at the other door
> Obsequious Darkness enters, till her hour
> To veil the heaven, though darkness there might well
> Seem twilight here.[87]

Now if all this interpretation be deemed sophistry, let us consider one more image. The principle of evil is very frequently associated with corruption—that is, with slime, excrement, mud, worms, and everything that might be described as "goo." One of the common beliefs about Satanism and witchcraft is that it involves transformations of the human form so that it flows from shape to shape, assuming such aspects as one sees in the diabolical figures of Bosch and Breughel. The only thing to be done with the final, stinking, green goo to which all this leads is to burn it up; and that leaves us with nice, clean, dry ashes. On the other hand,

---

* The symbolism is Jesus's own, in John 3:14, "And as Moses lifted up the serpent in the wilderness, even so must the Son of Man be lifted up, that whosoever believeth may in him have eternal life."

the principle of goodness is commonly associated with structure—with that which is clear and firm, organized and reliable, crystalline and pure. Goo is the flesh and structure is the spirit. Soul, according to Aristotle, is the form of the body. As the corruptible and impermanent, matter tends toward goo. But as the perfect and eternal, spirit tends toward purely abstract structure.

The trouble with pure structure, with ashes, bones, crystals, and perfect abstractions, is that it is quite dead. It is not truly spiritual at all because it is completely static and comprehensible. On the other hand, the greenest and sloppiest goo is a sort of compost from which living forms will again emerge. The body, just because it is impermanent and corruptible, is the true expression of spirit. It is allied to the dynamic arts of music, dancing, and poetry because it comes and goes like the "wind that bloweth where it listeth," and cannot be trapped in any fixed form. The romantic will therefore tend to favor goo, and the classicist, structure. Likewise, mysticism is in the direction of goo, whereas moralism and dogmatism go toward structure. But the obvious truth of the matter is that life is always structured goo, or gooey structure. When analyzed to the limit, structures turn out to be random quanta, a sort of electronic goo. Under the microscope, goo is a system of minute and rapidly changing structures. Absolute goo or absolute structure would thus be total annihilation, and the same will be true of absolute evil and absolute goodness. These harsh alternatives exist only in the abstract. The real world is rather vibration and alternation, the wave that goes up and down at once.

In sum, then, the vast metaphysical schism which traditional Christianity proposes is redeemable only if there is a twinkle in the Father's eye comparable to the "fear-not" gesture of Shiva in his dance of world-destroying rage. The melodramatic choice between everlasting delight and everlasting torment, as also between taking it seriously or in play, is a test of nerve. There is ample precedent for this kind of thing in Holy Scripture, as witness the Lord's command to Abraham to offer up his son, Isaac, as a sacrifice. Obviously, the Lord calls it off at the last minute when it has become clear that Abraham is going to go through with it. The game involved is a celestial version of "Chicken."

The whole genius of Christianity is that by requiring its followers to accept impossible challenges it greatly intensifies human consciousness and self-knowledge. The first and greatest commandment, "Thou *shalt* love the Lord thy God," is just such an impossible challenge. For a resolute attempt to obey it reveals the illusory nature of the ego or conscious will as the effective agent in love, or in any other deeply spontaneous and creative activity. It is only by trying to love, or to be humble, with the Devil and all his angels in hot pursuit, that one discovers the full depth of self-interest and pride involved in the very attempt. The injunctions and prohibitions of Jehovah bear fruit in the subtle wisdom of Freud. This is perhaps why Western drama and fiction from Shakespeare onward display an understanding of human character without any parallel in the literature of the world.

5. Dismemberment Remembered

ONE OF THE MORE WIDELY DISTRIBUTED THEMES of mythology is that the universe arises from the sacrificial dismemberment of a divine being. In Hindu mythology the cosmic drama of the One, Brahman, pretending to be the many is called *atma yajna* or "self-sacrifice," meaning simultaneously that the plurality and differentiation of the world is the cutting up of a primal unity, and that the dismemberment is voluntary, for in the Godhead what happens and what is willed are one and the same. The obscure and unexplained reference in the Apocalypse to "the Lamb slain from the foundation of the world" has been worked up by theologians of the Eastern Orthodox Church into a whole doctrine of the creation of the world by kenosis, that is, the self-emptying or self-abandonment of God. The creation is seen as the same kind of divine action as the Incarnation, in which God the Son voluntarily lays aside his omnipotence and glory to "humble himself and become obedient unto death." In Babylonian mythology heaven and earth are created from the sliced body of the dragon Tiamat, slain in battle by Marduk, the hero of heaven. In Norse mythology, too, Othin, Vili, and

Ve create the world from the sundered body of Ymir, the her-maphroditic giant:

> Of Ymir's flesh the earth was fashioned,
>> And of his sweat the sea;
> Crags of his bones, trees of his hair,
>> And of his skull the sky.
> Then of his bones the blithe gods made
>> Midgard for sons of men;
> And of his brain the bitter-mooded
>> Clouds were all created.[88]

In Hesiod's *Theogeny* Ouranos and Gaia, Heaven and Earth, are separated by the titan Kronos, who castrates his father, Ouranos, with a sickle and pushes him up out of the way. So also in the Maori creation myth Tane mahuta, the son of the sky father, Rangi, and the earth mother, Papa, has to rend his parents apart in order to emerge from the womb.[89]

It follows quite logically, then, that where there is dis-memberment in the beginning there is remembrance at the end—that the fulfillment or consummation of the cosmic game is the discovery of what was covered and the recollec-tion of what was scattered. It is, perhaps, in the sense that we must understand the crucial moment of the Christian Mass when bread and wine are transformed into the Body and Blood of Christ in obedience to the commandment, "Do this in *remembrance* of me." Is not this, also, why all the disci-plines of spiritual integration are based on concentration or recollection for the purpose of overcoming scattered and dis-tracted thoughts? "If thine eye be single, thy whole body shall be full of light." Get with it. Pull yourself together. A house which is divided against itself cannot stand. Make up your mind. The choice is between paranoia, being beside yourself, and metanoia, being with yourself—ordinarily translated as repentance.

Joseph Campbell[90] has pointed out a curious contrast between the creation myths of the East and the West, namely, that in the East there is a primordial splitting apart of the Creator* whereas, in the West, the Creator remains entire and the split transpires within the creature. Actually, this split and nonsplit situation of the Creator corresponds with what, in Vedanta philosophy, is called the *nirguna* Brahman and the *saguna* Brahman—the Godhead without differentiated qualities and the Godhead with such qualities, or the unmanifest and manifest aspects of the supreme Self. The Godhead is simultaneously involved and not involved in the production of the world, responsible and not responsible for the mystery of iniquity, omnipotently controlling everything and yet open to surprise, granting the creature freedom of will.

Here then are two Western versions of the primordial split, the Hebrew and the Greek accounts of the division of the sexes, the former in Ginzberg's reconstruction of the Haggadah.

> When Adam opened his eyes the first time, and beheld the world about him, he broke into praise of God, "How great are Thy works, O Lord!" But his admiration for the world surrounding him did not exceed the admiration all creatures conceived for Adam. They took him to be their creator, and they all came to offer him adoration. But he spoke: "Why do you come to worship me? Nay, you and I together will acknowledge

---

* See above, pp. 83–84, the quotation from the *Brihadaranyaka Upanishad*.

the majesty and the might of Him who hath created us all. The Lord reigneth," he continued, "He is apparelled with majesty."

And not alone the creatures on earth, even the angels though Adam the lord of all, and they were about to salute him with "Holy, holy, holy, is the Lord of hosts," when God caused sleep to fall upon him, and then the angels knew that he was but a human being.

The purpose of the sleep that enfolded Adam was to give him a wife, so that the human race might develop, and all creatures recognize the difference between God and man. When the earth heard what God had resolved to do, it began to tremble and quake. "I have not the strength," it said, "to provide food for the herd of Adam's descendants." But God pacified it with the words, "I and thou together, we will find food for the herd." Accordingly, time was divided between God and the earth; God took the night, and the earth took the day. Refreshing sleep nourishes and strengthens man, it affords him life and rest, while the earth brings forth produce with the help of God, who waters it. Yet man must work the earth to earn his food.

The Divine resolution to bestow a companion on Adam met the wishes of man, who had been overcome by a feeling of isolation when the animals came to him in pairs to be named. To banish his loneliness, Lilith was first given to Adam as wife. Like him she had been created out of the dust of the ground. But she remained with him only a short time, because she insisted upon enjoying full equality with her husband. She derived her rights from their identical origin. With the help of the Ineffable Name, which she pronounced, Lilith flew away from Adam, and vanished in the air. Adam complained before God that the wife He had given him had deserted him and God sent forth three angels to capture her. They found her in the Red Sea, and they sought to make her go back with the threat that, unless she went, she would lose a hundred of her demon children daily by death. But Lilith preferred this punishment to living with Adam. She takes her revenge by injuring babies—baby boys during the first night of their life, while baby girls are exposed to her wicked designs until they are twenty days old. The only way to ward off the evil is to attach an amulet bearing the names of her three angel captors to the children, for such had been the agreement between them.

The woman destined to become the true companion of man was taken from Adam's body, for "only when like is joined unto like the union is indissoluble." The creation of woman from man was possible because Adam originally had two faces, which were separated at the birth of Eve.

When God was on the point of making Eve, He said: "I will not make her from the head of man, lest she carry her head high in arrogant pride; not from the eye, lest she be wanton-eyed; not from the ear, lest she be an eavesdropper; not from the neck, lest she be insolent; not from the mouth, lest she be a tattler; not from the heart, lest she be inclined to envy; nor from the hand, lest she be a meddler; not from the foot, lest she be a gadabout. I will form her from a chaste portion of the body," and to every limb and organ as He formed it, God said, "Be chaste! Be chaste!" Nevertheless, in spite of the great caution used, woman has all the faults God tried to obviate. The daughters of Zion were haughty and walked with stretched forth necks and wanton eyes; Sarah was an eavesdropper in her own tent, when the angel spoke with Abraham; Miriam was a talebearer, accusing Moses; Rachel was envious of her sister Leah; Eve put out her hand to take the forbidden fruit, and Dinah was a gadabout.

The physical formation of woman is far more complicated

than that of man, as it must be for the function of child-
bearing, and likewise the intelligence of woman matures more
quickly than the intelligence of man. Many of the physical
and psychical differences between the two sexes must be at-
tributed to the fact that man was formed from the ground and
woman from bone. Women need perfumes, while men do not;
dust of the ground remains the same no matter how long it is
kept; flesh, however, requires salt to keep it in good condition.
The voice of women is shrill, not so the voice of men; when
soft viands are cooked, no sound is heard, but let a bone be
put in a pot, and at once it crackles. A man is easily placated,
not so a woman; a few drops of water suffice to soften a clod
of earth; a bone stays hard, even if it were to soak in water for
days. The man must ask the woman to be his wife, and not the
woman the man to be her husband, because it is man who has
sustained the loss of his rib, and he sallies forth to make good
his loss again. The very differences between the sexes in garb
and social forms go back to the origin of man and woman for
their reasons. Woman covers her hair in token of Eve's having brought sin into the world; she tries to hide her shame;
and women precede men in a funeral cortege, because it was
woman who brought death into the world. And the religious
commands addressed to women alone are connected with the
history of Eve. Adam was the heave offering of the world, and
Eve defiled it. As expiation, all women are commanded to separate a heave offering from the dough. And because woman
extinguished the light of man's soul, she is bidden to kindle
the Sabbath light.

Adam was first made to fall into a deep sleep before the
rib for Eve was taken from his side. For, had he watched her
creation, she would not have awakened love in him. To this day
it is true that men do not appreciate the charms of women

whom they have known and observed from childhood up. Indeed, God had created a wife for Adam before Eve, but he
would not have her, because she had been made in his presence. Knowing well all the details of her formation, he was re-
pelled by her. But when he roused himself from his profound
sleep, and saw Eve before him in all her surprising beauty and
grace, he exclaimed, "This is she who caused my heart to throb
many a night!" Yet he discerned at once what the nature of
woman was. She would, he knew, seek to carry her point with
man either by entreaties and tears, or flattery and caresses. He
said, therefore, "This is my never-silent bell!"

The wedding of the first couple was celebrated with pomp
never since repeated in the whole course of history. God Himself, before presenting her to Adam, attired and adorned Eve
as a bride. Yea, He appealed to the angels, saying: "Come, let
us perform services of friendship for Adam and his helpmate,
for the world rests upon friendly services, and they are more
pleasing in My sight than the sacrifices Israel will offer upon
the altar." The angels accordingly surrounded the marriage
canopy, and God pronounced the blessings upon the bridal
couple....The angels then danced and played upon musical
instruments before Adam and Eve in their ten bridal chambers of gold, pearls, and precious stones, which God had prepared for them.[91]

There now follows the Greek version, which Plato puts
into the mouth of Aristophanes in the *Symposium*:

First let me treat of the nature and state of man; for the original human nature was not like the present, but different. In
the first place, the sexes were originally three in number, not
two as they are now; there was man, woman, and the union of
the two, having a name corresponding to this double nature;

this once had a real existence, but is now lost, and the name only is preserved as a term of reproach. In the second place, the primeval man was round and had four hands and four feet, back and sides forming a circle, one head with two faces, looking opposite ways, set on a round neck and precisely alike; also four ears, two privy members, and the remainder to correspond. When he had a mind he could walk as men now do, and he could also roll over and over at a great rate, leaning on his four hands and four feet, eight in all, like tumblers going over and over with their legs in the air; this was when he wanted to run fast. Now there were these three sexes, because the sun, moon, and earth are three; and the man was originally the child of the sun, the woman of the earth, and the man-woman of the moon, which is made up of sun and earth, and they were all round and moved round and round like their parents. Terrible was their might and strength, and the thoughts of their hearts were great, and they made an attack upon the gods; and of them is told the tale of Otus and Ephialtes who, as Homer says, dared to scale heaven, and would have laid hands upon the gods. Doubt reigned in the councils of Zeus and of the gods. Should they kill them and annihilate the race with thunderbolts, as they had done the giants, then there would be an end of the sacrifice and worship which men offered to them; but, on the other hand, the gods could not suffer their insolence to be unrestrained. At last, after a good deal of reflection, Zeus discovered a way. He said: "I have a notion which will humble their pride and mend their manners; they shall continue to exist, but I will cut them in two, and then they will be diminished in strength and increased in numbers; this will have the advantage of making them more profitable to us. They shall walk upright on two legs, and if they continue insolent and won't be quiet, I will split them again and they shall hop about on a single leg." He spoke and cut men in two, like a sorb-apple which is halved for pickling, or as you might divide an egg with a hair; and as he cut them one after another, he bade Apollo give the face and the half of the neck a turn in order that the man might contemplate the section of himself: this would teach him a lesson of humility. He was also to heal their wounds and compose their forms. Apollo twisted the face and pulled the skin all round over that which in our language is called the belly, like the purses which draw in, and he made one mouth in the centre, which he fastened in a knot (this is called the navel); he also moulded the breast and took out most of the wrinkles, much as a shoemaker might smooth out leather upon a last; he left a few, however, in the region of the belly and navel, as a memorial of the primeval change. After the division the two parts of man, each desiring his other half, came together, and threw their arms about one another eager to grow into one, and would have perished from hunger without ever making an effort, because they did not like to do anything apart; and when one of the halves died and the other survived, the survivor sought another mate, whether the section of an entire man or of an entire woman, which had usurped the name of man and woman, and clung to that. And this was being the destruction of them, when Zeus in pity invented a new plan: he turned the parts of generation round in front, for this was not always their position, and they sowed the seed no longer as hitherto like grasshoppers in the ground, but in one another; and after the transposition the male generated in the female in order that by the mutual embraces of man and woman they might breed, and the race might continue; or if man came to man they might be satisfied, and rest and go their ways to the business of life: so ancient is the desire of one another which is implanted in us, reuniting our original nature, making one of two, and healing the state of man. Each of us when separated is but the indenture of a man, having one side only like a flat fish, and he is always looking for his other half. Men who are a section of that double nature which was once called Androgynous are lascivious; adulterers are generally of this breed, and also adulterous and lascivious women: the women who are a section of the woman don't care for men, but have female attachments; the female companions are of this sort. But the men who are a section of the male follow the male, and while they are young, being a piece of the man, they hang about him and embrace him, and they are themselves the best of boys and youths because they have the most manly nature. Some indeed assert that they are shameless, but this is not true; for they do not act thus from any want of shame, but because they are valiant and manly, and have a manly countenance, and they embrace that which is like them. And these when they grow up are our statesmen, and these only, which is a great proof of the truth of what I am saying. And when they reach manhood they are lovers of youth, and are not naturally inclined to marry or beget children, which they do, if at all, only in obedience to the law, but they are satisfied if they may be allowed to live unwedded; and such a nature is prone to love and ready to return love, and always embracing that which is akin to him. And when one of them finds his other half, whether he be a lover of youth or a lover of another sort, the pair are lost in an amazement of love and friendship and intimacy, and one will not be out of the other's sight, as I may say, even for a moment: these are they who pass their lives with one another; yet they could not explain what they desire of one another. For the intense yearning which each of them has towards the other does not appear to be the desire of intercourse, but of something else which the soul desires and cannot tell, and of which she has only a dark and doubtful presentiment. Suppose Hephaestus, with his instruments, to come to the pair who are lying side by side and say to them, "What do you people want of one another?" they would be unable to explain. And suppose further, that when he saw their perplexity he said: "Do you desire to be wholly one; always day and night to be in one another's company? for if this is what you desire, I am ready to melt you into one and let you grow together, so that being two you shall become one, and, while you live, live a common life as if you were a single man, and after your death in the world below still be one departed soul instead of two—I ask whether this is what you lovingly desire, and whether you are satisfied to attain this?"—there is not a man among them when he heard this who would deny or who would not acknowledge that this meeting and melting in one another's arms, this becoming one instead of two, was the very expression of his ancient need. And the reason is that human nature was originally one and we were a whole, and the desire and pursuit of the whole is called love.[92]

In the *Brihadaranyaka Upanishad* it is the Lord himself who becomes male and female, but in the West this ultimate identity of the many with the one is concealed. Duality and multiplicity pertain to the creature, never to the Creator, which is only to say that the Western situation is more "far out," more adventurous, a more extreme dismemberment of the original unity, culminating as we have seen in the shrieking madness of everlasting damnation. In the Western mythologies man is more lost, more out on his own, and thus unaware of his fundamental identity with the eternal and indestructible Self of all selves. And for this very reason the culture of the West is more frantic, more exciting, and more active than any other culture in the world, whether Oriental or "primitive."

Nevertheless, "the desire and pursuit of the whole" remains and is, as a matter of fact, all the stronger in mythological traditions which veil the ultimate identity of the many and the One. Almost invariably, our mythologies preserve the hint of a way back to the lost unity, though the price that has to be paid for it is a form of death. It may be death in its most literal sense, as in the orthodox Christian belief that the Beatific Vision is available in its fullness only to those who have died. But in other traditions this death is metaphorical: it is a denial or simply an abandonment of oneself, a refusal to believe in anxiety, a disenchantment with the will-to-live as a compulsion. For if I feel that I *must* go on living at all costs, survival becomes then and there an insupportable drudgery. Death—the treatment of oneself as already dead—makes all time borrowed time, makes life unnecessary and purely gratuitous. Such are the only terms upon which life is worth living at all.

And that is the state of "paradise regained." For, as I tried to show in the Introduction, life is problematic and "fallen" so long as it seems that there is a real choice between the opposites. True integrity is therefore the recognition that it is simply impossible to take sides, except in play or illusion. To take the side of one's own advantage in the struggle to survive is not so much a wickedness as an impossibility, for no being lives (i.e., survives) except in relation to the whole community of being. Human history seems to be showing that a chronic anxiety to survive is a major threat to survival, for the individual whom it afflicts is tormented inwardly and provokes aggression outwardly. The practical politics of survival amounts all too often to the solution of today's problem at the cost of seven new problems to be solved tomorrow.

It is in contrast with such "practicality" that the sage often appears to be an idiot or "wild man." A Hindu verse says:

> Sometimes naked, sometimes mad,
> Now as a scholar, now as a fool,
> Thus they appear on earth—
> The free men!

The Taoist, Chuang-tzu, says:

> When a drunken man falls out of a cart, though he may suffer, he does not die. His spirit is in a state of security, and therefore he does not suffer from contact with objective existences. If such security may be gotten from wine, how much more from the spontaneity of Heaven?

Jesus says:

> The foxes have holes, and the birds of the air have nests, but the Son of Man has nowhere to lay his head.... Be not anxious for the morrow—what you shall eat, what you shall drink, or how you shall be clothed.... Sufficient to the day is the trouble thereof.

And Lao-tzu:

> Other people seem to have everything,
> And I alone am lacking,
> For I have the mind of a fool
> And am all muddled and vague.
> The people are so smart and bright,
> While I am just dull and confused.

> They are so competent and confident,
> Whereas I am stupid,
> Careless as the sea,
> Drifting without aim.

The sage seems to be insane because he does not take choosing seriously. Life is not a matter of life *or* death; it is a matter of life *and* death, and ultimately there is nothing to be dreaded. There is nothing outside the universe, against which it can crash. The "I" experience, which is just as much you as it is myself, keeps on playing hide-and-seek with itself in the darkness like the coming and going of myriads of stars—one and yet many, immortal and yet endlessly varied, able to continue because delivered from boredom by incessant death. And the sage does not see himself as a little thing thrown into a vast and alien space: for him, the thing-space is a unity as inseparable as life-death, up-down, back-front, or inside-outside. Because, then, he does not fundamentally and seriously take sides, he has to be regarded as a dreamer or a madman; otherwise the paint on our masks would begin to peel.

As he transcends metaphysical and moral dualities, he also transcends the sexual duality, returning to that primal innocence of which monkish and clerical celibacy is, at best, a parody. As Lao-tzu says again:

> He who knows the male
> And yet keeps to the female
> Becomes like the space containing the world.
> As space containing the world
> He has the eternal virtue (power) which leaves not,
> And he returns to the state of infancy.

Mythological images often imply that holiness is hermaphroditic, for if holiness is wholeness the complete human being is at once male and female—the man who has developed his feminine aspect, and the woman her masculine. In Buddhist iconography, therefore, the Bodhisattva is very frequently a hermaphrodite. One thinks in particular of the Bodhisattva Avalokiteshvara, who, though masculine in name, is always feminine or near-feminine in form, especially in the Far East, where he appears as Kwan-yin or Kannon— the "goddess" of mercy. The traditional thirty-two physical marks of a Buddha include the obviously androgynous symbol of the retractable penis, and it is not uncommon to find *ardhanari* or "half-woman" images of Shiva, in which the body is female on the left and male on the right.

In Christianity, likewise, there is preserved the idea that God the Son, the Second Person of the Trinity, is Logos-Sophia or Word-and-Wisdom, the latter referring back to the feminine personification of the Divine Wisdom who speaks in the Book of Proverbs.[93] What, furthermore, is the sense of Jesus's saying that in the kingdom of heaven we shall be "as the angels, neither marrying nor giving in marriage"? In Christian iconography the angel is almost invariably feminine in form though masculine in name, and this is characteristic equally of Persian (Islamic) and Hindu-Buddhist angels (*deva*).

The "square" or profane interpretation of this imagery is that holiness is sexlessness, and, similarly, that transcendence of the opposites, such as pleasure-and-pain or life-and-death, is mere detachment from physical existence. But if holiness is wholeness, the meaning of this imagery must be plus rather than minus, suggesting that innocence is not the absence of the erotic but its fulfillment. In the words of A.K. Coomaraswamy:

> He...who merely *represses* desire, fails. It is easy not to walk, but we have to walk without touching the ground. To refuse the beauty of the earth—which is our birthright—from fear that we may sink to the level of pleasure seekers—*that* inaction would be action, and bind us to the very flesh we seek to evade. The virtue of the action of those who are free beings lies in the complete coordination of their being—body, soul and spirit, the inner and outer man, at one.[94]

Hermaphroditic imagery suggests, rather, that there is a state of consciousness in which the erotic no longer has to be sought or pursued, because it is always present in its totality. In this state all relationship and all experience is erotic, for the lover and the beloved, the male and the female, the self and the other, have become one body. It is the mature adult's reacquisition of what Freud called the polymorphously "perverse" body of the child—that is, a body so keenly aware that its whole surface and every sense is an erogenous zone, restoring, too, the sensation of oneness with the external world which we have forgotten in learning to adopt our social roles.

Every initiation into what lies behind the passing show involves, therefore, an unmasking which is the same thing as the death of the role or identity that one has assumed in the sociopolitical game. For the individual is almost universally unaware that he has learned to confuse himself with a political and legal fiction, a theory of the individual without physical or biological foundation. His identity is thus a construct built up through years of self-dramatization between himself and his associates, that is, a purely artificial status or role. It is this role which he mistakes for his essential self and that he fears to lose in death. And because the role defines him as a *separate* individual and an *independent* agent, his identification with it blinds him to his union with the external world.

In almost all cultures there have been "mysteries"—initiations into the world behind the scenes of both the social and the cosmic drama. One of the purest forms of such initiation is found among the Hopi Amerindians, so much so that it is an exemplary archetype of the whole principle of initiation, of being able to look behind the scenes and yet refrain from giving the show away. A fractious or rebellious Hopi child is liable to a sudden visit by a masked goblin or kachina, who orders the mother to surrender her unruly brat to be taken away and eaten. But the mother pleads with the goblin and eventually bribes him with a gift to go away and leave the child unharmed. As soon as the goblin has left the mother can turn on her child and say, "Now do you see what it has cost me to save your life because of your naughtiness?" But as the child approaches puberty the naughty deeds pile up one after another. The day comes when the kachina goblin will not accept any bribe, and the child is taken away to the goblins' sanctuary. Upon arrival, the child finds that he is not alone; he is with a group of his peers, but they are all in the clutches of these murderous goblins. The children are told that they are going to be eaten, but first they are blindfolded and whipped. There is then the terrifying climax in which the children hear the sound of bull-roarers coming closer and closer, and just as they expect to feel the teeth of the goblins in their flesh there is a sudden unmasking. The blindfolds are taken off, the kachina masks are doffed, and there are fathers, uncles, and other brothers. Thus initiated, the adolescent children join with the kachinas in keeping up the pretense for their younger brethren.

There follow now three different types of initiation myth, each involving some sort of death or sleep, and each implying that penetration of the Wall of Paradise requires an understanding of the "coincidence of opposites," or what we have called the implicit unity of all poles.* The first is Lucius Apuleius's account of his initiation into the mysteries of Isis in *The Golden Ass*:

> Refreshed in mind by these and other benevolent injunctions of the high goddess, I shook off slumber almost before light of day, and hastened immediately to the priest's abode. I fell in with him just as he was coming out of his bedchamber and saluted him. I made up my mind to urge my request with greater constancy than usual, as an act of obedience due to the sacred mysteries.
>
> But he was the first to speak. "Oh, my Lucius!" he said, as soon as he saw me. "How happy, how blessed you are, to whom the august divinity condescends so far and bends so propitious a will!...And why," he went on, "do you now stand idle and put delays in your own way? The day on which you have set your constant hopes is now at hand. The day on which, through the divine commands of the goddess of a thousand names, you may be introduced by these hands of mine to her most holy and sacred mysteries!"
>
> The affable old gentleman put his right hand through mine, and led me straightway to the portal of the glorious

---

* According to Nicholas Cusanus, *De Visione Dei*, 9. II, the *coincidentia oppositorum* is the wall which makes God invisible to man.

temple. Then when the Service of Opening had been celebrated in solemn rite and the morning sacrifice had been
offered, he brought forth from the interior of the sanctuary
certain books, written in unknown character. This consisted
partly of figures of animals of various kinds, which suggested
in an abbreviated form the words that corresponded to the
ideas of a discourse, and partly of knotted letters, which
twirled round in circular form and were condensed into corru-
gations, so as to preserve the reading from the curiosity of the
profane. He announced to me from this book what I should
have to get ready for use in my initiation ceremony.

I set to with a will and a certain amount of liberality and
procured what was to be bought, partly by myself and partly
through my associates.

And now, as the priest said, the time pressed. He led me es-
corted by the religious cohort to the nearest baths, where I was
first of all treated with ordinary washing, and then, after asking
leave of the gods, sprayed over with a most pure ablution. I was
led back to the temple after two parts of the day had already
passed, and placed at the goddess's feet. He then enjoined certain things upon me secretly, things too holy for utterance, but
ordained in the hearing of everyone that I should restrain all
pleasure in meats for ten successive days, eating the flesh of no
animal and refraining absolutely from wine.

These days were duly passed in worshipful continence.
The day approached for the redemption of the divine pledge,
and the sun bent low to lead in Vesper by the hand. Lo, the
congregation flowed in from all parts, and according to the
ancient mystic rite everyone brought a present in my honor.
All the profane were removed to a distance. I was clothed in a
rude vesture of linen, and the priest led me by the hand to the
very innermost sanctuary.

You may now perchance ask with some anxiety, studious reader, what was thereupon said, what done. I should tell you, were telling lawful. You should know, if you could lawfully hear. But both ears and tongue would incur the like guilt of rash curiosity. But I shall not prolong the tortures you may feel perchance in the suspense of your religious desire. Hear then, but believe what is the truth.

I neared the confines of death. I trod the threshold of Proserpine. I was borne through all the elements and returned. In the midst of night I saw the sun beaming in glorious light. I stood before the gods of heaven and the gods of the lower world, and adored as I stood close to them.

See, I have told you all, which you may hear but still be in ignorance of. Consequently I shall only relate what may be announced to the profane intelligence without sin.

It was morning. The rites were concluded. I walked forth, hallowed in twelve *stoles*, a garb abundantly religious, which I am prohibited by no tie from mentioning, for there were many present who beheld it. I was set in the very centre of the sacred edifice before the image of the goddess, and stood as I was ordered upon a wooden tribunal, conspicuous in my garb, which was of plain silk, but embroidered in bright colors. There hung from my shoulders down my back as far as my heels a costly chlamys.* Wherever the eye fell upon me it encountered the varied colors of animals with which I was decorated on every side. Here were Indian dragons, there hyperborean griffins, which the other world brings forth, in semblance like birds with wings. This stole bears among the consecrated the name of the *Olympiac*. In my right hand I bore a torch in full flame, while my head was gracefully encircled in a crown of shining palm-leaves, which stood forward like rays.

---

* The chlamys is a long white linen robe, similar to the alb worn by Catholic priests.

When I was thus adorned to resemble the sun and set up there like a statue, the veils were suddenly drawn apart and the people wandered in to see the sight.[95]

The "threshold of Proserpine" is of course the entrance to Hades, since for six months of the year Proserpine, the daughter of Ceres, must stay underground as the bride of Pluto, for she is indeed the seed of all plants. The point is that through his initiatic death Lucius finds the sun at midnight, light in the depths of darkness. The two are mutual: without light there is no darkness, for the blind have no knowledge of the dark. Lucius has therefore solved the riddle of the Emerald Tablet of Thoth, or Hermes Trismegistus:

> Heaven above, heaven below;
> Stars above, stars below;
> All that is over, under shall show.
> Happy who the riddle reads!

The Christian tradition, both orthodox and heretical, abounds with similar "paradoxes of transformation."

> Whosoever would save his soul shall lose it.
> Unless a grain of corn fall into the ground and die, it remains no more than itself. But if it dies, it brings forth much fruit.
> The last shall be first, and the first last.

There is the same basic theme of transformation through death and the discovery of light in the very depth of darkness. Hence the Vesper antiphon of Christmas:

> While all things were in quiet silence, and night was in the midst of her course, thine almighty Word, O Lord, came down from thy royal throne: alleluia!

On the homeopathic principle of *similia similibus curantur*—
like things are cured by like—death is overcome by death
and darkness by darkness. Thus the preface of the Mass at
Passiontide speaks of God

> who didst set the salvation of mankind upon the tree of
> the cross, so that whence came death (i.e., from the Tree of
> Knowledge), thence also life might rise again, and he that by
> the tree was vanquisher (i.e., Satan), might also on the tree be
> vanquished.

There follows, then, as the next initiatic myth, the story of
the crucifixion of St. Peter from the apocryphal Acts of Peter,
a Greek text of the third century, which is one of the most
remarkable examples of this particular use of paradox in
Christian literature.

> "I beseech you the executioners, crucify me thus, with the
> head downward and not otherwise: and the reason wherefore,
> I will tell unto them that hear."
>
> And when they had hanged him up after the manner he
> desired, he began again to say: "Ye men unto whom it belon-
> geth to hear, hearken to that which I shall declare unto you
> at this especial time as I hang here. Learn ye the mystery of
> all nature, and the beginning of all things, what it was. For
> the first man, whose race I bear in mine appearance (*or*, of
> the race of whom I bear the likeness), fell (was born) head
> downwards, and showed forth a manner of birth such as was
> not heretofore: for it was dead, having no motion. He, then,
> being pulled down—who also cast his first state down upon
> the earth—established this whole disposition of all things,
> being hanged up an image of the creation wherein he made
> the things of the right hand into left hand and the left hand
> into right hand, and changed about all the marks of their

nature, so that he thought those things that were not fair to be fair, and those that were in truth evil, to be good. Concerning which the Lord saith in a mystery: "Unless ye make the things of the right hand as those of the left, and those of the left as those of the right, and those that are above as those below, and those that are behind as those that are before, ye shall not have knowledge of the kingdom."

"This thought, therefore, have I declared unto you; and the figure wherein ye now see me hanging is the representation of that man that first came unto birth. Ye therefore, my beloved, and ye that hear me and that shall hear, ought to cease from your former error and return back again. For it is right to mount upon the cross of Christ, who is the word stretched out, the one and only, of whom the spirit saith: For what else is Christ, but the word, the sound of God? So that the word is the upright beam whereon I am crucified. And the sound is that which crosseth it, the nature of man. And the nail which holdeth the cross-tree unto the upright in the midst thereof is the conversion and repentance of man.

"Now whereas thou hast made known and revealed these things unto me, O word of life, called now by me wood (or, word called now by me the tree of life), I give thee thanks, not with these lips that are nailed *unto the cross*, nor with *this* tongue by which truth and falsehood issue forth, nor with this word which cometh forth by means of art whose nature is material, but with that voice do I give thee thanks, O King, which is perceived (understood) in silence, which is not heard openly, which proceedeth not forth by organs of the body, which goeth not into ears of flesh, which is not heard of corruptible substance, which existeth not in the world, neither is sent forth upon earth, nor written in books, which is owned by one and not by another: but with this, O Jesu Christ, do I give thee thanks, with the silence of a voice, wherewith the spirit that is in me loveth thee, speaketh unto thee, seeth thee, and beseecheth thee. Thou art perceived of the spirit only, thou art unto me father, thou my mother, thou my brother, thou my friend, thou my bondsman, thou my steward: thou art the All and the All is in thee: and thou ART, and there is nought else that IS save thee only."[96]

The martyrdom here is quite obviously an initiatic death, and the text is clearly of a Christian Gnostic type similar to the recently discovered Gospel According to Thomas, a Coptic text of the second century, which the Acts of Peter seems to quote:

> They said to Him: Shall we then, being children,
> enter the Kingdom? Jesus said to them:
> When you make the two one, and
> when you make the inner as the outer
> and the outer as the inner and the above
> as the below, and when
> you make the male and the female into a single one,
> so that the male will not be male and
> the female (not) be female, when you make
> eyes in the place of an eye, and a hand
> in the place of a hand, and a foot in the place
> of a foot, (and) an image in the place of an image,
> then shall you enter [the Kingdom].[97]

And again:

> Jesus said: I am the Light that is above
> them all, I am the All,
> the All came forth from Me and the All
> attained to Me. Cleave a (piece of) wood, I

am there; lift up the stone and you will
find Me there.[98]

St. Peter's interpretation of the symbolism of the Cross
recalls the vision of the cross of light in another second-
century text, the apocryphal Acts of John, a vision said to
have been revealed to St. John at the time of the Crucifixion
of Jesus.

> This cross of light is sometimes called the word by me [Jesus
> is speaking] for your sakes, sometimes mind, sometimes Jesus,
> sometimes Christ, sometimes door, sometimes a way, some-
> times bread, sometimes seed, sometimes resurrection, some-
> times Son, sometimes Father, sometimes Spirit, sometimes
> life, sometimes truth, sometimes faith, sometimes grace. And
> by these names it is called as toward men: but that which it is
> in truth, as conceived of in itself and as spoken of unto you,
> it is the marking-off of all things, and the firm uplifting of
> things fixed out of things unstable, and the harmony of wis-
> dom, and indeed wisdom in harmony. There are (the places) of
> the right hand and the left, powers also, authorities, lordships
> and demons, workings, threatenings, wraths, devils, Satan, and
> the lower root whence the nature of the things that come into
> being proceeded. This cross, then, is that which fixed all things
> apart by the word, and separated off the things that are from
> those that are below, and then also, being one, streamed forth
> into all things (*or*, compacted all into one).[99]

There is a glimpse here of God as a cross at once centrifu-
gal and centripetal, whereby the opposites—including the
angels and the demons—are simultaneously set apart and
reconciled.

The third initiation myth is Islamic—the story of

the Prophet Muhammed's visit to heaven as quoted in a seventeenth-century Iranian text entitled *Dabistan-ul-Mazahab* or "The School of Religious Doctrines."

> One night I slept in the house of my father's sister; it was a night of thunder and lightning; no animal uttered a sound; no bird was singing; no man was awake; and I slept not, but was suspended between sleep and waking; the secret meaning of this might have been, that it was a long while before I became desirous of understanding of divine truth. Under the shield of the night, men enjoy greater freedom, as the occupations of the body and the dependence of the senses are broken. A sudden night fell then, and I was still between sleep and waking; that is, between reason and sensuality. I fell into the sea of knowledge; and it was a night with thunder and lightning, that is, the seven upper agents prevailed, so that the power of human courage and the power of imagination sunk from their operation, and inactivity manifested its ascendancy over activity. And lo! Jabrííl* came down in a beautiful form, with much pomp, splendor, and magnificence, so that the house became illuminated..."whiter than snow, with a lovely face, black hair, and on his forehead the inscription: 'There is no God but one God'; the light of his eyes charming, the eyebrows fine, having seventy thousand curls twisted of red rubies, and six hundred thousand pearls of a fine water,"...And such were the charms of the angel that, if one possessed seventy thousand curls, he would not attain to his beauty; and such was his rapidity, that thou wouldst have said, he was flying with six hundred wings and arms, so that his progress knew neither space nor time.†
>
> What he said came upon me, and he took me to his

---

*   The Iranian form of Gabriel.
†   In other words an angel is pure thought and travels with the speed of thought.

bosom, and gave me kisses between the eyes, and said: "O thou sleeper, how long sleepest thou? rise!" That is, when the power of holiness came upon me, it caressed me, opened the road of its revelation, and exalted me; a certain delight which I cannot describe diffused itself in my heart and transported me to devotion. The angel then continued: "How long sleepest thou?" that is, "why indulgest thou in the delusions of false-hood? thou art attached to the world, and, as long as thou remainest in it, and before thou awakest, knowledge cannot be obtained; but I, from compassion toward thee, shall be thy guide on the road. Rise." I trembled at his words, and from fear jumped up from my place; that is, from timid respect for him no reflection remained in my heart and mind. He further said: "Be calm, I am thy brother, Jabrííl"; thus, by his kindness and revelation, my terror was appeased. But he unfolded more of his mysteries, so that fear returned upon me. I then said: "O brother, I feel the hand of an enemy." He replied: "I shall not deliver thee into the hand of an enemy." I asked: "Into whose?" He answered: "Rise, and be glad, and keep thy heart within thyself": that is, "preserve thy memory clear, and show obedience to me, until I shall have removed the difficulties before thee." And as he spoke I became entranced and trans-ported, and I proceeded on the footsteps of Jabrííl; that is, I forsook the sensual world, and by the aid of natural reason, I followed the footsteps of holy grace.

When I left the mountains, I went on until I reached the house of sanctity (Jerusalem); and as I entered it, a person came to me, and gave me three cups—the one of wine, the second of water, and the other of milk. I wished to take that of wine, but Jabrííl forbade it, and pointed to that of milk, which I took and drank....When I arrived there I entered the mosque, and the crier called to prayer; and I stepped forward.

I saw an assembly of prophets and angels standing to the right and left; every one saluted me, and made a new covenant with me....When I became free, I raised my face upward, and I found a ladder, one step of which was of silver and the other of gold.

[Here Jabrííl took Muhammed upon his wings and flew with him to the gate of Paradise, which was guarded by a legion of angels. In the first heaven he saluted Adam, who sat between two gates, and was looking now to the right, now to the left; when to the right, he laughed, when to the left, he wept, for the right hand led to heaven, the left to hell: the first father's joy or sadness followed his children going to either side.]

I arrived at the heaven of the universe; the gates yielded and I entered. There I saw Ismâíl seated upon a throne, and a crowd before him, with their eyes fixed upon his face. I made my salute, looked at him, and went on...I entered the second heaven; there I saw an angel excelling all others; by his perfect beauty, he captivated the admiration of the whole creation; one half of his body was of ice and the other half of fire; and yet there was no counteraction nor enmity between them. He saluted me, and said: "Be welcome! All things and riches are thine.".…When I arrived into the third heaven, I there saw an angel, equal to whom in excellence and beauty I had seen none, placid and joyful, he was seated upon a throne; and a circle of angelic effulgency was diffused about him....When I entered the fourth heaven, I there saw an angel, surrounded with royal pomp, seated upon a throne of light; I made my obeisance, to which he replied with entire haughtiness, and, from pride and majesty, he bestowed neither word nor smile upon any body about him. When he answered my salute, he said: "O Muhammed, I see all things and riches in thee: glory and happiness to thee.".…When I arrived at, and entered, the fifth heaven, I happened to have a view of hell; and I saw a black region, and on its borders was seated a terrific and dark angel, who was engaged in the business of punishing bad men.…Moreover, when I entered the sixth heaven, I saw an angel sitting upon a throne of light, occupied with counting his prayers by beads, and with uttering benedictions; he had wings, and curls set with jewels, pearls, and rubies. I bowed before him, to which he returned blessings and congratulations, and wishes of joy and prosperity, and said: "I give thee perpetual blessing.".…When I attained the seventh heaven, I saw an angel seated upon a throne of red rubies; not every one had access to him, but he who approached him found a kind treatment. I made my reverence, and he returned an answer by blessing me.

When I proceeded, I arrived at the heavenly mansion of the angel Jabrííl; I saw a world full of light and splendor, and such was the effulgency that my eyes were dazzled. To the right or left, to whatever side I turned my looks, they met with angelic spirits, engaged in devotion. I said: "O Jabrííl, who are this class of beings?" He answered: "these know of no other fixed business but praying, counting their beads, and visiting churches.".…I saw five mansions greater than anything else, which spread their shade over earth and heaven.…When I proceeded, I saw four seas, the waters of each being of a different color.…I saw angels much occupied with beads and prayers and all taken up with the precious sentence, *There is no God but one God*.

…When I left this assembly, in my progress I arrived at a sea without borders; howsoever I strained my sight, I could not perceive any boundary or shore; and at this sea I saw a river, and an angel who was pouring the seawater into the river,

and from thence the water ran to every place....On the level
of that sea, I perceived a great desert, greater than which I
had never seen any space, so that, in spite of my endeavor, I
found neither the beginning nor the end of it....On the level
of the sea and the desert, I saw an angel surrounded with every
grandeur, splendor, and pomp, who guarded both halves with
facility; he called me to him, and having joined him, I asked:
"What is thy name?" He answered: "Mikáíl:* I am the greatest
of all angels; whatever is difficult, ask it from me: I will satisfy
all thy wishes."...When I had set myself free from saluting and
questioning, I said: "To arrive at this place I experienced much
trouble, and my purpose in coming here was to attain knowledge, and the sight of God Almighty. Grant me guidance, that
I may satisfy my desire, and then return home."...That angel
took me by the hand, and gave me a passage through several
thousand curtains into a world, where I saw nothing like what
I had seen before, until he brought me at last near the Lord of
glory; then the command came to me: "Approach."...In that
majesty I immersed my sense and motion, and found entire
relaxation, contentment, and tranquility....From fear of the
Lord I forgot all things I had seen and known before, and I
felt such an exaltation, inspiration, and inward delight, that
thou wouldst have said: "I am intoxicated." I felt some impres-
sions of God's proximity, so that I was seized with trembling;
and I heard the command: "Proceed," and I proceeded. Then
came the word: "Fear not nor be disquieted."...I trembled at
the boldness of my journey, which had attained such a height
and distance; and I apprehended failing in the proof of the
unity; but I heard the words: "Come nearer"; that is: dismiss

*   That is, Michael.

thy pondering, fear, and terror; for such is the proper state of
a believer in the unity of God, to be continually immersed
in a spiritual ecstasy, so that he may never fall back into the
disgrace of brutishness, and fear and hope belong to the state
of brutishness.

Moreover: I drew nearer, and upon me came the blessing
of the Lord, such as I never had heard before...Further: The
command came: "Say thy prayer": I replied: "I cannot; for thou
art thyself such as thou hast said.."...

The word came to me: "What dost thou wish?" I said:
"Leave to ask whatever comes into my mind, so that my difficulties may be removed."...

When I had performed all this, and returned home, on
account of the rapidity of my journey, I found the bedclothes
still warm.[100]

The Prophet finds entrance to the vision in a state between sleep and waking, reason and sensuality, and the whole
journey is undertaken in a flash of time. The great Awakening, according to the Hindu-Buddhist tradition, is to be
found in the interval between two thoughts. This is also the
theme of Symplegades, of the clashing rocks through which
Jason sailed the *Argo*, a theme which appears in a surprising
variety of forms all over the world. For this is the Active Door,
the Strait Gate, which is sometimes a portcullis, or the jaws
of a beast, or a whirling sword such as is said to guard the
gates of Paradise. The point is that the hero-initiate has to
leap through without hesitation, that is, without stopping to
choose between the opposites. Usually the hero loses something in his leap. The *Argo* lost its rudder, and bird or hare
heroes get their tails docked. Is it, as Coomaraswamy[101] suggested, that the price of the leap into Paradise is the loss of

one's ego? The two aspects of Adam's face recall the Haggadah that he was originally two-faced in his hermaphroditic state before the creation of Eve. The Angel of the Second Heaven combines fire and ice without enmity, Michael guards both halves, that is sea and desert, with facility, and what concerns Muhammed most in the divine presence is to attain the unity of God beyond and above the brutish opposites of hope and fear.

As prophets, visionaries, and seers enter the innermost sanctuary of Heaven to behold the ultimate Unity they are apt to fall silent. It is not only that the show must not be given away; it is also that the glory is too great for words. Dante's "vision failed the lofty fantasy"; Muhammed described his own peace and ecstasy but said nothing of his vision, save that it was unlike anything he had seen before; Lucius was under oath not to reveal it; the author of the *Apocalypse* says only that he who sat upon the throne was "like unto a jasper and sardine stone." But the art of the poet is just to say what cannot be said, and to describe what cannot be described.

An unknown Indian, Buddhist, writer living, perhaps, in the first century AD had no such lack of tongue. There follow certain passages from the *Amitayur-dhyana-sutra* which describe the Pure Land, Sukhavati, presided over by the Buddha Amitayus or Amitabha—the personification of Boundless Light. Amitabha is, in Buddhist mythology, the most popular of the five so-called Dhyani Buddhas—transcendental beings who represent five aspects of the Universal Consciousness in which the worlds are forever appearing and disappearing like dreams. Amitabha is thus the nearest thing in Buddhism to a God. The devotees of Amitabha believe

that in some immeasurably distant time he made the vow
that he would not attain Buddhahood, or Perfect Enlightenment, unless—at the mere repetition of his name—any person however evil would be transported at death to his Pure
Land. They believe that the world is now so evil and human
psychology so trapped in vicious circles that even the most
heroic efforts to attain Buddhahood have become nothing
but spiritual pride, tightening the knots of *karma*. There is
then no hope except trust in Amitabha's liberating vow—to
claim no merit for oneself, but simply to say his name and be
reborn in the Pure Land where the attainment of Buddhahood is so simple as to be a certainty.

Here, then, is the vision of Amitabha, the Sun Buddha,
described as the highest beatitude to which life can attain
and yet, simultaneously, as the root and ground of one's own
being. The vision belongs to a class of images which have
been called mandala—the Sanskrit term for symbols of uni-
versality or wholeness, which Auboyer has described as follows:

> An esoteric diagram, consisting of a series of circular or quad-
> rangular zones surrounding a mysterious center, residence
> of the divinity. The one who meditates on a *mandala* must
> "realize" through meditative effort and prayer the divinities
> belonging to each zone. Progress is toward the center, at which
> point the person meditating attains mystical union with the
> divinity.[102]

The passage quoted above from the Acts of John, concerning the vision of the cross of light, likewise described a mandala. The account of the Heavenly City in the *Apocalypse*,
and Dante's visions of the Mystic Rose and of the Trinity in

the *Paradiso* have also the mandala form. The mandala is the typical symbol of reconciliation and harmony, of the cosmic order in which all deviations are balanced and all conflicts subordinated to a superior unity. It is the archetype par excellence of the implicit, polar unity of opposites.

The words that follow—instructions for meditating upon the Buddha Amitabha—are put into the mouth of Gautama, the historical Buddha, as a sermon to Vaidehi, the queen of Rajagriha.

"All beings, if not blind from birth, are uniformly possessed of sight, and they all see the setting sun. Thou shouldst sit down properly, looking in the western direction, and prepare thy thought for a close meditation on the sun; cause thy mind to be firmly fixed (on it) so as to have an unwavering perception by the exclusive application (of thy thought), and gaze upon it (more particularly) when it is about to set and looks like a suspended drum.

"After thou hast thus seen the sun, let (that image) remain clear and fixed, whether thine eyes be shut or open;—such is the perception of the sun, which is the First Meditation.

"Next thou shouldst form the perception of water; gaze on the water clear and pure, and let (this image) also remain clear and fixed (afterwards); never allow thy thought to be scattered and lost.

"When thou hast thus seen the water thou shouldst form the perception of ice. As thou seest the ice shining and transparent, thou shouldst imagine the appearance of lapis lazuli.

"After that has been done, thou wilt see the ground consisting of lapis lazuli, transparent and shining both within and without. Beneath this ground of lapis lazuli there will be seen a golden banner with the seven jewels, diamonds and the rest, supporting the ground. It extends to the eight points of the compass, and thus the eight corners (of the ground) are perfectly filled up. Every side of the eight quarters consists of a hundred jewels, every jewel has a thousand rays, and every ray has eighty-four thousand colours which, when reflected in the ground of lapis lazuli, look like a thousand millions of suns, and it is difficult to see them all one by one. Over the surface of that ground of lapis lazuli there are stretched golden ropes intertwined crosswise; divisions are made by means of (strings of) seven jewels with every part clear and distinct.

"Each jewel has rays of five hundred colours which look like flowers or like the moon and stars. Lodged high up in the open sky these rays form a tower of rays, whose storeys and galleries are ten millions in number and built of a hundred jewels. Both sides of the tower have each a hundred millions of flowery banners furnished and decked with numberless musical instruments. Eight kinds of cool breezes proceed from the brilliant rays. When those musical instruments are played, they emit the sounds 'suffering,' 'non-existence,' 'imperma- nence,' and 'non-self';*—such is the perception of the water, which is the Second Meditation.

"When this perception has been formed, thou shouldst meditate on its (constituents) one by one and make (the im- ages) as clear as possible, so that they may never be scattered and lost, whether thine eyes be shut or open. Except only during the time of thy sleep, thou shouldst always keep this in thy mind. One who has reached this (stage of) perception is said to have dimly seen the Land of Highest Happiness (Sukhavati).

"One who has obtained the Samadhi (the state of super- natural calm) is able to see the land (of that Buddha country)

---

* The terms used by the Buddha for the "marks of becoming"—that is, the basic characteristics of life as we live it in the vicious circle of samsara.

clearly and distinctly: (this state) is too much to be explained fully;—such is the perception of the land, and it is the Third Meditation.

"Thou shouldst remember, O Ananda, the Buddha words of mine, and repeat this law for attaining to the perception of the land (of the Buddha country) for the sake of the great mass of the people hereafter who may wish to be delivered from their sufferings. If any one meditates on the land (of that Buddha country), his sins (which bind him to) births and deaths during eighty millions of kalpas* shall be expiated; after the abandonment of his (present) body, he will assuredly be born in the pure land in the following life. The practice of this kind of meditation is called the 'right meditation.' If it be of another kind it is called 'heretical meditation.'"

Buddha then spoke to Ananda and Vaidehi:† "When the perception of the land (of that Buddha country) has been gained, you should next meditate on the jewel-trees (of that country). In meditating on the jewel-trees, you should take each by itself and form a perception of the seven rows of trees; every tree is eight hundred yoganas high, and all the jewel-trees have flowers and leaves consisting of seven jewels all perfect. All flowers and leaves have colours like the colours of various jewels:—from the colour of lapis lazuli there issues a golden ray; from the colour of crystal, a saffron ray; from the colour of agate, a diamond ray; from the colour of diamond, a ray of blue pearls. Corals, amber, and all other gems are used as ornaments for illumination; nets of excellent pearls are spread over the trees, each tree is covered by seven sets of nets, and

---

*   A day of Brahma, or 4,320,000 years.
†   Ananda is the young disciple of the Buddha who has a strong personal attach-
     ment to the master. Queen Vaidehi is the wife of King Bimbisara of Rajagriha,
     the city in which this discourse is set.

between one set and another there are five hundred millions of palaces built of excellent flowers, resembling the palace of the Lord Brahman; all heavenly children live there quite naturally; every child has a garland consisting of five hundred millions of precious gems like those that are fastened on Sakra's (Indra's) head, the rays of which shine over a hundred yoganas, just as if a hundred millions of suns and moons were united together; it is difficult to explain them in detail. That (garland) is the most excellent among all, as it is the commixture of all sorts of jewels. Rows of these jewel-trees touch one another; the leaves of the trees also join one another.

"Among the dense foliage there blossom various beautiful flowers, upon which are miraculously found fruits of seven jewels. The leaves of the trees are all exactly equal in length and in breadth, measuring twenty-five yoganas each way; every leaf has a thousand colours and a hundred different pictures on it, just like a heavenly garland. There are many excellent flowers which have the colour of Gambunada gold and an appearance of fire-wheels in motion, turning between the leaves in a graceful fashion. All the fruits are produced just (as easily) as if they flowed out from the pitcher of the God Sakra. There is a magnificent ray which transforms itself into numberless jewelled canopies with banners and flags. Within these jewelled canopies the works of all the Buddhas of the Great Chilicosm appear illuminated; the Buddha countries of the ten quarters also are manifested therein. When you have seen these trees you should also meditate on them one by one in order. In meditating on the trees, trunks, branches, leaves, flowers, and fruits, let them all be distinct and clear—such is the perception of the trees (of that Buddha country), and it is the Fourth Meditation.

"Next, you should perceive the water (of that country). The perception of the water is as follows:—

"In the Land of Highest Happiness there are waters in eight lakes; the water in every lake consists of seven jewels which are soft and yielding. Deriving its source from the king of jewels that fulfills every wish, the water is divided into fourteen streams; every stream has the colour of seven jewels; its channel is built of gold, the bed of which consists of the sand of variegated diamonds.

"In the midst of each lake there are sixty millions of lotus-flowers, made of seven jewels; all the flowers are perfectly round and exactly equal (in circumference), being twelve yoganas. The water of jewels flows amidst the flowers and rises and falls by the stalks (of the lotus); the sound of the streaming water is melodious and pleasing, and propounds all the perfect virtues (Paramitas), 'suffering,' 'non-existence,' 'impermanence,' and 'non-self'; it proclaims also the praise of the signs of perfection, and minor marks of excellence of all Buddhas. From the king of jewels that fulfills every wish, stream forth the golden-coloured rays excessively beautiful, the radiance of which transforms itself into birds possessing the colours of a hundred jewels, which sing out harmonious notes, sweet and delicious, ever praising the remembrance of Buddha, the remembrance of the Law, and the remembrance of the Church*—such is the perception of the water of eight good qualities, and it is the Fifth Meditation.

"Each division of that (Buddha) country, which consists of several jewels, has also jewelled storeys and galleries to the number of five hundred millions; within each storey and gallery there are innumerable Devas engaged in playing heavenly music. There are some musical instruments that are hung up in the open sky, like the jewelled banners of heaven; they emit

---

* "Church" should be translated "Order" or "Brotherhood," since it refers to the *sangha* or brotherhood of those who follow the Buddha's method of liberation.

musical sounds without being struck, which, while resounding variously, all propound the remembrance of Buddha, of the Law and of the Church, Bhikshus,* etc. When this perception is duly accomplished, one is said to have dimly seen the jewel-trees, jewel-ground, and jewel-lakes of that World of Highest Happiness (Sukhavati);—such is the perception formed by meditating on the general (features of that Land), and it is the Sixth Meditation.

"If one has experienced this, one has expiated the greatest sinful deeds which would (otherwise lead one) to transmigration for numberless millions of kalpas; after his death he will assuredly be born in that land.

"Listen carefully! listen carefully! Think over what you have heard! I, Buddha, am about to explain in detail the law of delivering one's self from trouble and torment. Commit this to your memory in order to explain it in detail before a great assembly." While Buddha was uttering these words, Buddha Amitayus stood in the midst of the sky with Bodhisattvas Mahasthama and Avalokitesvara, attending on his right hand and left respectively. There was such a bright and dazzling radiance that no one could see clearly; the brilliance was a hundred thousand times greater than that of gold (Gambunada). Thereupon Vaidehi saw Buddha Amitayus and approached the World-Honoured One, and worshipped him, touching his feet; and spoke to him as follows: "O Exalted One! I am now able, by the power of Buddha, to see Buddha Amitayus together with the two Bodhisattvas. But how shall all the beings of the future meditate on Buddha Amitayus and the two Bodhisattvas?"

Buddha answered: "Those who wish to meditate on that

---

*   A *bhikshu* or "monk" is a member of the *sangha*.

Buddha ought first to direct their thought as follows: form the perception of a lotus-flower on a ground of seven jewels, each leaf of that lotus exhibits the colours of a hundred jewels, and has eighty-four thousand veins, just like heavenly pictures; each vein possesses eighty-four thousand rays, of which each can be clearly seen. Every small leaf and flower is two hundred and fifty yoganas in length and the same measurement in breadth. Each lotus-flower possesses eighty-four thousand leaves, each leaf has the kingly pearls to the number of a hundred millions, as ornaments for illumination; each pearl shoots out a thousand rays like bright canopies. The surface of the ground is entirely covered by a mixture of seven jewels. There is a tower built of the gems which are like those that are fastened on Sakra's head. It is inlaid and decked with eighty thousand diamonds, Kimsuka jewels, Brahmamani and excellent pearl nets.

"On that tower there are miraculously found four posts with jewelled banners; each banner looks like a hundred thousand millions of Sumeru mountains.

"'The jewelled veil over these banners is like that of the celestial palace of Yama, illuminated with five hundred millions of excellent jewels, each jewel has eighty-four thousand rays, each ray has various golden colours to the number of eighty-four thousand, each golden colour covers the whole jewelled soil, it changes and is transformed at various places, every now and then exhibiting various appearances; now it becomes a diamond tower, now a pearl net, again clouds of mixed flowers, freely changing its manifestation in the ten directions it exhibits the state of Buddha;—such is the perception of the flowery throne, and it is the Seventh Meditation."

Buddha, turning to Ananda, said: "These excellent flowers were created originally by the power of the prayer of Bhikshu,

Dharmakara.* All who wish to exercise the remembrance of that Buddha ought first to form the perception of that flowery throne. When engaged in it one ought not to perceive vaguely, but fix the mind upon each detail separately. Leaf, jewel, ray, tower, and banner should be clear and distinct, just as one sees the image of one's own face in a mirror. When one has achieved this perception, the sins which would produce births and deaths during fifty thousand kalpas are expiated, and he is one who will most assuredly be born in the World of Highest Happiness.

"When you have perceived this, you should next perceive Buddha himself. Do you ask how? Every Buddha Tathagata† is one whose (spiritual) body is the principle of nature (Darmadhatu-kaya),‡ so that he may enter into the mind of any beings. Consequently, when you have perceived Buddha, it is indeed that mind of yours that possesses those thirty-two signs of perfection and eighty minor marks of excellence (which you see in Buddha). In fine, it is your mind that becomes Buddha, nay, it is your mind that is indeed Buddha. The ocean of true and universal knowledge of all the Buddhas derives its source from one's own mind and thought. Therefore you should apply your thought with an undivided attention to a careful meditation on that Buddha.... In forming the perception of that Buddha, you should first perceive the image of that Buddha; whether your eyes be open or shut, look at an image like Gambunada gold in colour, sitting on that flower (throne).

"When you have seen the seated figure your mental vision will become clear, and you will be able to see clearly and

---

*   The name of Amitabha before he attained Buddhahood.

†   Tathagata, one who comes or goes "thus," is a usual title for a Buddha. *Tatha*, "thus," or *Tathata*, "thusness," is a Buddhist term for the highest and purest reality.

‡   The Dharmadhatu-kaya (lit., "realm-of-Dharma body") is the universe considered as a completely integrated system of relativity.

distinctly the adornment of that Buddha country, the jewelled ground, etc. In seeing these things, let them be clear and fixed just as you see the palms of your hands. When you have passed through this experience, you should further form (a perception of) another great lotus-flower which is on the left side of Buddha, and is exactly equal in every way to the above-mentioned lotus-flower of Buddha. Still further, you should form (a perception of) another lotus-flower which is on the right side of Buddha. Perceive that an image of Bodhisattva Avalokitesvara is sitting on the left-hand flowery throne, shooting forth golden rays exactly like those of Buddha. Perceive then that an image of Bodhisattva Mahasthama is sitting on the right-hand flowery throne.

"When these perceptions are gained the images of Buddha and the Bodhisattvas will all send forth brilliant rays, clearly lighting up all the jewel-trees with golden colour. Upon every tree there are also three lotus-flowers. On every lotus-flower there is an image, either of Buddha or of a Bodhisattva; thus (the images of the Bodhisattvas and of Buddha) are found everywhere in that country. When this perception has been gained, the devotee should hear the excellent Law preached by means of a stream of water, a brilliant ray of light, several jewel-trees, ducks, geese, and swans. Whether he be wrapped in meditation or whether he has ceased from it, he should ever hear the excellent Law.

"Thou shouldst know, O Ananda, that the body of Buddha Amitayus is a hundred thousand million times as bright as the colour of the Gambunada gold of the heavenly abode of Yama; the height of that Buddha is six hundred thousand niyutas of kotis of yoganas* innumerable as are the sands of the river Ganga.

---

* A number denoting the immeasurably vast, but indeterminate, since the *niyuta* may be 100,000 or 1,000,000 or even 10,000 × 10,000,000.

"The white twist of hair between the eyebrows all turning to the right, is just like the five Sumeru mountains.

"The eyes of Buddha are like the water of the four great oceans; the blue and the white are quite distinct.

"All the roots of hair of his body issue forth brilliant rays which are also like the Sumeru mountains.

"The halo of that Buddha is like a hundred millions of the Great Chiliocosms; in that halo there are Buddhas miraculously created, to the number of a million of niyutas of kotis innumerable as the sands of the Ganga; each of these Buddhas has for attendants a great assembly of numberless Bodhisattvas who are also miraculously created.

"Buddha Amitayus has eighty-four thousand signs of perfection, each sign is possessed of eighty-four minor marks of excellence, each mark has eighty-four thousand rays, each ray extends so far as to shine over the worlds of the ten quarters, whereby Buddha embraces and protects all the beings who think upon him and does not exclude (any one of them). His rays, signs, etc., are difficult to be explained in detail. But in simple meditation let the mind's eye dwell upon them.

"If you pass through this experience, you will at the same time see all the Buddhas of the ten quarters. Since you see all the Buddhas it is called the Samadhi* of the remembrance of the Buddhas.

"Those who have practised this meditation are said to have contemplated the bodies of all the Buddhas. Since they have meditated on Buddha's body, they will also see Buddha's mind. It is great compassion that is called Buddha's mind. It is by his absolute compassion that he receives all beings.

"Those who have practised this meditation will, when they die, be born in the presence of the Buddhas in another

---

*   *Samadhi* denotes any state of transcendental consciousness in which dualities
     (e.g., of subject and object) are resolved.

life, and obtain a spirit of resignation wherewith to face all the consequences which shall hereafter arise.

"Therefore those who have wisdom should direct their thought to the careful meditation upon that Buddha Amitayus. Let those who meditate on Buddha Amitayus begin with one single sign or mark—let them first meditate on the white twist of hair between the eyebrows as clearly as possible; when they have done this, the eighty-four thousand signs and marks will naturally appear before their eyes. Those who see Amitayus will also see all the innumerable Buddhas of the ten quarters. Since they have seen all the innumerable Buddhas, they will receive the prophecy of their future destiny (to become Buddha), in the presence of all the Buddhas.".…

"If there be any one who commits evil deeds, and even completes the ten wicked actions, the five deadly sins and the like; that man, being himself stupid and guilty of many crimes, deserves to fall into a miserable path of existence and suffer endless pains during many kalpas. On the eve of death he will meet a good and learned teacher who will, soothing and encouraging him in various ways, preach to him the excellent Law and teach him the remembrance of Buddha, but, being harassed by pains, he will have no time to think of Buddha. Some good friend will then say to him: 'Even if thou canst not exercise the remembrance of Buddha, thou mayst, at least, utter the name, "Buddha Amitayus."' Let him do so serenely with his voice uninterrupted; let him be (continually) thinking of Buddha until he has completed ten times the thought, repeating (the formula), 'Adoration to Buddha Amitayus' (Namo-mitayushe Buddhaya). On the strength of (his merit of) uttering Buddha's name he will, during every repetition, expiate the sins which involve him in births and deaths during eighty millions of kalpas. He will, while dying, see a golden lotus-flower like the disk of the sun appearing before his eyes; in a moment he will be born in the World of Highest Happiness."[103]

Some speculations on the meaning of this vision are certainly in order, even though it takes us far beyond the present competence of scientific psychology. For the vision is at once mythological and psychophysiological. Its point of departure is the instruction to gaze directly into the setting sun, and it is well known that many states of paranormal consciousness may be induced by this type of stimulation. For gazing at the sun so excites and energizes the optical nervous system that the seeing process becomes, in a special and unusual way, aware of itself. Patterns, mosaics, kaleidoscopic designs, and sparkling clusters of jewel-forms appear before the eyes, and these must undoubtedly correspond to and be based upon structures within the eye and the optic nerves. The sense of sight is, as it were, turned in upon itself, and this kind of intense and concentrated self-awareness is often a trigger for visionary and mystical experiences. Compare the case of Jacob Boehme:

> Sitting one day in his room his eyes fell upon a burnished pewter dish, which reflected the sunshine with such marvellous splendor that he fell into an inward ecstasy, and it seemed to him as if he could now look into the principles and deepest foundation of things. He believed that it was only a fancy, and in order to banish it from his mind he went out upon the green. But here he remarked that he gazed into the very heart of things, the very herbs and grass, and that actual nature harmonized with what he had inwardly seen. He said nothing of this to anyone, but praised and thanked God in silence.[104]

Or a more generalized form of turning awareness back upon itself, as described by Tennyson:

> A kind of waking trance I have frequently had, quite up from boyhood, when I have been all alone. This has often come upon me through repeating my own name to myself silently, all at once, as it were, out of the intensity of the consciousness of individuality, the individuality itself seemed to dissolve and fade away into boundless being; and this not a confused state, but the clearest of the clearest, the surest of the surest, the weirdest of the weirdest, utterly beyond words, where death was an almost laughable impossibility, the loss of personality but the only true life.[105]

The marvelously ordered, luminous complexity of the Buddhist vision has its parallel in many more recent accounts of similar phenomena:

> Now came a period of rapture so intense that the universe stood still, as if amazed at the unutterable majesty of the spectacle. Only one in all the infinite universe! The All-loving, the Perfect One....In that same wonderful moment of what might be called supernal bliss, came illumination. I saw with intense inward vision the atoms or molecules, of which seemingly the universe is composed—I know not whether material or spiritual—rearranging themselves, as the cosmos (in its continuous, everlasting life) passes from order to order. What joy when I saw there was no break in the chain—not a link left out—everything in its place and time. Worlds, systems, all blended in one harmonious whole.[106]

Or compare this:

> Everything "breathed," but breathed with that "one breath" which is the universal inspiration and expiration expressed

in the cardinal opposites of day and night, male and female, summer and winter. Indeed the wonderful and awe-inspiring livingness of everything seemed to be part of the interrelatedness of everything; within the one thing which the entire universe was, the multitudinous aspects of it enjoyed a living relationship both to one another and to the totality, and this in an extraordinary complexity which at the same time was an extraordinary simplicity....Things were related to one another which to ordinary thinking would have no connection whatever, and related to one another in ways which we cannot normally conceive. Things which we should call far apart, whether in space or time or by their nature, here interpenetrated; things which we should call wholly different from one another became one another....

One knew and understood this different world as a spectator of it, recognizing it as the object of one's apprehension, but at the same time knew and understood that it existed within oneself; thus one was at once the least significant atom in the universal whole and that universal whole....The sum of things appeared before my inward eyes as a living geometrical figure, an infinitely complicated and infinitely simple arrangement of continually moving, continually changing golden lines on a background of darkness....This living geometrical figure seemed to be telling me that everything is in order, that everything works according to an ineluctable pattern, and that, since all things are under the sun's almighty eye, nothing need ever be wholly meaningless, even on earth, where we live so far from the central and perfect unity. Provided that we bear the pattern's existence in mind, even pain...can have meaning; so can death; so can the worst that we may have to endure; while the possibility of discerning this meaning is itself the divine mercy.[107]

The scientific temperament is biased toward descriptions—if not explanations—of these visions in naturalistic terms. L. L. Whyte[108] has pointed out that human consciousness is a monitoring system with almost the sole function of calling attention to unusual changes and disturbances in the environment. It has, therefore, an extremely superficial, restricted, and, shall we say, one-sidedly anxious apprehension of all that is going on in the organism-environment field. In particular, it is ignorant of the unbelievable harmoniousness and perfection of our constant and basic psychophysiological functions, and of their exquisitely complex ties and balances with the outside universe. It is possible, then, that any method of turning the senses back upon themselves will restore awareness of this ignored aspect of life, for consciousness is thereby led back to its own organic roots. The extreme subtlety and beauty of these processes thereupon invade consciousness like a vision from heaven.

Furthermore, we have seen throughout these pages that conscious thinking and attention is ordinarily restricted (a) to inspection of "bits" of the world in a one-at-a-time linear series, and (b) to symbolic systems, such as language, which are clumsy in the expression of polar relationships. It is much easier to think in terms of either/or than of both/and, of A causing B than of A and B as mutually interdependent. But it is obvious that the organism-environment cannot function intelligently by any such cumbersome method. There is far, far too much going on at once for anything so slow as conscious attention to regulate. Again, then, one might suggest that when consciousness is turned back upon its own organic basis, it gets some apprehension of that "omniscience" which is the body's total, organizing sensitivity. In the light of this deeper and more inclusive sensitivity, it becomes suddenly clear that things are joined together by the boundaries we ordinarily take to separate them, and are, indeed, definable as themselves only in terms of other things that differ from them. The cosmos is seen as a multidimensional network of crystals, each one containing the reflections of all the others, and the reflections of all the others *in* those reflections....In the heart of each there shines, too, the single point of light that every one reflects from every other.

There is a Hassidic saying, "If I am I because you are you, and if you are you because I am I, then I am not I, and you are not you."

Acknowledgments

FOR PERMISSION TO REPRINT EXCERPTS from source materials in this volume, the author is indebted to the following:

George Allen & Unwin Ltd. for selection from *The Upanishads* translated by S. Radhakrishnan.

The American-Scandinavian Foundation for selection from *Prose Edda* translated by A.G. Brodeur.

The American Scholar for selection from "The Vedanta and Western Tradition" by A. K. Coomaraswamy, *American Scholar*, Spring, 1939.

Ernest Benn Ltd. for selection from *Early Zoroastrianism* translated by J. H. Moulton.

Bollingen Foundation—for selections from *The King and the Corpse* by Heinrich Zimmer; *Philosophies of India* by Heinrich Zimmer; and Mircea Eliade for selection from his "La Coincidentia Oppositorum" in the *Eranos-Jahrbuch*, 1959; and Routledge & Kegan Paul Ltd. for selection from *Freud and Psychoanalysis*, Vol. 4 of *Collected Works of C. G. Jung*.

E. J. Brill Ltd. for selections from *The Gospel according to Thomas* translated by Guillaumont, Puech, Quispel, Till, and 'Abd al Masih.

Cambridge University Press for selections from *Science and Civilisation in China* by Joseph Needham.

Clarendon Press, Oxford for selections from—*The Apocryphal New Testament* translated by M. R. James; *The Book of Enoch* translated by R. H. Charles; *Sacred Books of the East*, vol. xlix, translated by J. Takakusu; and *Zurvan*, translated by R.C. Zaehner.

Miss S. E. Collins and J. M. Dent & Sons Ltd. for "The Skeleton" from *The Wild Knight and Other Poems* by G. K. Chesterton.

Columbia University Press for selection from *Sources of the Chinese Tradition* edited by De Bary, Chan, and Watson.

E. P. Dutton & Co. Inc. for selection from *Cosmic Consciousness* by Richard Maurice Bucke.

Farrar, Straus & Company, Inc. for selection from *The Dance of Shiva* by Ananda K. Coomaraswamy.

Victor Gollancz Ltd. for selection from *A Drug-Taker's Notes* by R. H. Ward.

Holt, Rinehart, and Winston, Inc. for selection from *William Blake* by Mark Schorer.

The Jewish Publication Society of America for selections from *The Legends of the Jews* by Louis Ginzberg.

Alfred A. Knopf, Inc.—and The Richards Press Ltd. for "The White People" from *Tales of Horror and the Supernatural* by Arthur Machen. Copyright 1948 by Alfred A. Knopf, Inc.; and Andre Deutsch Ltd. Publishers—for selection from *Yesteryear* by Kurt Marek. © 1961 by Alfred A. Knopf, Inc.

Lili Kohler for selection from *Jewish Theology* by K. Kohler.

Luzac & Company Ltd. for selection from *Man and His Becoming* by R. Guénon.

Oriental Art magazine for selection "Moudrâ et hasta ou le langage par signes" by J. Auboyer, *Oriental Art*, 1951.

Oxford University Press (Bombay) for selections from *The Thirteen Principal Upanishads* translated by R.E. Hume.

Oxford University Press for selections from *The Tibetan Book of the Dead* by W.Y. Evans Wentz.

Pantheon Books, Inc. for selections from *The Divine Comedy*, translated by Lawrence G. White. Copyright 1948 by Pantheon Books Inc. Reprinted by permission of Pantheon Books, a division of Random House, Inc.

Princeton University Press for selections from *Heraclitus* by Philip Wheelwright. Copyright © 1959 by Princeton University Press.

Arthur Probsthain (London) for selections from *World Conception of the Chinese* translated by A. Forke.

Ramakrishna-Vivekananda Center for selections from *The Gospel of Sri Ramakrishna* translated by Swami Nikhilananda.

Routledge & Kegan Paul Ltd. for selections from *The Trickster* by Paul Radin; and *The Secret of the Golden Flower* translated by R. Wilhelm.

University College Oxford and Christ's College Cambridge for selections from *From Fetish to God in Ancient Egypt* by E.A. Wallis Budge, actual translation by Alan Gardiner. By permission of the Estates Bursar, University College, Oxford.

Vedanta Centre (Massachusetts) and Ananda Ashrama, Inc. for selections from *Bhagavad-Gita* translated by Swami Paramananda.

A. Watkins, Inc. and David Higham Associates, Ltd. for selection from *The Next Development in Man* by L.L. Whyte. © 1948 Lancelot Law Whyte.

John M. Watkins Publishers for selection from *Fragments of a Faith Forgotten* by G.R.S. Mead.

Notes on the Plates
(following page 128)

PLATE

1. *Lingam* and *Yoni*. Sculpture in stone, Cambodia. The union of the male (*lingam*) and female (*yoni*) principles, the phallus and the vagina, seen as from within the body of the female—i.e., from within this world. Liberation, the attainment of nirvana or moksha, is thus equated by analogy with birth and not, as in the Freudian mystique, with return to the womb.

2. Kali. A tenth-century figure from South India, Chola Dynasty. The dark, all-devouring Mother who, as the consort or Shakti of Shiva, represents the very abyss of the destructive principle. But for this reason she is "the darkness before the dawn" and thus the Mother of light, and her front right hand is raised in the gesture of "Fear not." The image is somewhat unusual. (See text, pp. 94–96.)

3. Black Madonna. Polish School, undated. This is the Christian equivalent of Kali; the Black Madonna has been venerated in Europe for many centuries. This version is dated as far back as the eleventh century, although the dating is uncertain. There are some two hundred shrines to her cult in Western Europe alone. Although dark, the Black Madonna is—like Kali—a symbol of the creative force of the negative. The image reflects certain liturgical texts, taken originally from the *Song of Songs*:

"Who is she that riseth up as the morning, fair as the
moon, clear as the sun, and terrible as an army with banners?"

"I am black, but comely. O ye daughters of Jerusalem;
therefore the King delighteth in me, and hath brought me
into his chambers." (Antiphons from the *Roman Breviary*,
Common of the BVM.)

4. Yamantaka. Tibetan painting, eighteenth or nineteenth century. Not a devil in the Western and Christian sense, but the
   wrathful form of the Bodhisattva Manjusri, and sometimes of
   the Buddha Amitabha. Yamantaka is also known as Yamari.
   (Tib., *gsin-rje gsed*. Jap., *Dai Itoku Myo-o*.) He has nine heads,
   of which the chief is in the form of a bull, thirty-four hands,
   and sixteen feet, and is shown here embracing his Shakti, or
   female counterpart, Pashadhari from whose girdle swings
   a cluster of severed heads. The name Yamantaka means
   "Destroyer of the Lord of Death (Yama)," and this is the form
   which Manjusri assumes for penetrating the illusion of death.
   Manjusri stands for *prajña*, the intuitive wisdom of a Buddha,
   which enables him to see through the apparent dualities of
   experience.

5. St. Michael and the Dragon. Fourteenth century, Sienese. We
   pass now to a series of plates where the Image of Darkness
   appears in the Western form of unrelieved diabolism, a thing
   to be hated and crushed without quarter. The emergence of
   the informal, realistic techniques of Western painting give the
   artist unparalleled opportunities for elaborating images of
   pure horror.

6. The Descent of Christ into Hell. Pieter Breughel, sixteenth
   century. Engraving by Hieronymus Cock. In the interval
   between the Crucifixion and the Resurrection, Jesus is said
   to have descended into Hades to liberate, from Adam on, all
   those who would have followed him had they lived after the

founding of the Church. Here a master fantast shows Hell, not only as a realm of physical agony, but also of terrified screaming insanity. Note, however, that the artist draws for his effect upon the ordinary materials of nature: the orgiastic postures of the figures in the foreground, and the predatory activities of fish and reptiles. By contrast (cf. plate 9) the figures of Christ and his angels in the central capsule are utterly without verve or interest.

7. The Inferno. Coppo di Marcovaldo, thirteenth century. It is easier to depict the "face" of evil in terms of violence inflicted upon living bodies. And yet Satan—chewing Judas with his mouth, and Cassius and Brutus with the serpent heads emerging from his thighs—looks curiously detached. He is the dutiful servant of God, carrying out rather distasteful orders. Even the serpent heads do not seem to be enjoying their meals. The most sinister elements are perhaps the frog forms, later to be exploited so horrendously by Breughel.

8. Detail from The Temptation of St. Anthony. Mathias Grünewald, the Isenheim Altar, fourteenth century. The temptation of the desert hermit, St. Anthony, has been one of the favorite themes for the painter's display of diabolic imagination. The puzzle—is it merely aesthetic or is it also moral—is, can one depict an absolutely evil countenance? (See the discussion in the text, p. 165–66.) Is Grünewald showing us evil, in the full theological sense of perfected malice, or do we have here merely the grotesque, the lunatic, the animal, or even the clownish?

9. The Last Judgment. Hubert van Eyck, fifteenth century. Here again, one must note the astonishing contrast between the demure and characterless formality of the justified saints in Heaven, and the squirming vitality and variety of Hell. Above is the most stately gathering for Vespers or an ecclesiastical

convention. Below is a wriggling orgy in which naked bod-ies—some rather shapely—are being eaten forever and ever by worms, and it is simply obvious that the artist was far more inspired, and, indeed, had much more fun, in painting the lower part. If this is not a covert work of sadistic pornography (cf. also plates 6 and 7), what alternatives can we suggest?

Perhaps the artist has considered the possibility that *eternal* pain would be absolute ecstasy. It could neither harm nor destroy, for, as Scheeben (pp. 182–85) was careful to point out, the mangled and seared limbs are everlastingly restored.

10. Lucifer, King of Hell. Gustave Doré, 1833–1883.

11. The Saintly Throng in the Form of a Rose. Gustave Doré, 1833–1883. (See text, p. 40–41.)

12. Vision of the Throne of God. Illumination from a Flemish Apocalypse, c. 1400. The scene described in Revelation 4. To the left, St. John is being drawn up into the heavenly city by an angel to behold the vision of the King of Heaven, sur-rounded by the four cherubim: the Bull of St. Luke (Taurus), the Lion of St. Mark (Leo), the Eagle of St. John (Scorpio), and the Man of St. Matthew (Aquarius). The evangelical cheru-bim correspond to the four Fixed Signs of the Zodiac, here arranged in their correct order (which is somewhat rare). The eagle or phoenix was anciently an alternative symbol for the scorpion, and represents death-and-resurrection. The seven lamps of "the Seven Spirits of God" hang before the throne, and around are seated the "four and twenty elders" not iden-tified in the text. But the remarkable feature of this illumina-tion is the clarity with which it illustrates the polarity of the spiritual and the erotic, the heavenly and the earthy.

13. St. Michael. Andrea della Robbia, fifteenth century. The ideal of the androgyne. In the course of spiritual evolution the opposition of male and female seems to be transcended. (See text, pp. 208–9.)

14. The Cross as the Tree of Life. Mosaic, fourth century with additions, c. 1125. (See text pp. 215–18.) One of the most interesting representations of the Tree of the Cross as the Axle-Tree of the universe. In the original the crucifix is surmounted by an immense sunburst, suggesting the Hindu symbolism of the spinal tree. According to the cosmic anatomical system of Yoga, the work of spiritual liberation consists in the ascent of the spinal tree by the *kundalini* or "serpent-power," which ordinarily lies dormant at its base. (Cf. the plate here.) When awakened, the *kundalini* passes up through the various *chakras*, or centers of power believed to be located along the spine, until it reaches the *sahasrara chakra*—the thousand-petaled lotus in the head, a figure of the sun beneath the dome of the sky. The serpent-and-tree theme is also found in the Norse myth of the worm Nidhug who gnaws at the roots of Yggdrasil, and the Hebrew myths of (a) *nehushtan*, the brazen serpent of Moses, and of (b) the Tree of Life in the Garden of Paradise, which have always been regarded as prophetic "types" of the crucifixion. Note, in the accompanying plate, the four streams flowing from the base of the Cross, reminiscent of the Four Rivers of Eden.

15. Indian Tree of Life. Bronze, seventeenth century. Compare with the preceding plate. This is probably the Mucalinda Tree of Buddhist legend, where the Buddha sat in meditation for seven days shortly after his great Awakening. This tree was the home of the Serpent-King Mucalinda, the five-headed cobra here shown, who protected the Buddha from the elements with his hood.

16. Vishnu sleeping on Adhi Shesha, his snake bed, in the infinite sea of milk (Pierre Sonnerat, 1782). In the *pralaya*, or interval between manifestations of the universe, the Supreme Self, here personified as Vishnu, is said to rest upon the thousand-headed serpent Ananta, i.e., "Endless," the image of

eternity. When the time comes for a new cycle of manifestation, a golden lotus grows out from Vishnu's navel with
Brahma, the creator, seated upon it, and once again the play
of maya is set in motion. See text, pp. 75–83.

17. Amphisbaena. Aztec; mosaic in shell and turquoise. The
ambivalence of the serpent, who is both poison and medicine.
The amphisbaena appears also as a heraldic emblem in the
West, and was mentioned by Pliny and Lucanus as a creature
actually to be found in Libya. The serpent and the tree are
both mythologically associated with the homeopathic principle that "like cures like"—the hair of the dog that bit you. On
the Tree of Knowledge the serpent is Satan, but on the Tree
of the Cross it is Christ. "For as Moses lifted up the serpent
(*nehushtan*) in the wilderness, so also shall the Son of Man be
lifted up." Moses's serpent was apparently a talisman against
an infestation of the Israelite camp by snakes, and taking this
as a prophetic "type" of Christ, forms of the crucifix are found
showing a serpent entwined upon a T cross.

18. Symbolic door. Sona Masjid, at Gaur, NW Bengal. Sixteenth
century. The polarity of the double door, with one half the
mirror image of the other. This exquisite merging of Persian
Islamic and Hindu styles shows the Door (i.e., the entrance to
Heaven, *fana el fana*, or liberation) surmounted (top center)
by an emblem of the axle-tree of the world—a cypress above
an inverted (*skambha*) lotus—since the way out is always
through the center of the scene, not in flight from it. Furthermore, the Door of Heaven is usually "active," like a portcullis
or snapping jaws, or like the whirling sword of fire which
guards the entrance to the Paradise Garden. Whoever would
gain access must jump through "in a moment, in the twin-
kling of an eye," for if he stops to consider *when* is the right
moment to leap, he is always too late.

19. Brahma. Stone sculpture. South India, Chola Dynasty, tenth to

eleventh century. (See text pp. 89–97.) The One Actor behind all the manifold parts and roles of the universe—not just two-faced, like Janus, but four-faced so as to be looking in every direction, left and right, before and after.

20a and 20b. Two forms of the four-faced Brahma. *Left:* Standing Brahma (tenth to eleventh century), South India. *Right:* Statue of Hindu god Brahma. Rishikesh, Uttarankhand, India. For further elucidation of the symbolism of four faces, looking all ways, see pp. 99–100.

21. Shiva as Nataraja, King of the Dance. Bronze, eleventh century. South India, Chola Dynasty. (See text pp. 75–109.) The upper left hand holds a flame, symbol of creative dissolution and purgation. The upper right holds a drum, because the world is a manifestation of rhythm and vibration. The lower left hand points to the raised left foot, which, seeming to float above the ground, represents liberation. The lower right hand is in the gesture of *abhaya*, "Fear not." The right foot presses down upon the demon Apasmara, namely, forgetfulness—especially of one's own true nature. The ring of flames signifies the everlasting magic (maya) of the physical universe, produced by the dance as one creates the illusion of a circle by whirling a flaming torch.

22. Indian map of the world, of Jain origin but uncertain date. The world assimilated to the form of the *mandala.* At once the most preconceived, or unscientific, and the most profound image of the cosmos. The symbolism here is, however, no more geocentric than it is egocentric, for the world is centered upon an image of the *atman*, the Self within and beyond ego which unites the individual with the universal. The center is Mount Meru, the *axis mundi*, the pillar joining heaven and earth. Around it, within the first dark circle, is the Jambud-vipa, sometimes considered as the world of human beings and sometimes as just the subcontinent of India. The dark,

ribbonlike markings are rivers, and the dark rings, with their
fish, are the oceans. Beyond the Jambudvipa lie two other
"continents," separated by still another circular ocean. This is,
therefore, not the world as seen externally, from the standpoint of the geographer, but the world as seen in another kind
of space, or hierarchy of values, whose center is not terrestrial
but metaphysical.

23. Amitayus Mandala. Tibetan painting, probably eighteenth
century. This mandala, or circle of perfection and wholeness,
has been selected as an appropriate illustration for the passages from the *Amitayur-dhyana-sutra* quoted on pp. 226–35.
Like all mandalas of this general form, it represents the union
of the *vajradhatu* (*vajra* = diamond = thunderbolt, *dhatu*
= realm or sphere) and the *garbhadhatu* (*garbha* = womb),
that is, of consciousness and form, yang and yin, the cosmic
male and the cosmic female. In the center it shows Amitayus
(Amitabha), the Dhyani-Buddha of Boundless Life and Light,
surrounded by eight replicas of himself upon the petals of a
lotus. In the T-shaped areas at the four points of the compass
are the four *lokapalas*, or Guardians of the Cardinal Points—
Vaishravana to the North, Virudhaka to the South, Dhritarashtra to the East, and Virupaksha to the West. Between
the outer circle and the inner square is Sukhavati, the Pure
Land over which Amitayus presides, with its flowers, banners,
clouds, Bodhisattvas, and celestial dancing-girls (*apsara*).

Immediately outside the mandala (above) are the Eight
Glorious Emblems: the banner of victory, the conch-shell,
the covered vase, the canopy of protection from the heat of
passions, the two fishes of happiness and utility or wisdom
and compassion, the lotus, the endless knot, and the wheel
of the doctrine (*dharmachakra*). Immediately below are the
Seven Jewels. The five figures at the top are the Bodhisattvas

Sitatapatra and Manjusri, the Buddha Amitabha, and the Bodhisattvas Shadakshari and Ushnishavijaya. The five below are two *yi-dam*, or tutelary gods, Jambhala and Sitajambhala, the Guardian God (*dharmapala*) Hayagriva, protector of horses, the *yi-dam* Kalajambhala, and the female Bodhisattva Vasudhara. For the descriptive information I am indebted to Antoinette Gordon's *Iconography of Tibetan Lamaism* (Charles E. Tuttle Co., 1959), esp. pp. 27–28.

Endnotes

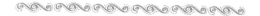

1. A.W. Watts, *Myth and Ritual in Christianity*. Vanguard. New York, 1954, p. 7.
2. Mark Schorer, *William Blake*. Holt. New York, 1946.
3. Cited by Arthur Machen in *Tales of Horror and the Supernatural*. Knopf. New York, 1948, pp. 301–2.
4. Thomas Traherne, *Centuries of Meditations*. Dobell. London, 1948, pp. 152–53.
5. H. Ostermann, "The Alaskan Eskimos," in Joseph Campbell, *The Masks of God*, vol. 1. Viking. New York, 1959, p. 350.
6. W.Y. Evans Wentz, *The Tibetan Book of the Dead*. Oxford, 1957, p. 146.
7. C.G. Jung, *Collected Works*, vol. 4, *Freud and Psychoanalysis*. Bollingen. New York, p. 332.
8. A.K. Coomaraswamy, *Hinduism and Buddhism*. Philosophical Library. New York, 1943, p. 33, n 21.
9. In G.R.S. Mead, *Fragments of a Faith Forgotten*. Watkins. London, 1931, p. 223.
10. *Paradiso* 33, 142.
11. Philip Wheelwright, *Heraclitus*. Princeton, 1959, p. 29.
12. *Dhammapada*, 153–54.
13. S. Radhakrishnan (tr.), *The Upanishads*. Allen & Unwin. London, 1953, p. 279. *Brihadaranyaka*, iv. 4, 22.

14. G.K. Chesterton, *Collected Poems*. Dodd, Mead. New York, 1932, p. 305.

15. In Paul Radin, *The Trickster*. Routledge. London, 1956, p. 185.

16. Mircea Eliade, "La Coincidentia Oppositorum." *Eranos Jahrbuch*, vol. XXVII. Rhein-Verlag, Zurich, 1959, pp. 202–5.

17. S. Freud, *On Creativity and the Unconscious*. Harper. New York, 1958, p. 55.

18. G.R. Taylor, *Sex in History*. Vanguard. New York, 1954, p. 121.

19. M. Garcon and J. Vinchon, *The Devil*. Gollancz. London, 1929. Quoted in (18), p. 121.

20. K. Kohler, *Jewish Theology*. Macmillan. New York, 1923, p. 176.

21. Kurt Marek, *Yestermorrow*. Knopf. New York, 1961, p. 23.

22. Tr. Philip Wheelwright, *Heraclitus*. Princeton University Press. Princeton, 1959.

23. Revelation 21:4.

24. *Tao Te Ching* 2. Tr. A.W.W.

25. Joseph Needham (tr.) in *Science and Civilisation in China*, vol. 2. Cambridge University Press. Cambridge, 1956, p. 326.

26. De Bary, Chan, and Watson (eds.), *Sources of the Chinese Tradition*. Columbia University Press. New York, 1960, pp. 211–12.

27. J. Needham (25), pp. 460–61.

28. A. Forke (tr.) in *World Conception of the Chinese*. Arthur Probsthain. London, 1925, p. 37.

29. A. Forke (28), p. 56.

30. A. Forke (28), p. 68.

31. A. Forke (28), p. 217.

32. A. Forke (28), p. 220.

33. H.A. Giles (tr.) *Chuang-tzu*. Kelly & Walsh. Shanghai, 1926, p. 228. Tr. mod. by A.W.W. *Chuang-tzu* 18.

34. H.A. Giles (33), p. 278. *Chuang-tzu* 22.

35. H.A. Giles (33), pp. 19–21. Tr. mod. by A.W.W. *Chuang-tzu* 2.

36. H.A. Giles (33), pp. 211–212. *Chuang-tzu* 17.

37. J. Needham (25), p. 333.

38. R. Wilhelm and C.G. Jung, *The Secret of the Golden Flower.* Kegan Paul. London, 1931, pp. 26–27. *T'ai I Chin Hua Taung Chi* 2.

39. Wilhelm and Jung (38), p. 36. *T'ai I Chin* 3.

40. H.A. Giles (33), pp. 43–44. Tr. mod. by A.W.W. *Chuang-tzu* 4.

41. *Bhagavad-Gita*, x. 20, 31–34, 36, 38–42, xi. 1–5, 7–21, 23–34. Tr. Swami Paramananda. Vedanta Centre Inc., Cohasset, Mass.

42. *Brihadaranyaka Upanishad*, 1.4. 1–5. Tr. F. Max Müller in *The Upanishads*, vol. i. Sacred Books of the East, vol. i. Oxford, 1900.

43. *Brihadaranyaka Upanishad*, 3.6 and 3.8. Tr. R.E. Hume, *The Thirteen Principal Upanishads*. Oxford, 1931, pp. 113–14, 117–19.

44. *Kalika Purana*, 1. 1–5, 10. Tr. Heinrich Zimmer (ed. Joseph Campbell) in *The King and the Corpse*. Pantheon Books, Bollingen Series XI, New York, 1956, pp. 241–42.

45. H. Zimmer (44), pp. 243, 245.

46. H. Zimmer (44), pp. 246–47.

47. Swami Nikhilananda (tr.), *The Gospel of Sri Ramakrishna.* Ramakrishna-Vivekananda Center. New York, 1942, p. 619.

48. Nikhilananda (47), pp. 134–36.

49. Nikhilananda (47), p. 136.

50. H. Zimmer (44), *Kalika Purana*, 17. 1–9, 13, p. 306.

51. Commentary on *Kena Upanishad*. In R. Guénon, *Man and His Becoming*. Luzac. London, 1945, p. 114.

52. A.K. Coomaraswamy, "The Vedanta and Western Tradition." *The American Scholar*, viii. 1939, p. 223.

53. *Vishnu Purana*, i. 6. Tr. H.A. Wilson in *Works*, vol. vi. Trübner. London, 1864, pp. 100–104.

54. *Vishnu Purana*, i. 8. (54), pp. 118–20.

55. *Mahabharata*, 12. 281. 1 to 282. 20. Tr. Joseph Campbell in *The Masks of God*, vol. ii. Viking. New York, 1962, pp. 184–87.

56. W.Y. Evans Wentz (tr.), *The Tibetan Book of the Dead*. Oxford, 1957, pp. 95–96, 104.

57. Evans Wentz (57), pp. 105–7.

58. Evans Wentz (57), pp. 131, 137, 146–47.

59. E.A. Wallis Budge, *From Fetish to God in Ancient Egypt*. Oxford, 1934, pp. 450–52, 452–54, 456–57. Actual trs. by Alan Gardiner.

60. Heinrich Zimmer (tr.) (ed. J. Campbell) in *Philosophies of India*. Pantheon Books (Bollingen Series). New York, 1951, pp. 185–87, 188–90, 190–91, 192–93, 195–200, 201–3.

61. Louis Ginzberg, *The Legends of the Jews*. Simon & Schuster for the Jewish Publication Society of America. New York, 1961, pp. 54–58. (This is an abridged edition of a seven-volume work of the same title first published in 1909, giving in detail the rabbinical or patristic sources for each incident.)

62. R. H. Charles (tr.), *The Book of Enoch*. Oxford, 1912, p. 56.

63. *Gathas*, yasna 30. J.H. Moulton (tr.), in *Early Zoroastrianism*. Williams & Norgate. London, 1913, pp. 349–51.

64. *'Ulema i Islam*, 8–10. In R.C. Zaehner (tr.), *Zurvan*. Oxford, 1955, p. 410.

65. Eznik of Kolb, *De Deo*. French text in Zaehner (64), tr. A.W.W.

66. Theodore Abu Qurra, *On the True Religion*. In Zaehner (trs.) (64), p. 429.

67. *Selections of Zatspram*, 35. In Zaehner (trs.) (64), p. 351.

68. *Cambridge Ancient History*, vol. 4, pp. 207, 616.

69. J. Scheftclowitz, *Die altpersische Religion und das Judentum*. Giessen, 1920.

70. Th. Gaster, *The Dead Sea Scriptures*. Anchor. New York, 1956.

71. Watts, *The Supreme Identity*. Pantheon. New York, 1950. Noonday (paper). New York, 1958.

72. Watts, *Myth and Ritual in Christianity*. Vanguard. New York, 1953. Grove Press (paper). New York, 1960.

73. L. Ginzberg (62), pp. 34–35.

74. Matthias Joseph Scheeben, *Die Mysterien des Christentums*. Quotation tr. by Inge Sammet. Herder & Co., G.m.b.H., Freiburg im Breisgau, 1941, pp. 232–33.

75. Milton, *Paradise Lost*, v. 577–617.

76. *Paradise Lost*, v. 657–93.

77. *Paradise Lost*, v. 743–802.

78. *Paradise Lost*, vi. 824–77.

79. *Paradise Lost*, i. 44–74.

80. *Paradise Lost*, i. 242–70.

81. Arthur Machen, "The White People" in his *Tales of Horror and the Supernatural*. Knopf. New York, 1948, pp. 116–23.

82. *Vishnu Purana*, vi. 5. Wilson (54), pp. 207–8.

83. M.R. James (tr.), *The Apocryphal New Testament*. Oxford, 1926, pp. 508–10, 517–18.

84. Robert Cardinal Bellarmine, *On the Ascent to God*. Tr. T.G. Gent, 1616. London, 1928.

85. M.J. Scheeben (74), pp. 614–16.

86. Dante, *Inferno* 34. Tr. Lawrence G. White, *The Divine Comedy*. Pantheon Books. New York, 1948.

87. *Paradise Lost*, vi. 4–12.

88. A.G. Brodeur (tr.), *Prose Edda*, "Gylfaginning," iv–viii. American-Scandinavian Foundation. New York, 1916.

89. Cf. Joseph Campbell, *The Hero with a Thousand Faces*. Pantheon. New York, 1949, pp. 282–83.

90. Joseph Campbell, *The Masks of God*, vol. ii, "Oriental Mythology." Viking. New York, 1962. See ch. 1.

91. L. Ginzberg (61), pp. 34–36.

92. *Symposium*, 189–92. B. Jowett (tr.), *The Dialogues of Plato*, vol. i. Scribner. New York, 1889, pp. 483–86.

93. Proverbs 8:1 to 9:2.

94. A. K. Coomaraswamy, *The Dance of Shiva*. Noonday Press. New York, 1957, p. 130.

95. L. Apuleius, *The Golden Ass*. Tr. Harold Berman. Privately printed, 1930, pp. 287–89.

96. M. R. James (tr.), *The Apocryphal New Testament*. Oxford, 1924, pp. 334–35. Acts of Peter, 31 *ad fin.* to 39.

97. Guillaumont, Puech, Quispel, Till, and 'Abd al Masih (tr.), *The Gospel According to Thomas*. Harper. New York, 1959, pp. 17–19.

98. Guillaumont, et al. (97), p. 43.

99. M. R. James (96), pp. 254–55. *Acts of John*, 98–99.

100. David Shea and Anthony Troyer (trs.), *The Dabistan*. Tudor. New York, 1937 (repr.) First edn., 1843, pp. 398–410.

101. A. K. Coomaraswamy, "Symplegades."

102. J. Auboyer, "Moudrâ et hasta ou le langage par signes." *Oriental Art*, iii. London, 1951, pp. 153–61.

103. J. Takakusu (tr.), *Buddhist Mahayana Texts*. Sacred Books of the East, vol. xlix. Oxford, 1894, pp. 169–79, 180–81, 197–98.

104. H. L. Martensen, *Jacob Boehme: His Life and Teaching*. Tr. T. Rhys Evans. Hodder & Stoughton. London, 1885.

105. *Alfred, Lord Tennyson: A Memoir by His Son*. Macmillan. London, 1897, vol. i, p. 320.

106. R. M. Bucke, *Cosmic Consciousness*. Dutton. New York, 1923, p. 326.

107. An experience under the influence of nitrous oxide, in R. H. Ward, *A Drug-Taker's Notes*. Gollancz. London, 1957, pp. 26–31.

108. L. L. Whyte, *The Unconscious Before Freud*. Basic Books. New York, 1960.

Index

Page references followed by an italicized *fig.* indicate illustrations or material contained in their captions. A bold **pl.** indicates plates found in the insert after page 128.

seasons, 61, 64

Sekhmet (Egyptian deity), 118, 118n

Self, 12–13, 28, 28n, 255n22. *See also* Supreme Self (*Paramatman*)

self: essential, 77; not-self vs., xv, 71–72

selfishness, 29

self-love, 20–21

self-othering, 43

sensuality, 89–90

Septuagint, 178n

Serpent: ambivalence of, 254n17, **pl. 17**; artistic representation of, 253–54nn14–17, **pls. 14–17**; in Christian mythology, 19, 136, 253n14, **pl. 14**; in Hindu-Buddhist mythology, 128, 131–32, 133–34, 253–54nn15–16, **pls. 15–16**

Sesa (Jaina mythological figure), 132

Set (Egyptian deity), 116, 119n. *See also* Horus and Set myth

Seven Jewels, 256n23

sexes, division of: in Greek mythology, 201–5; in Hebrew mythology, 197–201; hermaphroditism and transcendence of, 208–10, 252n13;

in Hindu mythology, 83–85, 101–3, 249n1, **pl. 1**; transcendence of, 252n13, **pl. 13**. *See also* yin-yang

sexuality, 65, 70, 71

Shadakshari (Bodhisattva), 257

shadow, 115, 149

Shaktis (feminine symbols of maya), 90–94, 95, 110n, 249n2, 250n4

Shankara (Hindu philosopher), 99

Shekinah (radiance of God), 152, 152n

Shiva (Hindu deity), 92; Brahma vs., 89–90, 93–94, 96, 98, 101–3; consorts of, 96, 97, 249n2, **pl. 2**; cosmic battle and, 104–5; cosmic dance of, 255n21, **pl. 21**; hermaphroditic images of, 209; human passions of, 98

Shiva as Nataraja, King of the Dance (sculpture; anon.), 255n21

sibling rivalry, 115

sin, 154–55, 186

Sitajambhala (Buddhist god), 257

Sitatapatra (Bodhisattva), 257

"Skeleton, The" (poem; Chesterton), 29

About the Author

ALAN WATTS IS BEST KNOWN AS AN INTERPRETER of Zen Buddhism in particular and of Indian and Chinese philosophy in general. He earned the reputation of being one of the most original and unfettered philosophers of the twentieth century. He was the author of more than twenty books, including *The Way of Zen*, *The Wisdom of Insecurity*, *Does It Matter?*, *Psychotherapy East and West*, *The Book*, *This Is It*, *The Joyous Cosmology*, *In My Own Way*, and *Tao: The Watercourse Way* (with Chungliang Al Huang). He died in 1973.